Questions & Answers
Torts

FOURTH EDITION

Multiple Choice, Short Answers, Essay Issue-Spotters, and
90-Minute Practice Final Exam

Anita Bernstein
ANITA AND STUART SUBOTNICK PROFESSOR OF LAW
BROOKLYN LAW SCHOOL

CAROLINA ACADEMIC PRESS
Durham, North Carolina

W0009846

Copyright © 2018
Anita Bernstein
All Rights Reserved

ISBN 978-1-5310-0500-9
e-ISBN 978-1-53100-501-6

Carolina Academic Press, LLC
700 Kent Street
Durham, North Carolina 27701
Telephone (919) 489-7486
Fax (919) 493-5668
www.cap-press.com

Printed in the United States of America

In memory of David P. Leonard 1952–2010

Contents

Preface: How to Use This Book

The law of torts deals with a broad range of human conduct. From punches in the nose to automobile accidents; from affronts to dignity to environmental pollution; from defective products to infliction of emotional distress. Not only must rules of tort law regulate vastly different types of potentially harmful behavior, but they must also be flexible enough to account for the almost limitless variety of fact patterns within each type. No two punches in the nose are exactly alike. At the same time, the rules ought to make the law at least reasonably predictable and the results of the cases both fair to individuals and conducive to social prosperity.

With these far-reaching goals in mind, modern rules of tort law are written in broad strokes. They seldom seek to prescribe or proscribe specific behavior in specific circumstances (always stop, look, and listen before crossing a railroad track). Rather, they set forth general principles to guide behavior in a variety of circumstances (always exercise reasonable care). Instead of purporting to tell us exactly what to do, they provide us with standards against which our conduct may be measured.

The generality of tort rules is what makes the study of tort law difficult. But tort is not unstructured. Every claim for relief and every affirmative defense has a set of required *elements*. These elements tell lawyers what they must allege and prove in order to demonstrate their clients' entitlement to relief or why their clients should not be held responsible. It is your task to learn what these elements are and how to apply them to real and hypothetical fact patterns.

How can *Questions and Answers: Torts* help you in this task? Recognizing that torts coverage varies somewhat from school to school, instructor to instructor, and even day to day in the same course, this book follows a comparably varied path to give you what you need.

You will find a range of difficulty. Some questions are tough while others are pretty easy. In the subject-specific chapters, most of the time the questions start relatively easy and get harder. The difficulty order on the Practice Final Exam is (purposely) random.

Multiple-choice questions, which predominate in this book, always offer four alternatives and only rarely resort to something like "none of the above." They might ask you to pick the best of a list, the worst of a list, the correct one of two contrary outcomes accompanied by the best rationale, or the story that illustrates a point of doctrine most effectively, as well as other routes to mastery of the material. Short-answer questions ask you to analyze scenarios or communicate discrete points. A little (simple) arithmetic comes up now and then—just as it does for practicing lawyers. The Practice Final Exam simulates tort litigation in the real world by not announcing up front, the way the chapter headings do, which topics are at issue. Whether you're in your beginning or ending stage of pulling torts material together, then, you'll find coverage at a level suited to that need.

This edition adds two new features to the book. First, "Zoom Out" is designed for when you've examined more than one topic in depth and want to confirm your understanding about how the two (or more) relate to each other. You'll need that skill on your final exam, because exam questions do not point you to a particular chapter or passage in your syllabus. Second, multiple-choice questions that unite around the same fact pattern are identified and characterized. You'll know what to expect from these joined questions.

Like most torts classes, the book emphasizes black-letter law but also goes beyond it. While most of its questions use the familiar issue-spotter approach to doctrine—an approach you can probably expect to see on your final—a number of questions will help you review social policy, economic theory, fairness, and the insights of famed common law judges. Most torts teachers expect you to think about torts at this more conceptual level while also mastering rules and elements. Questions that fall in this "policy" category are identified at the end of the Index.

Despite its wide swath, this book is neither a casebook nor a treatise. Its purpose is to help you test your comprehension of the elements of the most important tort claims and defenses. It does not purport to teach you the law in the first instance: that is the purpose of your torts class. Therefore, you should not attempt to answer the questions in any particular part of this book until you have studied the applicable law.

Once you have completed an area of study, you can work your way through the problems in that part of the book to test your understanding of the subject matter. Take your time. Try to answer each question before reviewing the answers and the explanations they provide. If the question calls for a response in your words, write something before reviewing the answer—at least an outline. Don't just suppose what you would say. It's too easy to think you have the perfect response in your mind. Your instructor will grade what you produce, not what you intend.

When you reach the end of the semester, consider taking the Practice Final Exam. Give yourself 90 minutes to answer it and do so under conditions of the kind your instructor imposes—for example, closed book or open book depending on what you'll face. If the question tests on something you didn't cover, you'll know and can skip it. Try to avoid the temptation to peek at the answers until after you've finished. This exercise can give you a better idea of how to allocate your study time before your actual final.

Many people helped me and my much-missed co-author of the first and second editions, David P. Leonard, to reach the point where we could put these questions before you with confidence that you will benefit from them. First to be thanked are the Torts students who over many years challenged me, and David too, to dig deeper into the whys and wherefores of this fascinating subject. Some multiple-choice questions in this book originated in their ideas. Robin Deis, Maria Raneri, and Joanne Tapia worked on the manuscript. Jennifer Fried, Jack Berry, and Veronica Mishkind provided research assistance. Keith Rowley and Heather Dean got the book started. Carolina Academic Press, publisher of the Q&A series since 2016, offered a welcoming and supportive new environment.

ANITA BERNSTEIN
Brooklyn, New York

About the Author

Anita Bernstein, Anita and Stuart Subotnick Professor of Law at Brooklyn Law School, has also taught at Chicago-Kent, Cornell, Emory, Fordham, Iowa, Michigan, New York, and Seton Hall law schools. She served as chair of the Torts & Compensation Systems section of the Association of American Law Schools, and has published extensively on the relation between torts and other subjects including feminist theory, legal history, comparative law, and the sociology of products liability. Her torts books include *Understanding Torts* (with John L. Diamond and Lawrence C. Levine) and *A Products Liability Anthology*.

Zoom Out

When you've finished studying a unit and want to relate it to something else you've reviewed, consider the multiple-choice questions below, which cover intersections between two or more topics.

Q 1: **Battery** without **assault**

Q 2: **Intentional torts** and **defenses to intentional torts**

Q 58: Breach: **Negligence per se** or **res ipsa loquitur?**

Q 65: Breach: Choose **res ipsa loquitur**, the **locality rule**, the **Hand formula**, or **custom.**

Q 71: Breach: What **circumstantial evidence** means

Q 98: Which **plaintiff's conduct defense** applies?

Q 104: Which fits better, **strict liability** or **negligence?**

Q 110: Choose **nuisance, negligence, strict liability,** or **trespass to land.**

Q 117 and 118: Contrast *Rylands v. Fletcher* with the Second Restatement treatment of **strict liability**

Q 122: Choose **negligence, express warranty, strict products liability,** or **absolute liability.**

Q 162: Connect **assault** and **battery** with **intentional infliction of emotional distress.**

Q 170: Which **negligent infliction of emotional distress** topic is not like the others?

Q 172: Does this scenario raise **intentional misrepresentation** or **negligent misrepresentation?**

Q 186: Which issue related to **discounting to present value** is not like the others?

Q 194: Which of the following is not **vicarious liability?**

Q 212: A **medical** operation goes badly. Which claim fits best?

Q 216: Another **medical** operation goes badly. Which claim fits best?

Q 223: Which fits better, **battery** or **negligence?**

Q 224: Which "**advanced torts**" rubric fits best?

Q 228: Distinguish **intentional** from **negligent defamation.**

Q 234: Is the problem with this claim **duty, breach, causation,** or a **plaintiff's conduct defense?**

Multiple-Choice Problems That Use the Same Fact Pattern

Topic	Questions
Duty to rescue	41 and 42
Duty of an **architect**	46 and 47
Office visit to a **doctor** gone wrong	65 and 66
Negligently contaminated oysters: two **breach** questions	68 and 69
Res ipsa loquitur, with variations	72, 73, and 74
Combine **comparative negligence** with **assumption of risk**	89 and 90
Combine **comparative negligence** with **assumption of risk** in a very different setting	91 and 92
Contrast *Rylands v. Fletcher* with the **Second Restatement** treatment of **strict liability**	117 and 118
Products liability, two issues	125 and 126
Products liability that tests engagement with a factual variation	132 and 133
Factual variations in **bystander negligent infliction of emotional distress**	167, 168, and 169
Workers compensation and **respondeat superior**	204 and 205
LSAT-style reasoning by analogy; asks you to ascertain relevance	208 and 209
Contrast outcomes when **a jurisdiction observes the categories of trespasser, licensee, and invitee,** and when it **merges these categories**	213 and 214
Scenario that starts with **duty, then moves to breach,** then onto **assumption of risk**	218, 219, and 220
Assault followed by **self-defense**	221 and 222
Land visitor duty along with **custom** as a **breach** topic	229 and 230
Duty, breach, and two tests for **proximate cause: directness and the risk rule**	234, 235, and 236
Variations on **informed consent**	240, 241, and 242

Questions

Intentional Torts: Battery and Assault

1. Which of the following scenarios illustrates a claim for battery without an accompanying claim for assault?

   (A) Plaintiff Letitia, riding her motorcycle, was hit by motorist Mart and knocked unconscious. Dr. Doolittle, a physician who was walking near the scene of the accident, rendered emergency care to Letitia without her consent.

   (B) Before undergoing general anesthesia, plaintiff Sharon reached an agreement with her surgeon, Dr. Spurgeon, saying that she consented to having her appendix removed. Sharon consented to the removal of no other organs. While she was unconscious, Dr. Spurgeon removed her gallbladder as well.

   (C) Despite being rich, plaintiff Patrick habitually refused to pay his medical bills. His physician, Dr. Proctor, became infuriated by this practice. When Patrick lay on Dr. Proctor's examining table, Dr. Proctor brandished a scalpel and shouted, "I'm going to amputate your left eye!" Patrick was able to deflect Dr. Proctor with the help of a well-aimed judo chop.

   (D) Plaintiff Cankersore recovered slowly from a back injury with the help of opioid painkillers, to which he became addicted. His treating physician, Dr. Milquetoast, obtained sexual gratification from touching Cankersore, along with threatening to withhold prescriptions for the painkillers. Cankersore agreed to Dr. Milquetoast's touchings believing he would be in grave pain if he did not consent.

2. Dr. Ozzzz, an ophthalmologist, undertook to perform laser surgery to correct nearsightedness in the right eye of Boomhauer. Boomhauer and Ozzzz agreed that the operation would occur under general anesthesia, with Boomhauer unconscious. While Boomhauer was unconscious, Ozzzz decided that Boomhauer's left eye, though less nearsighted, should get laser surgery first. Ozzzz operated on the left eye and did not touch Boomhauer's right eye during this surgery, following his policy of always operating on only one eye at a time unless an emergency existed. The surgery went fine and Boomhauer now has excellent vision in his left eye. Boomhauer nevertheless is considering a tort action against Ozzzz.

   Which of the following statements is most accurate?

   (A) Such a claim would be good, because the surgery on the left eye was a wrongful touching.

   (B) Such a claim would be good, because the surgery on the left eye was an unreasonable medical choice.

(C) Such a claim would be bad, because the surgery inflicted no pain on Boomhauer.

(D) Such a claim would be bad, because neither purpose nor substantial certainty is present.

3. Which of the following scenarios best illustrates the tort of battery?

(A) Jorge gets on a train during rush hour and is pushed into Pedro by the oncoming rush of people attempting to get on the train.

(B) Gary fouls off a curveball during a regular season game against the Florida Marlins and the baseball strikes a spectator in the eye.

(C) Lawrence tackles Joe during a football game, causing Joe's leg to break.

(D) At halftime, all the players return to their locker rooms where quarterback Bill, in a rage, throws his helmet at Kevin's head.

4. Spiderman, Superman, the Incredible Hulk, Batman, and Mary Jane are in a bar. Spiderman sees Batman gazing intensely at Mary Jane as she gets up to leave. Spiderman has been upset with Batman for a while, and has had a bad day. Spiderman threatens Batman: "You ever look at Mary Jane like that again, I'll end you." Hearing the threat and thinking he needs to protect Batman, the Hulk pulls back his fist in Spiderman's direction. Spiderman's "spidey sense" tingles, giving him an intuition of what is about to happen, and he ducks Hulk's punch. Superman is struck in the face by the Hulk's fist and is knocked off his chair, breaking his back.

Can the Hulk be liable to Superman for battery?

(A) No, because the Hulk did not intend to punch Superman.

(B) No, because Superman did not see the punch coming and therefore was not placed in apprehension of harmful contact.

(C) Yes, because the Hulk's intent to punch Spiderman transferred to Superman.

(D) No, because Superman consented to the touching by hanging out with the volatile Hulk.

5. Defend the position, endorsed by several courts, that a five-year-old child may be liable for battery.

ANSWER:

6. Which of the following claims for assault is most likely to succeed?

(A) In order to collect on a debt, Jane approaches Narcissa and takes out a gun, which she points at Narcissa's chest, warning Narcissa that if she doesn't give her the money, she knows the consequences.

(B) Ian and Tom are in the park tossing a football back and forth. Ian throws the ball harder than he intended. Tom misses it, causing Meghan, who is sitting on the grass eating her lunch, to fear that the ball will hit her. The football misses her head by about two feet.

(C) Damon, a very large man, was getting annoyed while waiting in line with three friends to get into a nightclub. After waiting in line for more than 20 minutes he approached the bouncer and said, "If you don't let us in within the next 10 minutes, you'll be sorry. I've got four inches and 80 pounds on you."

(D) Jed and Edgar, old friends, are working together at a neighbor's house helping out with the installation of a tile floor. Edgar, wearing headphones, is listening to his iNoize music system while working. Jed, meanwhile, adjusts a temporary light fixture overhead. Jed accidentally loosens the fixture too much and it falls, hitting Edgar on the head. Edgar never hears or sees the fixture approaching him.

7. Elise, a college student, thought it would be funny to blow cigarette smoke in the faces of the staunchest anti-smokers she knew. The flaw in her plan was she was a novice who did not know how to smoke—how to hold a cigarette, what it means to inhale. Elise thought she could start with basic smoking and then move to blowing smoke in rings. She acquired a package of cigarettes and, sitting on her dormitory bed, lit one to practice this new activity. Lighting a cigarette, as Elise knew, violated dormitory rules: Elise thought she was alone and that nobody would know what she was doing. Elise found inhalation difficult and decided to abandon her malevolent plan, but not before her cigarette smoke wafted into a nearby room occupied by Johanna. Johanna experienced coughing and shortness of breath.

Would Johanna have a good battery claim against Elise?

(A) Yes, because Johanna's inhalation of particulate matter constituted harmful contact.

(B) Yes, because Elise intended harmful contact.

(C) No, because the battery was inchoate: Elise failed at the task of smoking.

(D) No, because Elise lacked the intent to inflict harmful contact.

8. On a beautiful summer afternoon, Kerys lay on the grass in Graceland Park, using a smartphone to watch television. Kerys watched a Channel 7 News report that a criminal named Faith, red-haired and more than six feet tall, was on the loose and dangerous. The image of Faith on the phone screen was small and blurry. Looking up, Kerys saw an unusually tall red-haired woman running on the jogging path alongside Kerys, coming close. The woman wore jeans rather than exercise clothes. In a sincere belief that this woman was the missing Faith and running to flee rather than for leisure, Kerys leaped from the grass and grabbed the tall woman's leg, causing her to fall and break her wrist. The woman—only 5'11" as it turned out—proved to be someone other than Faith. Though she wore jeans, she had been innocently running for exercise.

Which of the following statements is most accurate?

(A) Despite having desired a benign result, Kerys had the intent to support a claim of battery by the tall woman.

(B) The tall woman has a claim of battery not only against Kerys but against Channel 7 News.

(C) Under the circumstances related, the contact that Kerys inflicted on the tall woman was not harmful.

(D) Under the circumstances related, the contact that Kerys inflicted on the tall woman was accidental rather than intentional.

9. Siobhan, hating Puckaluck and wishing him dead, had no reason to have confidence in her bomb-building skills. She had flunked high school chemistry. Nevertheless, she found on the Internet a set of directions for making a crude explosive device, and followed them as best as she could to create a letter bomb. She mailed Puckaluck this letter bomb, laughing at herself for attempting such a futile experiment. Against all odds, the letter bomb exploded in Puckaluck's hands, killing him.

    Can Siobhan be liable to Puckaluck's estate for battery?

    (A) Yes, because Siobhan's purpose is sufficient to establish intent, and she fulfilled the other requirements of battery as well.

    (B) Yes, because Siobhan acted with substantial certainty, and she fulfilled the other requirements of battery as well.

    (C) No, because, although Siobhan's actions fulfilled elements of a battery claim, Siobhan lacked substantial certainty that harmful contact would result.

    (D) No, because, although Siobhan's actions fulfilled the elements of a battery claim, causation in fact is absent.

10. Can a defendant be liable for assault if in fact she is not capable of inflicting harmful contact on the plaintiff? Explain.

    ANSWER:

11. Which of the following reflects a change in the *Restatement (Third) of Torts* from the Second Restatement's treatment of assault?

    (A) The Third Restatement adds a requirement of physical harm.

    (B) The Third Restatement permits recovery for a threatened battery in the future, such as domestic violence.

    (C) The Third Restatement substitutes "anticipation" for "apprehension."

    (D) The Third Restatement replaces the subjective standard with an objective standard.

12. Zebbia lives in the residential unit of Upsala Hospital, a large institution that offers treatment for many conditions. Zebbia suffers from dementia associated with Alzheimer's disease. According to her medical chart, Zebbia is capable of aggression against young children because a delusion causes her to believe that children are dangerous. Doctors recommend that Zebbia be kept from children; staffers of Upsala Hospital have done a good job in following this recommendation. Unfortunately, one day eight-year-old Brion, while visiting his grandmother in the residential unit, managed to flee from his parents and run through the corridor where Zebbia resided. After colliding with Brion as she walked out of her room, Zebbia angrily punched Brion several times on the top of Brion's head, causing injury. (Colliding with Zebbia, however, caused no injury to Brion.)

    Brion's parents wish to bring an action on Brion's behalf against Zebbia for battery. Which of the following statements is most accurate?

(A) Regardless of Zebbia's actual intent, Zebbia will be held liable both to encourage her family to take better care of Zebbia and to compensate an innocent plaintiff.

(B) Even if Zebbia's mental illness deprived her of control over her arm and hand when she struck Brion, she will be liable.

(C) Even if Zebbia's mental illness caused her to suffer a delusion that Brion was dangerous to her, she will be liable.

(D) Because Zebbia's mental illness removed any moral fault from her actions, she cannot be held liable for an intentional tort such as battery.

13. For purposes of liability for assault, what is the difference between fear and apprehension?

ANSWER:

14. Sam and Rebecca, teenagers, were playing tag in the park. Rebecca was "it," and within a few minutes caught Sam. Rather than lightly tapping him, however, she hit him in the jaw with her fist, breaking one of his teeth. She had not intended to break a tooth, only to smack him in fun. Sam brings a battery action against Rebecca to recover for his broken tooth.

Which of the following statements is most accurate?

(A) Sam will prevail because Rebecca, in exercising her right of self-defense, exceeded the force reasonably necessary to repel Sam's attack.

(B) Sam will prevail because Rebecca, by striking him so hard, exceeded the scope of his consent to a touching.

(C) Rebecca will prevail because, by agreeing to play the game, Sam consented to touches that would otherwise constitute batteries.

(D) Rebecca will prevail because she did not intend to break Sam's tooth.

Intentional Torts: Invasions into Land, Harm to Property, and False Imprisonment

15. Which of the following invasions would *not* be actionable under the tort of trespass to land?

    (A) Sound engineer/computer programmer Klutzmonkey experiments with digital recordings of harsh-sounding musical instruments, trying to write programming code that captures the range of what these bizarre instruments produce. In these experiments, Klutzmonkey makes unpleasant sounds that disturb his neighbors.

    (B) Motivated by malice, Yodel removes the lids of his filled trash cans and lays the cans on their sides, hoping that the wind will blow his trash onto the lawn of his neighbor. It does.

    (C) Adele, Bittybop, and Chichi own adjacent houses in a chic urban brownstone district. Each lot is only 20 feet wide. Adele and Chichi have been living there for years; Bittybop recently moved into the middle house. In the back of their houses, Adele and Chichi like to toss a football from Adele's lot to Chichi's lot and back. Their ability to throw a football has improved, and ever since Bittybop moved in, the ball has never landed in Bittybop's yard.

    (D) The Historic Pumpkinsburg Association, Inc. (HPA), an incorporated neighborhood association in the town of Pumpkinsburg, asked homeowner Dingaling if he would be willing to hang the HPA flag from his flagpole during Civic Pride Week, running from October 17–24. Dingaling told the HPA staff that he would be willing to fly this flag during this week provided that HPA would assume responsibility for removing the flag on October 25. It is now October 28 and HPA still has done nothing to remove the flag.

16. Describe the types of property that are covered under the tort of conversion and the types of property that are not.

    ANSWER:

17. Olivia Reynolds and John Wharton, law professors, were attending a rural academic retreat. John was staying in a cabin close to the meeting facility. John invited some colleagues to his cabin the night before he was to present an innovative paper he had published. He was especially excited about the presentation because Ramona Mills, of Lasser, Snell & Mills, LLP, a top law firm, would be in attendance to size him up for a job. The job would mean a substantial pay increase for John and it was all but certain he would get it. By 11:00 P.M., everyone

had gone back to their own cabins, except Olivia. Olivia and John wound up getting into a heated argument. She walked out the door and slammed it behind her. John was agitated, but wanted to get a good night's sleep so he retired. The next morning, as John was getting ready to leave his cabin, he saw that the door lock was jammed. Olivia's slamming of the door had caused the door to stick. John began to panic. He went to the phone to call for help but found that the line was dead. Locked in his room, John was not able to give his presentation, and he lost his job opportunity.

If John brings an action against Olivia for false imprisonment, his claim will likely

(A) succeed, because Olivia slammed the door, causing John to be confined overnight.

(B) succeed, because Olivia was negligent and failed to exercise reasonable care when closing the door.

(C) fail, because Olivia did not intend to confine John.

(D) fail, because John's failure to check if the door was jammed vitiates his claim.

18. Agathon decided to invite some friends over one night to drink and discuss the nature of love. During the party his friend, Phaedrus, had a few too many sheepskins of wine and passed out on the sofa. The next day, Phaedrus woke up with a splitting headache, and refused to get off the sofa despite Agathon's assertion that he was no longer welcome. "You don't even own this land, Agathon, your father does," said Phaedrus. (Phaedrus was right about that.) "I'm sure that if he were here he would want me to stay and rest."

If Agathon brings an action against Phaedrus for trespass, the court will likely find that

(A) Phaedrus did not trespass because he was invited.

(B) Phaedrus did not trespass because the landowner's consent is unknown.

(C) Phaedrus committed a trespass because he never received the consent of Agathon's father.

(D) Phaedrus committed a trespass because Agathon revoked his consent.

19. For purposes of trespass law, how does sub-surface entry differ from entry into land by air?

ANSWER:

20. When Potter stopped his car at a red light, Denny ran up to the car, forced open the driver's door, ordered Potter to move over, and got in. He then brandished a knife and ordered Potter to turn over his wallet and get out. Potter refused, and started screaming for help. Denny then, with Potter in the passenger seat, took off. Potter remained in the car even when Denny had to stop several times for traffic lights. Finally, Denny abandoned the car in a remote location with Potter still inside.

If Potter brings an action against Denny for false imprisonment, which of the following statements is correct?

(A) Potter has a strong false imprisonment case.

(B) Potter's case is weak because he chose to remain in the car rather than follow Denny's order to turn over the wallet.

(C) Potter's case is weak because the more appropriate action is for assault.

(D) Potter's case will fail because the more appropriate action is for conversion.

21. Store detective Escamillo observes Angie slip five small objects from a display shelf into her large leather purse. Angie is about to walk out the store door into a crowded parking lot. Escamillo wishes to protect the store's property but does not want to be liable, or make his employer liable, for the tort of false imprisonment.

How should Escamillo proceed?

ANSWER:

22. Rhonda and Remus, teenage hikers, came upon a small abandoned barn. While Rhonda explored the interior of the barn, climbing into a hayloft, Remus explored the exterior. He noticed that a horizontal two-by-four slab of wood could seal the only door to the barn from the outside, preventing anyone inside the barn from exiting. Moving this slab into place, Remus locked Rhonda into the barn and called good-bye to her, ignoring her cries for help and pleas for release. Hoping to gain the attention of a potential rescuer, Rhonda leaned into a crack in the barn wall, calling out for help. About a half hour after Remus walked away, passerby Pia heard Rhonda's cries, but decided to ignore them.

An action by Rhonda against Pia for false imprisonment should fail because

(A) Pia did not confine Rhonda.

(B) Remus is the proper defendant for a claim of false imprisonment.

(C) Rhonda entered the barn voluntarily.

(D) Rhonda was a trespasser.

23. During a commercial flight, one of the plane's three engines stopped working. The captain, disclosing this news over the loudspeaker, assured the passengers that the plane could fly safely on its remaining engines and said the plane would continue to its scheduled destination. One of the passengers, Frank, was not reassured, and demanded that the plane land at the first available airport. The captain refused, even though the plane's flight path would take it close to another airport. The plane continued on course and landed on time one hour later at its scheduled destination. Frank brings an action against the airline for false imprisonment.

Of the following, which constitutes the airline's strongest argument?

(A) Because the plane landed on time at its original destination, there was no confinement.

(B) Because Frank was the only passenger who wanted to land earlier, to have done so would have falsely imprisoned all the other passengers by taking them where they did not want to go.

(C) Frank's confinement was not unlawful.

(D) Frank was not physically harmed by the confinement.

24. Marylebone Island, a small, rustic bit of land connected to a mainland town only by a rickety bridge, attracts occasional explorers. Hurley was fond of driving her 15-year-old automobile over the bridge and strolling around the island. Her enemy, Hommyside, decided to kill her by connecting a bomb to her automobile ignition while Hurley was away exploring the island. Hommyside's plan was that, on her return, Hurley would turn the ignition key and the bomb would go off, killing her. The plan didn't work. Between the time that Hommyside wired the explosive and Hurley's return to her car, a severe storm pounded Marylebone Island. Because of the age of the car, the hood was not watertight. Rainwater got under the hood, ruining Hommyside's rewiring. When Hurley attempted to start her car, the wet, exposed ignition wires would not send current to the engine and the car simply failed to start, trapping Hurley on Marylebone Island for several hours.

Has Hommyside's conduct fulfilled a prima facie case for false imprisonment?

(A) Yes, because Hommyside's rewiring created a physical barrier that confined Hurley to Marylebone Island.

(B) Yes, under transferred intent: Hommyside intended to commit a battery and the consequences of false imprisonment resulted.

(C) No, because Hommyside intended harmful bodily contact, not unlawful confinement.

(D) No, because Hurley voluntarily entered the island and assumed the risk of automobile failure.

25. Which of the following is *not* an example of a behavior that can constitute conversion?

(A) Wrongful transfer

(B) Negligent alteration

(C) Theft

(D) Bona fide purchase of stolen goods

26. Sheldon, a graduate student studying theoretical physics, used an old laptop computer with a laughably archaic operating system. Despite some teasing from his social circle, he was content with this laptop. His engineer friend Howard could not imagine how anyone could tolerate such low speed, poor screen resolution, and frequent system failures. One Wednesday, when Howard knew Sheldon was at his weekly comic book store visit, Howard went to Sheldon's apartment. Howard told Sheldon's roommate Leonard that he had come to upgrade Sheldon's laptop. "About time," said Leonard, admitting Howard to the room. Howard remained there, installing the new system. He had it ready to go by the time Sheldon returned from the comic book store. Much to Howard's disappointment, Sheldon expressed displeasure about Howard's behavior. It turned out that Sheldon had planned to enter his laptop in a competition called "The World's Greatest Clunker," which featured prizes in various categories for archaic computers. Sheldon can prove that he probably would have won.

Does Sheldon have a tort claim against Howard?

(A) No, because any potential claim is eliminated by Leonard's consent.

(B) No, because Sheldon experienced only benefit, and no detriment, from Howard's behavior.

(C) Yes, for trespass to chattels, if Howard's upgrade lowered the value of the laptop in the "World's Greatest Clunker" competition.

(D) Yes, for trespass to land, if Sheldon can establish that Leonard did not have authority to approve entry to the dormitory room for this purpose.

27. At 3:50 A.M., the night manager of the Empire Hotel got a call from the police informing her that Pushkin, a hotel guest, was a terrorist. The caller asked the manager to detain Pushkin for a few hours until the police could arrange a reliable and safe way to arrest him. The manager agreed. From the late hour, the manager assumed that Pushkin was in the room. She then ordered two custodians to move an enormous bureau against what she believed was Pushkin's door. The custodian complied. Two hours later, she discovered that she had barred the door to Peter's room instead of Pushkin's. Peter slept through the whole thing, but when he found out that he'd been barricaded in his room, he brought an action against the Empire Hotel for false imprisonment.

Which of the following statements is correct?

(A) Peter will prevail because he was actually confined.

(B) Peter will prevail if his distress on learning of his prior confinement was severe.

(C) Peter will lose because he was unaware of the confinement until later, and he suffered no physical harm as a result of his confinement.

(D) Peter will lose because the manager did not intend to confine him.

28. "Whoever owns the soil, it is theirs all the way up to Heaven and down to the depths," according to a medieval legal maxim. (In Latin: *Cujus est solum, ejus est usque ad coelum et ad inferos.*) Why did trespass doctrine move away from allowing land possessors to bring a claim for trespass to land when entries occur high above the surface?

ANSWER:

29. Grudgepudge, a Web designer, accepted an offer from Sparky to visit Sparky's home office. The purpose of this meeting was for Sparky to consider hiring Grudgepudge to design a new website for Sparky's business. Grudgepudge brought his laptop computer to the meeting and demonstrated some interactive features of websites that Grudgepudge had designed. About an hour into the meeting, Grudgepudge excused himself to make several business calls to other clients of his. When he returned to Sparky's office, Sparky smirked, "Soooo — where's your laptop, buddy?" Grudgepudge looked around; it was not in sight. Sparky had hidden the laptop somewhere in his office while Grudgepudge was away. Grudgepudge demanded to know why Sparky had hidden the laptop, but Sparky refused to answer. Grudgepudge remained at Sparky's office for another two hours, attempting to regain his laptop.

An action by Grudgepudge against Sparky for false imprisonment should

(A) fail, because Sparky had a privilege to claim temporary possession of Grudgepudge's laptop.

(B) fail, because Sparky did not confine Grudgepudge.

(C) succeed, because Sparky wrongfully withheld Grudgepudge's property and departing from Sparky's office would have meant leaving the laptop behind.

(D) succeed, because Sparky had no privilege to claim temporary possession of Grudgepudge's property and Grudgepudge felt reasonable compulsion to remain.

Defenses to Intentional Torts

30. Which of the following scenarios illustrates valid and express consent to an act that would otherwise be actionable as an intentional tort?

   (A) Stage magician Gethsemane asks the audience for a volunteer to lie down inside a dark wooden coffin and have the lid lowered. Volunteer Victor gets into the coffin and leaps out instantly, having discovered that the bottom of the coffin is lined with spikes. Victor brings an action against Gethsemane for battery.

   (B) Bodybuilder Jean, proud of her abdominal muscles, invites Ralph to swing back and punch her with all his might. Ralph does so. Jean is for the most part unharmed, although the punch leaves her out of breath and a little sore for a few minutes. Jean brings an action against Ralph for battery.

   (C) Nurse Nottingham comes to office worker Dilbert's cubicle and asks Dilbert if he wants to be vaccinated against influenza. Dilbert, wearing a T-shirt and talking on the phone, raises his left arm. Nottingham infers that Dilbert has consented, and injects him. It turns out that Dilbert did not want to be vaccinated. Dilbert brings an action against Nottingham for battery.

   (D) Easley is a commercial cultivator of roses. A path through some of his plants, on his property, has become a kind of informal shortcut for children headed from middle school to a soccer field. Easley has long been aware of this entry into his land, and never stopped the children from taking this shortcut. Easley now brings an action against the children for trespass to land.

31. Tort law has long taken an interest in "spring guns" and similar devices that protect unoccupied property by setting up a tripwire that an intruder sets off by crossing some threshold. By rigging the wire to a firearm, the property owner can arrange for the intruder to be shot before he or she can enter. Tort law generally frowns on this self-help measure. Suppose no liability rules exist on the subject. For this question you are to write your own doctrine.

   In which of the following settings would a spring-gun trap for intruders make the most sense, suggesting a relatively good case for no liability to intruders who get injured while invading?

   (A) A remote, unoccupied building containing valuable physical items.

   (B) A home with vulnerable family members living inside.

   (C) A commercial warehouse amenable to private patrols by security personnel.

   (D) An abandoned house that drug users have taken over for sales and shelter.

32. If consent to what would otherwise be an intentional tort is obtained by the defendant's fraud, is the consent invalid, restoring the prima facie case for an intentional tort and making the defendant liable? Explain.

    ANSWER:

33. One rainy evening, Norris, who was recovering from a severe heart attack, went to the local multiplex to see *Screech 2*, a scary movie. During a particularly tense moment, when the slasher was stalking one of his young victims in a dark house, Ivanka, who was sitting behind Norris, tapped Norris's shoulder to request that he move his head out of her sight line. Believing he was being attacked, Norris reached into his pocket, withdrew a switchblade, and swung it behind him, slashing Ivanka's arm.

    If Ivanka brings an action against Norris for battery, which of the following arguments offers Norris a reasonable chance of avoiding liability?

    (A) If Norris reasonably believed Ivanka was attacking him, he acted in justifiable self-defense.

    (B) Because of his state of mind, Norris was afflicted by temporary insanity, and cannot be held liable.

    (C) Because Norris's reaction to Ivanka's touch was not volitional, there was no "act," and Norris cannot be held liable.

    (D) Because Norris's heart attack deprived him of the ability to control his movements, he cannot be held liable.

34. Which of the following statements best distinguishes public necessity from private necessity?

    (A) Public necessity entitles a plaintiff to just compensation as provided by the Fifth Amendment to the U.S. Constitution; private necessity does not.

    (B) Public necessity is a qualified privilege; private necessity is an absolute privilege

    (C) Public necessity arises when harm to a large number of people is threatened; private necessity is a defense offered on behalf of individuals or families

    (D) Public necessity permits the destruction of human life; private necessity does not.

35. Late one night, a sneak thief named Rugrat broke a window to enter the home of Joplin, a bachelor who lived alone. Rugrat used a chisel to gain entry. Holding the chisel, Rugrat began roaming through Joplin's dark house, hoping to spot a wallet or a purse in easy view. Joplin was awakened by the noise and, after retrieving a pistol he kept under his bed, walked to the door of his bedroom. Joplin saw Rugrat just as a beam of light from the street illuminated the chisel. Joplin thought the chisel was a handgun and promptly shot Rugrat in the chest, injuring Rugrat severely.

    In a battery action by Rugrat against Joplin, Joplin ought to prevail because

(A) although Joplin had a duty to retreat before injuring Rugrat preemptively, Joplin fulfilled this duty by remaining inside his bedroom.

(B) Joplin had no duty to retreat and reasonably believed that Rugrat threatened his life.

(C) Joplin did not have the mental state to sustain a prima facie claim of battery by Rugrat.

(D) Rugrat's status on the land was that of a criminal trespasser.

36. Horace owns a lively, friendly dog named Tangyfangy. Between the suburban homes of Horace and Dr. Yertle stands a wire mesh fence. Over the years, the fence, owned by Dr. Yertle, deteriorated. It now has a few holes.

One morning, Tangyfangy, romping in the yard with Horace, managed to squeeze through a hole in the fence and run onto Dr. Yertle's property. Horace had noticed the hole but had believed it to be too small for Tangyfangy to pass through. Horace realized it was likely that Tangyfangy would harm Dr. Yertle's elaborate flower garden. He called out for Dr. Yertle but heard nothing. Hurrying to bring Tangyfangy home, Horace enlarged the fence hole with a pair of garden shears he had at hand so that he could get through. He reclaimed Tangyfangy before Tangyfangy could do any harm to the garden.

Dr. Yertle, who received an estimate from a fence-maker of what the repair would cost, has asked you to give advice about a possible action for trespass against Horace. You will explain the relevant law of trespass. Which of the following observations that you might make to Dr. Yertle is most correct?

(A) Horace's conduct fulfilled the prima facie elements of trespass to land, and Horace is liable for harm to the fence and harm to the garden.

(B) Horace's conduct fulfilled the prima facie elements of trespass to land, and Horace has no privilege of necessity.

(C) Horace's conduct fulfilled the prima facie elements of trespass to land, but Horace had a privilege to enter. He will be required to pay for his enlarging the hole in the fence.

(D) Horace's conduct did not fulfill the prima facie elements of trespass because Horace entered Dr. Yertle's land under the privilege of necessity.

37. In the tort action of *Omar v. Stringer*, Omar seeks compensation for the destruction of his dog, a large Great Dane/Labrador mix named McNulty. Stringer does not deny that he shot McNulty to death with a rifle. He says he "had no choice," having caught McNulty on his property when McNulty had just killed three chickens in Stringer's large coop and was attacking a fourth. Before he shot McNulty, Stringer had suspected that this dog had killed other chickens of his in the past, but he had never before caught McNulty in the act.

Which of the following statements, if correct, relates most closely to Stringer's defense?

(A) The chickens were more valuable than McNulty, in dollar terms.

(B) McNulty had a reputation for aggression.

(C) Stringer had previously asked Omar to restrain McNulty and Omar refused the request.

(D) McNulty was innocent, so to speak, in the earlier chicken-killings; Stringer's other chickens had been killed by coyotes.

38. Following a verbal dispute about the relative merits of two professional volleyball teams, Rupert and Hannah engaged in a fistfight in an alleyway behind a bar. They pounded at each other until the police arrived. The police arrested them both for assault and disturbance of the peace. Both were injured by the other's blows.

Discuss their tort claims with reference to battery and consent.

ANSWER:

39. Imagine the following split-second scenario as if you had time to weigh all your options: You are in a cocktail lounge and you see a person at the crowded bar slipping a vial of some liquid into another person's drink, while the person about to drink is not looking. The person about to drink lifts her cocktail glass by the stem and opens her mouth, preparing to drink.

Does tort doctrine permit you to use force, or any kind of physical contact, to defend the drinker before she drinks the adulterated cocktail? If so, consider what you could do that would be both privileged and effective, and also state which tort(s) you could be accused of committing.

ANSWER:

40. In each of the following scenarios, suppose that the individual whose name begins the scenario is the plaintiff in a battery action. In which of them would the principle of consent implied by law suggest that the defendant ought to prevail?

(A) Axel, playing football for his high school team, was tackled by opposing lineman Tacky and suffered injury.

(B) Belinda's ophthalmologist asked her, during a routine eye examination, whether she would be willing to have the thickness of her cornea measured. This measure had no therapeutic benefit to Belinda; the ophthalmologist was measuring the corneas of all patients who came into the office because she hoped to correlate corneal thickness with other variables for a research study. Belinda agreed to the measuring. Belinda now believes that the measuring injured her eye.

(C) Currey gave consent for a hernia operation to Dr. Spongebath, a surgeon. Currey gave no other express consent. Dr. Spongebath not only operated on Currey's hernia but also removed Currey's gallbladder.

(D) Dauphine became unconscious while riding an escalator and collapsed into the steps. She appeared not to be breathing and had only a faint pulse when a physician's assistant, Pallowag, standing on the escalator nearby, saw her collapse. Pallowag carried Dauphine off the escalator and applied mouth-to-mouth resuscitation.

Negligence: The Duty of Care

41. Law school buddies Adam and Eve scaled a construction fence intending to play a prank by spray-painting one of the construction vehicles. While on the construction site, Adam fell and hit the ground hard, knocking himself out. Seeing this, Eve ran away because she didn't want to be caught. She did not report the accident, and Adam was not discovered until the next morning, when a construction worker found him on the ground. By that time, Adam had suffered additional injury from exposure. Adam has brought an action against Eve for negligence, claiming that she should have assisted him.

    Which of the following constitutes Adam's strongest argument for liability?

    (A) Eve's going to the scene with Adam was an act of misfeasance for which she should be held liable.

    (B) As a joint venturer, Eve is vicariously liable for the harm Adam suffered.

    (C) Eve is in a special relationship with Adam as a result of their joint venture, imposing on her an obligation to take affirmative steps to assist Adam.

    (D) Because the harm to Adam was the direct and proximate result of Eve's failure to assist him, Eve is liable.

42. Same facts as above. Sara, the construction worker who found Adam early in the morning, knew Adam was in need of medical care. Sara had arrived at the site before anybody else. She carefully placed Adam in the passenger seat of her pickup truck and headed for the nearest hospital. On the way, the pickup ran out of gas—not an uncommon experience for Sara, who had a limited budget for pickup-truck expenses. Sara grabbed an empty gas can from the vehicle's bed, ran to a gas station, filled the can, and returned as quickly as she could, but the delay cost Adam more blood and led to further physical injury.

    If Adam brings a negligence action against Sara, which of the following statements is most likely correct?

    (A) Because Sara undertook to assist Adam, she was obligated to complete her rescue effort successfully. Her failure to do so will make her liable.

    (B) Because Sara undertook to assist Adam, she was obligated to exercise reasonable care in the effort. If it was unreasonable to attempt to take Adam to the hospital in the pickup, Sara will be held liable for negligence.

    (C) Because Sara undertook to assist Adam, she was obligated to exercise reasonable care in the effort. Sara was acting in an emergency situation, however, and cannot be held liable even though her pickup ran out of gas on the way to the hospital.

(D) Because Sara did not place Adam in his perilous position and had no special relationship with Adam, statutes in most jurisdictions provide that she will not be liable unless she intentionally harmed Adam during her rescue effort.

43. Jojo, a graduate student halfway to an MBA in finance, frequently gave financial advice to his friends free of charge. The advice usually served his friends well. One startup business called Hooya caught Jojo's eye: Jojo thought Hooya would go public, thereby making money for investors. Jojo bought shares of Hooya and suggested that his girlfriend Alma, a physician's assistant, do so. Alma took this advice and invested. Hooya went out of business without ever going public. Jojo himself lost $10,000 on Hooya; Alma, the poorer of the two, feels worse about her loss of $2,500 and is thinking of litigation against Jojo. Assume that reasonable care by Jojo would have resulted in no investment in Hooya by either Alma or Jojo.

Is the duty element of a negligence claim against Jojo present under these facts?

(A) No, because in general, no duty of care is owed to avoid the risk of consequential economic loss to another.

(B) No, because Jojo, still a student, was not yet a professional financial adviser and cannot be held to a professional standard of care.

(C) Yes, because Alma relied on Jojo's superior knowledge about finances.

(D) Yes, because an undertaking is present, even though in general no duty of care is owed to avoid the risk of consequential economic loss.

44. Suppose negligence law were to impose a general duty to exercise reasonable care to avoid causing harm, through both affirmative conduct and failure to act. Why might it be unwise to impose this general duty, eliminating what are now sometimes called "no-duty rules"?

ANSWER:

45. You practice law in a state that has retained the common law categories of trespasser, licensee, and invitee; you have been approached by Natalia, a prospective client. Natalia wishes you to consider bringing a personal injury action on her behalf against Marie. Natalia tells you that Marie invited her to a party at Marie's home. Natalia did not want to go but because she, Natalia, had been thinking of asking Marie to invest in Natalia's start-up business, Natalia "felt [she] had no choice." Natalia suffered a head injury when she fell from a tree branch on Marie's property. Natalia had climbed the tree on a dare.

The main weakness in the duty element of a negligence claim by Natalia against Marie is

(A) Natalia's status as a trespasser.

(B) Natalia's status as a licensee: the danger of climbing onto the tree branch was not hidden.

(C) Natalia's status as a licensee: Marie acted with reasonable care.

(D) Natalia's status as an invitee: although Natalia was owed reasonable care, nothing in the facts indicates breach by Marie.

46. Archie, a licensed and qualified architect, designed a traditional theater with backstage entrances and a pit below for musicians. Unfortunately, in his plans he provided for joists that were not wide enough to support the standard, normal weight placed on a stage floor. The builders followed Archie's plans exactly. The stage floor remained intact for a year. It fell down unexpectedly one evening when the local community was using the stage to hold school board elections. At the time of the collapse, the total weight of persons and objects on the stage was about 1500 pounds, evenly distributed. Two residents of the neighborhood, waiting in line on stage to reach the voting machine, were injured when the floor collapsed and dropped them into the pit. They brought a negligence action against Archie.

    Did Archie owe these plaintiffs a duty of care?

    (A) Yes, because they were present on the stage for a lawful public purpose.

    (B) Yes, because physical injury to them as visitors based on Archie's misfeasance was foreseeable.

    (C) No, because Archie's duty arose under a contract between him and the builders of the theater.

    (D) No, because they were not actors, stagehands, or other persons foreseeably present on a performance stage.

47. Same facts as above. Suppose the court decided to review the contract between Archie and the developers of the theater to help determine the existence and scope of Archie's duty. Which of the following possible provisions in the contract would be most helpful to Archie's side of the dispute?

    (A) *Statement of purpose*: a provision to design a stage sufficient to support up to 800 evenly distributed pounds of weight on it.

    (B) *Indemnity*: a promise by the builders to share in any malpractice liability that Archie might face.

    (C) *Representations*: an assurance by Archie that he holds a license to practice architecture in the jurisdiction.

    (D) *Materials*: an assurance by the builders that they would obtain materials of suitable quality to carry out Archie's design.

48. Which of the following points is *not* a policy argument in support of the general rule that persons have no duty of care with respect to pure economic loss?

    (A) This duty is harder to administer than one relating to physical damage because financial connections can extend almost infinitely.

    (B) Recognizing this duty would permit liability far out of proportion to the breach.

    (C) In comparison to physical damage, pure economic loss is relatively unlikely to generate social loss.

    (D) Persons who suffer pure economic loss are relatively likely to share responsibility for their own injury.

49. Courts sometimes hold that a defendant owes no duty to an "unforeseeable plaintiff." What is an unforeseeable plaintiff?

ANSWER:

50. One Sunday, Hank was home with his son Bobby, age 10. Bobby was bored, so Hank decided to take him to Arlene's, a hardware store, where Hank planned to shop for a new drill. While Hank was looking over the selection of drills, Bobby wandered away into the power saw aisle. Bobby was touching a power saw hanging on a hook when the hook gave way and the saw fell, its blade cutting Bobby's arm. As it happens, the hook was loose. Bobby brings an action against Arlene's for negligence. Assume the jurisdiction follows the common law rule about plaintiffs as entrants to land. Arlene's moves for summary judgment.

Which of the following statements is most likely correct?

(A) Because Bobby was not in Arlene's for the purpose of purchasing anything, he will be classified as a trespasser. Because Arlene's only owed Bobby a duty to refrain from willful and wanton misconduct, and it is clear that no such conduct occurred, the court will grant Arlene's motion for summary judgment.

(B) Even though Bobby was not in Arlene's to purchase anything, he will be classified as an invitee to whom the store owes a duty of reasonable care. The court will deny Arlene's motion for summary judgment.

(C) Bobby's status in Arlene's was that of a licensee. Because Arlene's only owed Bobby a duty to warn of hidden dangers of which it was aware, and because there is no evidence that Arlene's knew the hook was loose, the court will grant Arlene's motion for summary judgment.

(D) Regardless of Bobby's status, the court will grant Arlene's motion for summary judgment because Hank's negligence in allowing Bobby to wander away superseded any potential liability of Arlene's.

51. Officer Krumpke went to Willie's home to investigate a claim that someone had broken into a residence. When the person who answered the door called for Willie, Willie came downstairs. As soon as he saw the uniformed Officer Krumpke, however, Willie ran back up the stairs. Krumpke could tell that the stairway was dangerous because of rotting wood, but pursued Willie, trying to avoid the worst spots. Unfortunately, Krumpke fell through one of the stairs and sustained a serious injury.

If Krumpke brings an action against Willie for negligence, which of the following statements is most accurate?

(A) Because Officer Krumpke was at Willie's home on police business and suffered an injury as a result of Willie's negligent maintenance of the stairway, Krumpke will recover.

(B) Because Officer Krumpke suffered an injury at Willie's home while conducting police business, he will not recover.

(C) Because Willie did not have an opportunity to warn Officer Krumpke of the dangerous condition of the stairs, Willie did not breach a duty of care, and Officer Krumpke cannot recover.

(D) Because Officer Krumpke failed to exercise reasonable care for his own safety, his recovery will be reduced.

52. On a commercial airline flight, things were going fine until the captain accidentally played for the passengers a pre-recorded announcement, an audio clip from a feature film that a friend had sent him, stating that the plane was about to crash into the sea. There was no actual emergency and after a short time, the captain realized the mistake and apologized over the sound system for the false alarm. Daphne, an elderly passenger, suffered a serious anxiety attack as a result of the erroneous announcement, and a flight attendant made an announcement asking whether a physician was on the plane. Dr. Gloucester, a physician, was there, but did not look up from his laptop and said nothing.

If Daphne brings an action against Dr. Gloucester for negligence, which of the following statements is most likely correct?

(A) Because Dr. Gloucester had the ability to assist, his failure to do so constituted actionable negligence.

(B) Because all the passengers were in a special relationship with one another, those with medical expertise had a duty to assist. Dr. Gloucester's failure to assist constituted actionable negligence.

(C) Because the passengers were in a special relationship with one another, those with medical expertise had a duty to assist. If, by assisting, Dr. Gloucester could have prevented some of the harm Daphne suffered, his failure to assist constituted actionable negligence.

(D) Dr. Gloucester will not be held liable for failing to assist.

53. In *Hart v. Cohle*, plaintiffs claim that Yvette Cohle negligently recommended her 17-year-old son, "True Detective," to the Harts, a married couple, when they were looking for a babysitter for their six-year-old twins. True Detective attacked both children, causing them injury. The twins are the named plaintiffs; the Hart parents, who are managing this litigation, wish to attribute responsibility to Cohle because True Detective has no assets and cannot pay damages or a settlement.

Did Cohle owe a duty of care to the Hart twins? Apply the Second Restatement.

(A) No. The claim is one of failure to rescue, a duty that negligence law does not impose.

(B) Yes. Reasonable care on Cohle's part would have reduced the risk of the injury that occurred.

(C) Possibly. Plaintiffs would have to show that Cohle had knowledge of True Detective's dangerousness and the ability to restrain him.

(D) Possibly. Plaintiffs would have to show an undertaking between Cohle and the Hart parents.

54. A driver negligently crashes her vehicle into one driven by a woman who is 32 weeks pregnant. The pregnant woman is slightly injured and the fetus suffers a more severe head injury. The fetus continues to develop and emerges into the world as a relatively healthy infant. Its parents wish to bring a lawsuit on behalf of the infant against the driver. Assume that the jurisdiction permits abortions for any reason through 36 weeks of pregnancy. If the parents bring this action, what argument about no duty could the driver raise, and on what basis would it fail?

ANSWER:

Negligence: Breach of Duty

55. In which of the following situations does the plaintiff have the strongest claim for res ipsa loquitur?

    (A) Danielle falls down the stairs in a restaurant after tripping over a wineglass left on the second step. She brings a negligence action against the restaurant.

    (B) Getting ready to drive to work one morning, Goop discovers a dent in his car. He brings a negligence action against his neighbor Patch, noting that Patch drives a maroon car and Goop found maroon paint in the dent.

    (C) While on a yacht during a fishing vacation, Mike falls overboard while leaning on a railing that gives way. He brings a negligence action against the fishing company.

    (D) Melissa and Murray go for a dinner date to an exotic restaurant where they eat food served in platters. The next day Melissa exhibits signs of severe food poisoning. She and Murray had eaten the same food, but Murray experiences no similar symptoms. Melissa brings an action for negligence against the restaurant.

56. When a child is a defendant in a negligence action, to what standard of care is the child held?

    ANSWER:

57. Rob operates Rob's Batting Practice (RBP), a business catering to children ages 8–14. Parents bring kids to RBP for about 45 minutes of being pitched to by a mechanical ball-thrower. Batted balls seldom escape the fenced space, but occasionally a ball will clear the fence around RBP and land outside. Concerned about liability should a ball hit someone or something, Rob is thinking of making the fence around RBP higher, but he knows that doing so will cost money.

    Which statement best describes the Hand Formula variables of this scenario?

    (A) *B* is the cost to Rob of raising the height of the fence around RBP, and *PL* is the cost of leaving the fence at its present height.

    (B) *B* is the cost to Rob of raising the height of the fence around RBP, and *PL* is the expected cost of injury that would be prevented by this action.

    (C) *B* is the likelihood that a batted ball will escape the RBP grounds, and *PL* is the expected cost of injury to someone or something outside.

(D) *B* is the burden of liability for Rob and RBP when a ball escapes, and *PL* is the cost, imposed on persons and property-holders outside, to take precautions in anticipation of this risk.

58. To reduce the risk of fire, by city ordinance the town of Elysium regulates the disposal of cigarette debris. Earl, a smoker, lives on the fifth floor of a condo building. He is in the habit of throwing still-lit cigarettes off his balcony, an act prohibited by the ordinance. His neighbor, Vanessa, who lives directly below him on the fourth floor, often finds his cigarette butts on her balcony. Vanessa has asked Earl repeatedly to stop tossing this debris. On one particularly windy evening Earl tossed one of his lit cigarettes off his balcony. This time the cigarette landed on Vanessa's balcony and fell where Vanessa had piled bags of trash from a party the prior evening. Vanessa would have brought the bags downstairs for disposal but the condo's maintenance staff was off that day, all the bins were full, and Vanessa didn't want to keep her garbage indoors because it smelled bad. Earl's cigarette ignited grease on one of the bags and started a fire that caused damage to Vanessa's condo.

If Vanessa brings a negligence claim against Earl, her action will most likely

(A) fail, because the wind that directed the cigarette onto Vanessa's balcony causing the fire originated in nature.

(B) fail, because Vanessa knew about Earl's habit of tossing his cigarettes onto her balcony and should have known better than to have kept trash on her balcony.

(C) succeed, because Earl's violation of the statute regulating cigarette disposal constituted negligence per se.

(D) succeed, under res ipsa loquitur.

59. What is the general standard of care for a physician in the practice of medicine?

ANSWER:

60. A state statute prohibits the wearing of headphones by any individual while riding a bicycle or motorcycle. Shimen, a bicycle messenger, generally obeys this law but finds it very burdensome, and one day he lapsed: While a song played loudly through his iMoozik headphones, Shimen could not hear a stranger yell "Look out!" His bicycle hit Phreddie, a homeless person sleeping near the sidewalk, whom Shimen hadn't seen. But for the headphones and the music playing, Shimen would have heard "Look out!" and had time to brake or steer away safely. Phreddie brings an action against Shimen for negligence. In a jurisdiction that follows the majority approach to negligence per se, which of the following statements is most accurate?

(A) Because Shimen violated a statute designed to protect a class of persons including Phreddie from the kind of harm that occurred in this case, Shimen was negligent.

(B) Because Shimen's violation of the statute is not sufficiently connected with the injury that occurred, Shimen's violation of the statute does not make him negligent.

(C) Because Shimen violated a statute designed to protect a class of persons including Phreddie from the kind of harm that occurred in this case, the jury will be permitted to take into account his violation in determining whether he breached his duty of care.

(D) Because safety is only one purpose of the headphone statute, this statute cannot of itself establish duty and breach by Shimen.

61. When Yarble was operating his motorboat at a dangerously fast speed, he found himself about to collide with another motorboat, operated by Mizuoko. Yarble did not have enough time to stop and his motorboat collided with Mizuoko's boat. Mizuoko brought an action against Yarble for personal injuries. Yarble argued that, under the emergency doctrine, he did not have enough time to prevent the collision, and so should not be liable.

Explain why Yarble's argument should fail.

ANSWER:

62. Ledger brought an action for negligence against Jetskidder Waterski Club, Inc., owner of an artificial lake that included a marina and a waterskiing facility. A beginner at waterskiing, Ledger suffered a severe spinal injury when he fell off his skis and hit his head on the bottom of the shallow lake. Ledger claimed that Jetskidder was negligent for having posted a sign at the lake's edge reading DEEP WATER. He said that if Jetskidder had not claimed that the water was deep and therefore safe to fall into, he would not have skied in that area. The lake was in fact only three feet deep. The DEEP WATER sign was posted in error; Jetskidder had prepared the sign in anticipation of building a channel for the benefit of boat traffic coming to its dock. An employee had been experimenting with locations for the sign and forgotten to remove it.

Ledger's claim that Jetskidder breached its duty of care to him is

(A) valid, because a reasonable person in Jetskidder's position should have known that the sign gave a false message of water depth that could induce someone to ski in the area.

(B) valid, because a lake depth of three feet is not reasonably safe for the activity of waterskiing that Jetskidder offered.

(C) not valid, because posting a sign about DEEP WATER reduces the risk of drowning, and drowning is more foreseeable than the injury Ledger suffered.

(D) not valid, because a lake depth of three feet is reasonably safe for the activity of waterskiing that Jetskidder offered.

63. A minority of jurisdictions hold that a defendant's violation of a relevant statute is not negligence per se, but merely evidence of negligence. Explain how this minority approach differs from the majority "negligence per se" approach.

ANSWER:

64. Which of the following 15-year-old individuals who injured a plaintiff named Moolalala through arguably negligent conduct is most likely to be held to the adult reasonable person standard of care, rather than a child standard?

    (A) Dennis: Without having good control of the wheel he drove a snowmobile into Moolalala, knocking her down.

    (B) Dee: He mishandled a rifle while hunting, causing it to discharge and fire a bullet into Moolalala's leg.

    (C) Mac: He built a campfire to roast marshmallows and then was unable to put it out; the fire burned Moolalala's property.

    (D) Charlie: Aware that the brakes on his bicycle had not been working well, he nevertheless bicycled down a steep hill and collided into Moolalala.

65. Claudia now regrets having seen Dr. Seuss for a gynecological checkup, but she had few doctors to choose from in her remote and low-income town. When Claudia told Dr. Seuss that she wanted oral contraception, Dr. Seuss wrote her a prescription for Estro-a-Gogo, a drug first patented in 1970, early in the Pill era. Estro-a-Gogo is today almost never used for birth control because its hormone quantities exceed what is considered safe and effective for this purpose. Taking Estro-a-Gogo made Claudia ill. Dr. Seuss acknowledged that the choice of Estro-a-Gogo was poor in hindsight, adding by way of explanation, "I'm just a country doc, I don't look at the Internet, I don't go to them fancy meetings."

    The issue raised by the remark of Dr. Seuss is

    (A) res ipsa loquitur.

    (B) the locality rule versus the national standard.

    (C) the Hand formula.

    (D) custom as either probative or dispositive.

66. Same office visit as above, but with no prescription. Dr. Seuss does not know much about today's oral contraceptives, but is well aware of the Pap smear, a diagnostic test commonly administered in gynecological checkups that looks for precursors to, and early signs of, cervical cancer. At the office visit, Dr. Seuss asked Claudia, "Do you want a Pap smear?" Claudia had had one before but forgotten what it was for. Thinking it would save time to decline something she didn't know much about, Claudia said no. "Okay," said Dr. Seuss, and concluded the examination, omitting this test.

    If Claudia should turn out to have had cervical cancer at the time of this office visit—at an early enough stage that it could have been treated but also a late enough stage that the Pap smear would have detected it—and this cervical cancer caused her an injury that could have been prevented by timely treatment, would Claudia have a good claim against Dr. Seuss?

    (A) No, because Dr. Seuss offered her the Pap smear and Claudia declined it.

    (B) No, because Dr. Seuss did not breach a medical duty to Claudia.

    (C) Yes, and the claim would be for failure to provide informed consent.

(D) Yes, and the claim would be for failure to perform the Pap smear with ordinary skill and care.

67. In an action for personal injuries, Bryna claims that Druze was negligent. Druze had consumed a full bottle of vodka before she engaged in the conduct at issue, motivated by curiosity about how this alcohol would make her feel. She was drunk when she engaged in the conduct. On what basis should the jury take into account Druze's intoxication?

(A) The jury should hold Druze to the standard of a reasonable intoxicated person.

(B) The jury should hold Druze to the standard of a reasonable sober person.

(C) The jury should hold Druze to the standard of a reasonable person with a mental deficiency.

(D) None; this question is not for the jury. Voluntary intoxication makes Druze negligent as a matter of law.

68. Walrus & Carpenter Co. (W&C) is a seafood cultivator and supplier that for the last 100 years has been growing oysters for human consumption in its privately owned Chucka Lake. It was recently sued by numerous consumers who became ill with Hepatitis A after eating oysters sold by W&C. Investigators determined that the cause of this outbreak of Hepatitis A was the consumption of contaminated W&C oysters: when they tested the flesh of W&C oysters, these investigators found very high levels of e.Coli, a bacterium that causes Hepatitis A. They do not know for sure how the oysters became contaminated, but suspect that unusually heavy rainfall in the month before the outbreak caused storm water drains in the region to overflow with human fecal matter containing the bacterium, and that this contaminated water made its way through the ground into the estuarine water at Chucka Lake in which the oysters grew. Assume it is not possible for an oyster cultivator to prevent contaminated groundwater from entering water in which it grows oysters and no feasible test exists to determine e.Coli contamination in estuarine water; only after-the-fact testing can identify contamination in the oysters themselves.

For an analysis of whether W&C may be liable in negligence for causing injury to the consumers who ate its oysters, which additional information is most pertinent?

(A) Medical histories of the plaintiffs, to determine whether they were unusually vulnerable to illness from contaminated food.

(B) The experience of W&C and similar oyster growers as suppliers, to determine whether W&C had reason to infer that heavy rainfall could result in contamination.

(C) The condition of nearby storm water drains, to determine whether they were obstructed or otherwise likely to spill e.Coli contamination into the nearby groundwater.

(D) The quality of other food that the plaintiffs consumed, to determine whether another source of contamination might have been the source of their illness.

69. Same facts as above. W&C could have conducted its business differently after the heavy rainfall. Which of the following courses of conduct available to W&C is LEAST likely to have prevented the plaintiffs from suffering their injury?

    (A)   Stop selling oysters harvested from Chucka Lake until oyster flesh tests indicated that the oysters were not contaminated.

    (B)   Continue selling oysters, but include a warning about the possibility of their contamination.

    (C)   Stop cultivating oysters in Chucka Lake altogether.

    (D)   Undertake tests of Chucka Lake water specimens to look for evidence of contamination.

70.   In the famous case of *United States v. Carroll Towing*, Judge Learned Hand spoke of three variables: (1) the probability of a bad outcome occurring, or *P*, (2) the severity of the outcome that would result, or *L*, and (3) "the burden of adequate precautions," or *B*. The events of *Carroll Towing* took place in New York harbor during World War II. The alleged negligence at issue was failure to have a person on board working as a barge attendant, and the injury was harm to a ship.

     The effect of wartime conditions on the variables, in comparison to the peacetime conditions that preceded the war, is to

    (A)   make *P* and *L* go up, but *B* go down.

    (B)   make *P* and *B* go up, but *L* go down.

    (C)   make *P, L,* and *B* all go up.

    (D)   make *P, L,* and *B* all go down.

71.   Which of the following negligence actions provides the best example of breach of duty demonstrated through circumstantial evidence?

    (A)   *Questo v. Quello*: Questo can prove that Quello, though blind, was not using a cane when he collided with Questo.

    (B)   *Pendayho v. Veruca*: An eyewitness testifies that when Pendayho was crossing the street, Veruca was driving at approximately 40 miles an hour in a 25-mph speed limit zone.

    (C)   *Gownad v. Bryant Motel*: After staying for several days at the Bryant Motel, Gownad experienced scabies, an intensely itchy skin condition caused by a burrowing mite.

    (D)   *Bettsee v. Yender's*: Bettsee slipped and fell into a puddle of shampoo in an aisle of Yender's supermarket. The spilled shampoo was grimy and mixed with grit.

72.   One Saturday, Lawrence took his daughter Naomi, age six, to an amusement park owned by AmuseCo to ride the carousel. Naomi climbed onto one of the wooden horses, and Lawrence attached the little safety belt around her waist. Naomi was the only rider on the carousel. Lawrence then stood at the side of the horse to hold Naomi in case she needed help. The music started and the carousel began to turn slowly. Instead of settling in at a constant rate of speed, the carousel continued accelerating. The carousel reached a speed of more than twice the rate it had reached the same day. Naomi was thrown from her horse onto the spinning platform, breaking her leg. Naomi brings an action against AmuseCo for negligence. She offers in evidence the facts just stated, and then rests. AmuseCo moves for a directed verdict on the ground that Naomi has not offered any evidence of negligence. Naomi responds that the court should deny the motion because of the doctrine of res ipsa loquitur.

Which of the following statements is most likely correct?

(A) Even if res ipsa loquitur applies, it can be used only to supplement other direct evidence pointing to negligence on defendant's part. Here, because no such evidence was offered, the court should grant AmuseCo's motion.

(B) While it is possible that res ipsa loquitur can be applied, expert testimony is always required when the issue concerns whether a malfunction in a mechanical device was caused by negligence. Because Naomi has not offered such evidence, the court should grant AmuseCo's motion.

(C) Because possibilities other than negligence can explain the accident, the doctrine does not apply, and the court should grant AmuseCo's motion.

(D) Because the circumstantial evidence supports the inferences necessary for application of res ipsa loquitur, the court would not err in denying AmuseCo's motion.

73. Same facts as in Question 72. Assume that the court denies AmuseCo's motion for directed verdict. AmuseCo offers no evidence to support its contention that it was not negligent in operating or maintaining the carousel. Assume the jurisdiction in which the action is filed does not hold that the res ipsa loquitur doctrine creates a presumption of negligence. Naomi now moves for a directed verdict on the issue of negligence.

Which of the following statements is most likely correct?

(A) Because AmuseCo failed to offer evidence of non-negligence, the court should grant Naomi's motion.

(B) Because the inference of negligence is overwhelmingly strong under the circumstances, the court should grant Naomi's motion.

(C) Because there is a jury question on the issue of negligence, the court should deny Naomi's motion.

(D) Because AmuseCo has better access to information concerning the cause of the accident, the court should grant Naomi's motion unless AmuseCo agrees to present evidence showing how the accident occurred.

74. Same facts as in Question 72. Assume again that, correctly or incorrectly, the court denies AmuseCo's motion. But instead of offering no evidence as it did in Question 73, at trial AmuseCo calls a witness who testifies that, just before Naomi got on the carousel, he saw a dirty, disheveled person appear to tinker with the carousel's apparatus and then run away. Naomi's lawyer, using rigorous cross-examination, attacks this testimony as not credible. Both parties then move for a directed verdict on the issue of negligence. A jury has heard the evidence.

Which of the following best represents what the court ought to do in response to the motions?

(A) Because AmuseCo was not negligent, the court should grant its motion for directed verdict. The court should deny Naomi's motion.

(B) Because AmuseCo was negligent, the court should grant Naomi's motion for directed verdict. The court should deny AmuseCo's motion.

(C) The court should gauge the credibility of the witness who said he saw the tinkering and then rule on the two motions accordingly — that is, granting Naomi's motion if the witness is not credible and granting AmuseCo's motion if the witness is credible.

(D) The court should deny both motions because there is evidence to support both positions on the question of negligence.

75. In contrast to duty, which is a question of law for the court, breach in the United States is a jury question. Which of the following descriptors of the breach element best explains why juries are tasked to determine whether it exists in a negligence action?

(A) The question of whether someone breached a duty of care is well-suited to expert resolution.

(B) Breach claims invite factfinders to bring their life experience to accounts of injury.

(C) One needs no education in the law to know whether persons breached their duty of care.

(D) Juries know more than judges about matters of fact, in contrast to judges, who know the law.

Negligence: Causation—Actual and Proximate

76. Which of the following is a criticism of the actual cause element of the prima facie case for negligence most likely to be endorsed by an economic analyst?

    (A) It is potentially unfair to plaintiffs as a group.

    (B) It is potentially unfair to defendants as a group.

    (C) Unlike duty, breach, and injury, the cause element requires litigants to prove something that cannot be known until the costly expenditure of discovery begins.

    (D) It impedes deterrence of wasteful conduct by permitting defendants to prevail even when plaintiffs can prove defendants engaged in this wasteful conduct.

77. Jocasta worried that the kitchen in the restaurant she owned, PlatterpusRex, might have a rat problem. She considered hiring an exterminator and/or setting traps in the kitchen, but she did not want her employees to know about her suspicion of rats. Jocasta concluded that the best thing to do was buy rat poison in powder form, store it in an unmarked jar, and wait for further evidence of rat infestation before making a decision about whether to use it. Jocasta intended to store the jar in a hall closet but distractedly placed it on a cabinet shelf in the PlatterpusRex kitchen. The rat poison looked like coarse kosher-style salt, a common ingredient in restaurant cooking. A week later when Sven, a health inspector, was visiting the PlatterpusRex kitchen, the unexpectedly stored jar of rat poison fell and landed on the expensive thermometer Sven had placed on the counter, damaging it. Sven brought a negligence action against Jocasta.

    Which of the following best describes the proximate cause issue raised in this scenario?

    (A) The misfit between what made the storage negligent and the injury that Sven experienced.

    (B) The unforeseeability of an expensive, fragile object being left on a restaurant kitchen counter by a visitor.

    (C) That although Jocasta's storage choice looks unreasonable in hindsight, it might have been the most reasonable course of action at the time she acted.

    (D) That Sven should have known that leaving an expensive, fragile object on a restaurant kitchen counter would put the safety of that object at risk.

78. Cooking at home, Gordon prepared beef Stroganoff using cream that he should have known was contaminated. He chose not to eat this entree because he was dieting; his guest, Wendy, suffered food poisoning when she consumed it. Gordon drove the violently ill Wendy to the

local emergency room, a freestanding clinic rather than a hospital. At this clinic Wendy received negligently administered care that caused her to acquire an infection. Just as Wendy was preparing to bring a personal injury action, she learned that the clinic had gone out of business. Gordon is now the only available defendant.

Which of the following statements is most accurate?

(A) Gordon may be liable for the food poisoning but not the infection.

(B) Gordon may be liable for both the food poisoning and the infection.

(C) Gordon may not be liable for the food poisoning or the infection because actual cause is not present.

(D) Gordon may not be liable for the food poisoning or the infection because proximate cause is not present.

79. Courts sometimes hold that a defendant is not liable despite having been negligent, on the ground that the defendant's negligence was superseded by subsequent wrongdoing by another person. They rule against the plaintiff on proximate cause grounds.

What type of subsequent wrongdoing most warrants such an outcome of non-liability? Give an example, being sure to mention both the initial negligence of the defendant and the subsequent wrongdoing of the other person.

ANSWER:

80. Granger owns a store that sells guns and sporting equipment. State law restricts the sale of guns to licensed dealers and requires dealers to complete a brief background check on all customers. Granger is a licensed dealer. On the day Granger sold a handgun to Esther, he got interrupted in the middle of the background check and never completed it. If Granger had fulfilled his obligation as a dealer, he would have learned that under federal law Esther could not buy a gun because she was a fugitive: she had neglected to appear in court in another state, and an arrest warrant was open. Although she flouted the law, Esther is a peaceful person. She bought the gun from Granger only for target practice, not to shoot anyone.

After Esther drove with the gun from Granger's store and parked near a restaurant for lunch, Andy broke into her car and stole items from the trunk, including the gun. Andy later used this gun to shoot Millard in a disputed drug deal. Millard survived the gun wound and brought a negligence action against Granger only, not Esther.

Millard's action will likely

(A) fail, because what makes selling a gun risky is the dangerousness of the buyer, and Esther was a peaceful person.

(B) fail, because although the sale was negligent, Andy's theft of the gun was a superseding cause.

(C) succeed, because both the federal and state laws described here have the purpose of reducing unauthorized gunfire and protecting a class of persons who include Millard.

(D) succeed, because Granger's violation of the state statute established proximate cause as a matter of law.

81. Courts sometimes describe a particular antecedent occurrence as "sufficient" to have caused harm, but not "necessary." Does such an antecedent occurrence fulfill the but-for test of causation? Explain.

ANSWER:

82. Umberto thought he might have a heart problem, and went to the emergency room. There, Doc diagnosed Umberto as suffering from fatigue, and sent him home. Umberto died that night. Doc's diagnosis was mistaken. Umberto had suffered a massive heart attack. It is undisputed that, if Doc had diagnosed him correctly, Umberto would have had about a 40 percent chance of surviving. Sending Umberto home reduced his chance of survival to near zero.

Which of the following statements is correct?

(A) In a jurisdiction adopting a traditional view of causation, Doc will be liable for Umberto's death.

(B) In a jurisdiction following a traditional view of causation, Doc will not be liable for Umberto's death.

(C) In a jurisdiction adopting a "lost chance of survival" theory, Doc will be liable for all damages resulting from Umberto's death.

(D) In either a traditional jurisdiction or one adopting a "lost chance of survival" theory, Doc will be liable for all damages resulting from Umberto's death.

83. Which of the following questions best asks what the "risk rule" or "scope of the risk" approach to proximate cause seeks to determine?

(A) "Is what happened to the plaintiff attributable to the negligent aspect of the defendant's conduct?"

(B) "But for the defendant's conduct, would the plaintiff have experienced the injury for which he or she seeks redress?"

(C) "Was the defendant's negligence a substantial factor in bringing about the injury for which the plaintiff seeks redress?"

(D) "Were the defendant's negligence and the plaintiff's injury closely linked in space and time, with no significant intervening force in between?"

84. In the classic merged-fires problem of accident law, a defendant carelessly starts a fire on its own property, or carelessly fails to contain a fire after building it. Call this fire F1. F1 leaves the defendant's land, headed in the general direction of the plaintiff's property. Along the way F1 merges with F2, a separate fire of innocent or unknown origin. The merged fire then arrives on the plaintiff's property, causing damage. Assume that either F1 or F2 would have been big and powerful enough to cause the plaintiff's damage by itself if the two had never merged.

The merged-fires problem is important to tort law because it challenges

(A) the doctrine of superseding cause.

(B) the but-for test for actual cause.

(C) the preponderance-of-the-evidence rule.

(D) the second injury rule of proximate cause.

85. In which of the following scenarios does the but-for approach to actual cause work just fine, needing no modification?

(A) Dr. Ticktock failed to follow her occupational standard of care when providing anesthesia to patient Phool. Phool had a heart attack on the operating table and died. If Dr. Ticktock had followed the standard of care, Phool would have had a 30 percent chance of survival. Phool's estate brought an action against Dr. Ticktock.

(B) Ursuline, an auto mechanic, negligently failed to secure the brakes she installed on Leandra's automobile. Before Leandra could pick up her car from Ursuline's garage, her enemy Anita slipped in and tampered with the brakes so that they would fail when used. As soon as Leandra drove out of the garage and tried to brake while exiting to the street, the brakes failed. Leandra's car hit a wall and Leandra suffered physical injury. Leandra brought an action against Ursuline.

(C) Snick, Inc., manufactured a cigarette lighter that, unlike other cigarette lighters, was easy for young children to (mis)use. Five-year-old Wilmot went into his mother's purse and found her Snick lighter. Wilmot started a house fire that led to injuries. His family brought an action against Snick, Inc.

(D) Gopher Industries manufactured an industrial solvent that is safe to use at full strength but becomes erratic and dangerous when mixed with water. At a manufacturing plant owned and operated by Skoliosis, managers made a careless decision to dilute the Gopher solvent in the hope of saving money. Workers suffered injury as a result and, unable to recover from Skoliosis due to the workers' compensation bar, brought an action against Gopher.

86. A car driven negligently by Danforth repeatedly struck Hester's car, causing damage and personal injury. Because she believed Danforth would assault her, Hester did not get out of her car to exchange information, and drove away from the scene. When a passerby saw Hester leave the scene, she reported Hester's license number to the police, and Hester was arrested and charged with hit-and-run driving. Hester was acquitted at trial. Hester now brings an action against Danforth, seeking, among other things, damages for emotional distress suffered as a result of her arrest and prosecution.

If Danforth claims his conduct was not a cause in fact of the damages resulting from Hester's arrest and prosecution, which of the following statements is most accurate?

(A) Unless Danforth could reasonably have foreseen Hester's arrest and prosecution, Danforth's conduct was not a cause in fact of these consequences.

(B) Because Hester would not have been arrested but for Danforth's conduct, Danforth's conduct was a cause in fact of the arrest and prosecution.

(C) Because Hester would not be able to "prove the negative" (what would have happened but for Danforth's conduct), the conduct was not a cause in fact.

(D) Because more than one factor contributed to Hester's arrest and prosecution, Danforth's conduct was not a cause in fact.

87. Which of the following negligence scenarios, all involving a pedestrian named Wolfe crossing the street, bears the strongest analytical resemblance to *Palsgraf v. Long Island Railroad Co.*?

(A) As Wolfe was crossing the street, a circus procession came into Wolfe's view. The procession was moving at an unreasonably high speed. Wolfe's long-suppressed phobia, a fear of clowns, was triggered and Wolfe suffered severe emotional distress. Wolfe brought an action against the circus.

(B) Careless driving by Edna resulted in a near collision between Edna's vehicle and Wolfe. Because Brad, a passerby, spotted Edna's oncoming car in time, Brad was able to push Wolfe out of the path of the car. Brad's push caused Wolfe to suffer minor bruises. Wolfe brought an action against Edna.

(C) Lee's car, driven by Lee at an unreasonably high speed, hit Wolfe. Wolfe's body went flying "like a field goal," as a witness later put it, and landed on another pedestrian, Dolores, standing 20 feet away on a sidewalk. Dolores brought an action against Lee.

(D) Fiddlehead, installing a sewer line under a sidewalk, negligently failed to fence off the worksite or post a warning sign. Pedestrians had little way to know about the hole in the ground Fiddlehead had dug. Wolfe fell into the hole. Because Wolfe suffers from a brittle bone condition, Wolfe's injury proved disabling for months. Ordinary pedestrians would have suffered much less severe injury if they had fallen into the hole. Wolfe brought an action against Fiddlehead.

88. Hannah suffered a heart attack. Her husband, Hardy, dialed 911, but was unable to get through because the telephone network had crashed due to a poorly performed maintenance check. Hannah died. Hardy has brought an action on behalf of the deceased Hannah against Phone Co. for negligence.

If Phone Co. claims that there was no cause-in-fact relationship between its conduct and Hannah's death, which of the following statements is most likely correct?

(A) To prevail, Hardy must prove that had the phone lines been open, Hannah would not have died, or that her life would have been extended in some meaningful way.

(B) To avoid being held liable, Phone Co. must prove that had the phone lines been open, Hannah would have died anyway, or that her life would not have been extended in some meaningful way.

(C) If it was not foreseeable that the phone network would be down and that a person would die because the 911 service would be unreachable, there was no cause in fact relationship between Phone Co.'s conduct and Hannah's death, and Hardy will not prevail.

(D) Because Phone Co. did not act, there is no cause in fact relationship, and Hardy will not prevail.

Defenses to Negligence

89. While shopping in Irving's Grocery Store (Irving's), Lina approached a display of glass jars of jam. The jars were stacked from waist height to six or seven feet from the ground and the rows were separated by corrugated cardboard. The display was unreasonably dangerous in an obvious way, being both too high and too precariously constructed. Lina decided to buy a few jars. She slowly began to pull the first jar out. Just before the jar was completely out, the display began to shake, and Lina stopped pulling out the jar. She was about to push it back into the stack when Robespierre, another shopper, accidentally bumped his cart into Lina. This contact caused Lina's hand to jolt forward, and the entire display fell over. Both Lina and Robespierre were knocked down and suffered glass cuts. Lina brought an action against Irving's for negligence; Irving's impleaded Robespierre. The jurisdiction, which prides itself on its modern tort law, long ago abolished the trespasser-licensee-invitee distinction for land-visitor plaintiffs and replaced contributory negligence with comparative negligence. On the question of apportionment, it treats assumption of risk the same as comparative negligence, using both as a basis for dividing damages rather than an absolute defense.

    Would it be correct for the court to reduce Lina's recovery by taking into account Lina's own responsibility for her injury?

    (A) No, because Lina was an invitee. Carelessness does not reduce the recovery of a visitor in this status category.

    (B) No, because a reasonable person would have had no awareness of the danger in Irving's display.

    (C) Yes, because the availability of Robespierre as a defendant means that the court must necessarily engage in apportionment.

    (D) Yes, because Lina failed to exercise reasonable care for her own safety and her conduct contributed to the fall of the display.

90. Same facts as above. If Irving's claims Lina assumed the risk of injury, which of the following statements is most accurate?

    (A) Lina will recover nothing only if the risk was inherent in the activity and Irving's was merely careless.

    (B) Lina will recover nothing if she appreciated the risk and voluntarily decided to confront it.

    (C) Lina's recovery will be reduced only if her conduct amounted to comparative negligence.

(D) Lina's recovery will be reduced only if she appreciated the risk and voluntarily confronted it.

91. At Coltrane College the trendy new drug is called Zip. An undergraduate named Alice came up with the formula and synthesizes it (illegally) in a campus laboratory, selling it to peers. People who take Zip enjoy gentle hallucinations and elevated mood. Zip is usually consumed in liquid form, mixed with vodka or a soft drink like soda or lemonade.

Alice has learned that Zip is partially neutralized by digestion before it reaches a user's bloodstream. Zip can be taken at full strength by injection, but most Coltrane undergraduates will not consume recreational drugs that require needles. Alice is working on a medium for Zip that will preserve its strength after oral consumption.

Mack, a classmate, approached Alice and said he wanted to buy "super Zip." Alice explained that for now the intense form of the drug could come only by injection. "No," said Mack, "just give me enough to make it super without needles. As much as I need." Alice did not know what dosage would "make it super." She estimated that four times the injectable amount in drinkable form would give Mack the same effect. Mack consumed the Zip that Alice sold him by mixing it with vodka. Unfortunately, Alice's estimate proved inaccurate and Mack suffered brain damage attributable to the size of his Zip dose. Mack brought an action against Alice. Assume that Alice's estimate was rendered negligently.

Is Mack's claim barred by assumption of risk?

(A) Yes, because Mack voluntarily consumed Zip.

(B) Yes, because Mack asked for a larger dose than what Alice normally sold.

(C) No, because as an addict Mack did not act voluntarily.

(D) No, because Mack lacked knowledge of the risk he was assuming.

92. Same facts as above except that Mack had a different experience with the large dose of Zip. Mack came home, took Zip with vodka, settled on the sofa near his girlfriend Isolde, and enjoyed intense hallucinations while watching a movie. No brain damage, but Mack suddenly thought if he leaped into the air he would float. He climbed onto the arm of the sofa and leaped, landing hard on Isolde and causing injury to her. In an action by Isolde against Mack and Alice, the defendants claimed that Isolde was comparatively negligent.

Which of the following points, assuming Isolde can support it, best strengthens Isolde's position with respect to this defense?

(A) Isolde did not know the effects of Zip on a user.

(B) Isolde did not know that Mack had taken any drug.

(C) Isolde had no reason to know that Mack had taken a drug.

(D) Isolde had no reason to know that Alice's assessment of how much Zip made the dose "super" was only a best-efforts estimate.

93. Pawel had never been horseback riding, but decided to try it after he began dating an avid equestrian. Pawel drove to Ed's Stables (Ed's), which was near his apartment. He approached an employee and mentioned that he'd never ridden a horse before but said he was anxious to

learn. The employee handed Pawel a form titled "Release," and told Pawel he'd have to sign it before he'd be allowed to ride. In part, the form stated:

> *I recognize that there are inherent risks in any horseback riding activity. I am also aware of the possible risks and dangers inherent in participating in such activities, including, but not limited to, possible injury or property damage from falling from my horse, collision with other riders, physical strain and injury due to unfamiliar or unexpected movements of the horse, biting or kicking by the horse, and allergic reaction to the horse, saddle and equipment, or vegetation and foliage encountered while riding.*
>
> *In consideration of Ed's making its facilities available to me for my use for horseback riding and activities related thereto, I hereby agree to and do hereby fully release Ed's and its agents and employees from any and all liability which they may have for injuries, death, or any other damages resulting from any injury which I may sustain while engaging in horseback riding and activities related thereto.*

Pawel skimmed the form quickly and signed it. He was then placed on a horse and began to ride. After two minutes, the horse suddenly took off at a full gallop and left the trail. She then reared up on her hind legs, throwing Pawel onto a cactus. He was seriously injured. The horse had never thrown a rider before. Pawel brought a negligence action against Ed's.

If Ed's defends on the ground that Pawel assumed the risk by signing the Release, which of the following statements is most likely correct?

(A) Because the document constituted an adhesion contract, it is unenforceable.

(B) Because the document did not specifically mention the risk of falling off the horse and landing on a cactus, it is unenforceable.

(C) Because Ed's knew Pawel was an inexperienced rider, the release is unenforceable.

(D) The release is probably enforceable.

94. While suffering from addiction to Opie, a drug, Philippa sought treatment from Dr. Mario, a psychiatrist. In one of their therapy sessions, Dr. Mario's phone alerted him to a text message from his daughter. Dr. Mario excused himself from the room, saying he would be back in a minute. Philippa felt she had a unique opportunity and dived into Dr. Mario's desk drawer where she found a small unlabeled plastic bottle of pills. Knowing nothing about what they were—they looked unfamiliar to her—Philippa took the bottle from the office and ingested most of the pills when she got home. The pills turned out to be sedatives whose overdose caused Philippa an injury. Philippa brought an action against Dr. Mario, alleging that it had been negligent for him to leave the room when the room contained drugs that Philippa could reach.

Should the court apply comparative negligence to Philippa's claim?

(A) Yes. It is unreasonable for any person, including a drug addict, to swallow mystery pills.

(B) Yes, because Dr. Mario's negligence is imputed to Philippa.

(C) No, because part of Dr. Mario's obligation to Philippa under the circumstances was to use care in anticipation of Philippa's drug addiction.

(D) No, because the therapeutic relationship between Philippa and Dr. Mario did not contemplate ingestion of the sedatives in question, but a different drug.

95. Which of the following statements about implied assumption of risk is *least* accurate?

(A) It must be voluntary.

(B) Many jurisdictions now regard it as comparable to comparative negligence.

(C) It must be manifested to the defendant.

(D) The plaintiff must have understood the risk.

96. Clinton went to a hockey game between the hometown team Mighty Chickens, which were owned by the Sidney Corp. (Sidney), and the Coyotes. His seat, which was only five rows off the ice, offered an excellent view even though it was in the area behind one of the goals. During the first period, a player hit a blazing shot toward the goal and, as often happens, the puck flew off the ice. The puck flew slightly left of the goal and struck the transparent barrier protecting the fans. Instead of bouncing off the barrier, the puck shattered it, sending sharp fragments flying. One fragment struck Clinton in the face and badly injured his eye. The barrier had been severely weakened from earlier collisions with pucks and players. Though the cracks in the barrier were not visible to fans, a reasonable inspection would have revealed that the barrier needed to be replaced. Sidney had not inspected the barrier.

If Clinton brings an action against Sidney for negligence, and Sidney claims Clinton assumed the risk, which of the following arguments constitutes Clinton's strongest response?

(A) Though the risk of this type of accident is inherent in sitting so close to the ice at a hockey game, Sidney's conduct was reckless, thus denying Sidney the assumption of risk defense.

(B) Though being hit by a flying puck is an inherent risk of sitting so close to the ice, the risk of being hit by flying fragments of the barrier is not. Clinton's recovery should only be reduced slightly.

(C) Though being hit by a flying puck is an inherent risk of sitting so close to the ice, the risk of being hit by flying fragments of the barrier is not. Clinton should recover fully.

(D) Because Clinton voluntarily chose to attend the game, he may not recover.

97. Three generations of the low-income Gramble family live in a tumbledown rented wooden house in the state of Pennsyltucky, which has adopted the "pure" form of comparative negligence. Under the terms of the lease the Grambles' landlord, Lester, is responsible for furnishing electricity and maintaining its supply safely. Careless maintenance of electric wires by Lester caused a fire. As the Grambles hurriedly fled the house, communications about who was with whom became confused and one family member, wheelchair-bound Grandpa, was left behind by mistake. Grandpa's teen granddaughter Natalie Gramble ran back into the burning house in an effort to rescue Grandpa. Natalie succeeded in publishing Grandpa out to safety, but the effort caused her to suffer burns.

Would Lester have a good implied assumption of risk defense in a negligence action by Natalie?

(A) Yes, because Natalie's encounter of the risk was knowing and voluntary.

(B) Yes, because a reasonable person in Natalie's position would have known of the danger.

(C) No, because the knowledge element is not present.

(D) No, because the voluntariness element is not present.

98. Same facts as above except family members push Grandpa out in his wheelchair just fine and all the other Grambles exit the burning house safely as well. As the fire burned and the house appeared about to topple, Natalie decided to enter the house for the smartphone she'd left behind in her bedroom. She retrieved the smartphone in time to save it, but the rescue effort caused her to suffer not only burns but a head injury when the frame above the front door collapsed on her.

Which of the following statements is most correct?

(A) Natalie has a negligence claim against Lester, and Lester can claim the defense of implied assumption of risk.

(B) Natalie has a negligence claim against Lester, and Lester can claim the defense of express assumption of risk.

(C) Natalie has a negligence claim against Lester, and Lester can claim the defense of comparative negligence by Natalie.

(D) Natalie does not have a negligence claim against Lester because she had the last clear chance to avoid the injury.

99. What is the difference between "primary" and "secondary" implied assumption of risk?

ANSWER:

100. Courts have been more willing to recognize mental deficiency in the context of contributory negligence than they have been in the context of primary (defendant) negligence. Explain why this inconsistency might not be unfair.

ANSWER:

101. Although most jurisdictions have replaced contributory negligence with comparative negligence, the continuing effect of contributory negligence has not entirely disappeared. Explain.

ANSWER:

102. A defendant could try to contend that because violation of a statute can establish negligence as a matter of law and thereby allow the plaintiff to prevail on the question of breach without having to persuade the factfinder that the defendant's conduct was careless, compliance with a statute ought to establish a defense to negligence. Courts in general do not accept this contention. Which of the following points notes the most important asymmetry between the

rule that violation of a statute is negligence per se and the hypothetical rule proposed here: compliance with a statute shows that the defendant was not negligent?

(A) The hypothetical rule would do a lot more work for defendants than negligence per se now does for plaintiffs.

(B) The hypothetical rule presumes that defendants know about statutory authority on point.

(C) Violation of a statute has more than one consequence in state courts: some states regard it as negligence per se, but others regard it as only evidence of negligence.

(D) When excused, violation of a statute does not constitute negligence per se.

Strict Liability and Nuisance

103. Which of the following is *not* a factor in the Third Restatement criteria for determining whether an activity qualifies for strict liability as abnormally dangerous?

    (A) The value of the activity to the community.

    (B) A foreseeable and highly significant risk of harm.

    (C) Whether the activity is a matter of common usage.

    (D) Whether the danger can be reduced or eliminated by reasonable care.

104. Working as a dog sitter while looking for employment as a lawyer, Maude arrived for the first time at the apartment of her new (dog-sitting) clients, Claude and Jeffrey. Claude and Jeffrey had said nothing to Maude about the temperament of their Rhodesian Ridgeback dog. As soon as Maude entered their apartment, the dog bit her. Maude is thinking about bringing a tort claim against Claude and Jeffrey. She believes Claude and Jeffrey might have been negligent for not having warned her of the Rhodesian Ridgeback's dangerous propensities, and also that they might be strictly liable for the attack.

    Assuming the jurisdiction follows the common law with respect to dog bites — meaning it has no statute providing for strict liability — which of the following statements is most accurate?

    (A) Strict liability is available; negligence is not.

    (B) Negligence is available; strict liability is not.

    (C) Both strict liability and negligence are available.

    (D) Neither strict liability nor negligence is available.

105. Merriweather, Inc., was developing a piece of land for residential housing, a task that required considerable earth and rock removal. It chose to use blasting for this purpose, and did so with reasonable care. One of its blasts created a strong shockwave that blew down a rickety old barn on property owned by Elizabeth.

    If Elizabeth brings an action against Merriweather, Inc., which of the following statements is most correct?

    (A) Strict liability applies.

    (B) Strict liability does not apply, but Elizabeth may have a negligence claim.

    (C) Strict liability would have applied if debris had landed on Elizabeth's property, but it does not apply to what she experienced, concussion damage.

(D) Strict liability does not apply because Elizabeth was contributorily negligent for keeping a rickety old barn on her property.

106. Ahmid was a sculptor who liked to work on big projects in his back yard shop in a residential subdivision. His specialty was fashioning three-dimensional "murals" on large concrete walls. Ahmid would first construct the thick concrete wall (the average size was about 15 feet long and about 10 feet high). Next, he would use chalk to sketch his designs on the wall. Finally, he would don a set of goggles and earplugs, start up his power tools, and begin to blast away at the smooth surface, creating within a matter of hours a monumental bas-relief sculpture.

One person's art is another person's headache. Rosa, an emergency room doctor, lived next door to Ahmid. Rosa's hours were somewhat erratic, and it was not unusual for her to be home until early afternoon and then to work a long shift at the hospital until late at night. When her schedule allowed, Rosa loved to sit on her back porch with a cup of decaf cappuccino and the morning paper, taking in the morning air. Doing so, however, was very difficult on days when Ahmid was creating his artwork. The noise from the power tools would be very loud, and concrete dust would fill the air for several blocks. After a while, Rosa found it impossible to spend time on her back porch, both because the noise bothered her and because she became concerned about the possible ill effects of ingesting concrete dust. She contacted a lawyer about the possibility of filing an action against Ahmid.

If Rosa brings a strict liability action against Ahmid for carrying on an abnormally dangerous activity, which of the following facts, if true, would impair her chances of recovering?

(A) Ahmid can avoid spreading dust into the air by enclosing his work area.

(B) Rosa can avoid the noise and dust by going inside when Ahmid is working.

(C) Rosa can enclose her back porch for less money than it would cost Ahmid to enclose his work area.

(D) Many other people in the neighborhood also suffered from the noise and dust as much as Rosa.

107. When courts apply strict liability rather than negligence to a particular activity, they

(A) discourage potential defendants from engaging in that activity.

(B) neither encourage nor discourage potential defendants from engaging in that activity.

(C) encourage potential victims to invest in safety, provided the costs of these investments do not exceed the value of foregoing precautions.

(D) encourage potential victims to invest in safety, regardless of whether the costs of their investments exceed the value of foregoing precautions.

108. Al owns a home next to the multi-story parking garage of Springfield Mall, owned and operated by the Peg Co. The parking structure is open at the sides, and it backs up to a narrow alley. Al's home is just across the alley. On days when Al works the late shift in the mall, he likes to sleep until noon. A recent rash of auto thefts has led the Peg Co. to install alarms on all 20 vehicles it uses for security at Springfield Mall. Almost every morning, one or more of the alarms activate when the vehicles are touched by mall patrons or when heavy delivery

trucks lumber by. The alarms make extremely loud siren-like sounds until mall employees turn them off, which sometimes takes 30 minutes. The sounds have caused Al to lose a great deal of sleep, and the Peg Co. has refused his requests to remove the alarm systems from the vehicles.

If Al brings an action against the Peg Co. for nuisance, which of the following statements is most likely correct?

(A) Because the noise from the car alarms harms the general public, the appropriate redress is through an action for public nuisance. Therefore, Al's action will fail.

(B) Because the Peg Co. does not intentionally set off the alarms, Al's action will fail.

(C) Because the sound from the alarms poses an abnormally high danger to Al and others in the community, Al's action will succeed.

(D) If the jury finds that the noise substantially interferes with Al's sleep and that a reasonable person could prevent the alarms from going off so easily or could arrange to have the alarms shut off more quickly, Al's action will succeed.

109. Compare and contrast the six-factor analysis for strict liability in *Restatement (Second) of Torts* § 520 with a negligence analysis.

ANSWER:

110. Ari, an amateur chemist, was working on an experiment in his home's basement designed to extract energy from a combination of water and the element palladium. At one point, just after Ari carefully uncorked a glass beaker containing the water and palladium, the contents unexpectedly and inexplicably became unstable. Ari ran for cover, and the entire apparatus exploded moments later, blowing out a window and sending a cloud of toxic matter into the neighborhood. The matter was heavier than the surrounding air, and soon deposited in and around the home of Curly, a nearby neighbor. Over the next several weeks, Curly became quite ill. Soon all of his hair fell out, and he gained 75 pounds.

Which of the following claims for an action by Curly against Ari best suits these facts?

(A) A private nuisance action.

(B) A strict liability action, alleging that Ari carried on an abnormally dangerous activity.

(C) A negligence action, alleging that Ari unreasonably permitted the container to explode.

(D) An action for trespass to land.

111. How do courts apply proximate cause to strict liability?

ANSWER:

112. GasCo was in the business of delivering gasoline to gas stations. For this purpose, GasCo used tanker trucks. An undetectable defect in the hitch mechanism caused the trailer on one

of its trucks to disengage while the truck was traveling along a highway. The trailer overturned and spilled much of its load. Within a few moments, a spark caused by a passing car ignited the gasoline vapors, and a huge fire broke out. Popper, driving another car, was unable to avoid the fire, and suffered significant burns when his car became engulfed in flames. Popper brings an action against GasCo.

Make an argument that GasCo should be held strictly liable for Popper's damage.

ANSWER:

113. Which of the following scenarios illustrates "coming to the nuisance"?

(A) Chasing his dream of producing nuclear fusion at room temperature, Humfrey obtained several gallons of D2O (known as "heavy water"), then set up a high-voltage electrical generator that would send a current through a large glass container filled with the D2O. Humfrey hoped to cause fusion of atoms in a palladium lattice immersed in the container.

(B) Margret built a tower on her property that blocked the view of her neighbor, Ann.

(C) Dollop, feeling driven out of his apartment by a drug-dealing neighbor who threatened his children, moved to a cheaper home near a hog feeding lot that emitted flies and bad odors.

(D) Taking advantage of a zoning loophole, Boomer Cement Company moved to a residential neighborhood where its operations caused cement dust to enter the one-family houses nearby.

114. To avoid being liable for breach of duty in negligence, exercise reasonable care; to avoid strict liability for an abnormally dangerous activity ...

(A) ... avoid engaging in the activity.

(B) ... take reasonable care when engaging in the activity.

(C) ... take cost-justified precautions when engaging in the activity.

(D) ... refrain from engaging in the activity in a place where it is not customary.

115. Darren owns First Step, a board and care facility for mental patients who have been confined in a state hospital but who have been deemed ready for a measure of independence. The 20 patients at First Step all have jobs during the day, but must return each evening by 6:00 and remain at First Step until 8:00 the next morning. First Step is located in a large converted house in a residential neighborhood. It is licensed and is not in violation of any zoning ordinances.

Recently, Samantha purchased the house next door to First Step. One window looks directly onto the First Step property, and from time to time, Samantha has seen First Step residents running around inside the building partly or fully naked, which she considers offensive.

If Samantha brings an action against Darren for nuisance, which of the following provides the strongest defense for Darren?

(A) Because Samantha can avoid being offended by simply not looking, her action must not succeed.

(B) Because First Step was operating before Samantha moved in, Samantha assumed the risk.

(C) Because these activities at First Step do not create a substantial and unreasonable interference with the use and enjoyment of her property, her action must not succeed.

(D) Because of the public interest in maintaining facilities such as First Step, Darren is not maintaining a nuisance.

116. The keeper of an animal known to be dangerous is generally held liable without fault for harms that the animal causes, when these harms relate to its dangerous propensities. Which situations present exceptions to this general rule?

ANSWER:

117. MotorCo was developing a new type of automobile engine at its plant in Humdrum City. Although the fuel source being tested was more explosive than gasoline, the engine, if successful, could help end the nation's dependence on oil as a fuel source. One day, a test car that was supposed to remain stationary while the engine ran suddenly shifted into gear, and the driverless car lurched forward, broke through a barrier separating the plant from the public highway, and struck a car driven by Potter that was traveling along the highway. Potter brings an action against MotorCo on a theory of strict liability. Assume the case was being decided by Justice Blackburn, who wrote one of the opinions in *Rylands v. Fletcher*.

Which of the following statements best approximates what Justice Blackburn would say?

(A) Traffic on the highways cannot be conducted without exposing those upon them to the inevitable risk of accident. In the absence of negligence, therefore, MotorCo cannot be held responsible to Potter.

(B) Because MotorCo carried on its business in a densely populated part of River City, it was engaging in what might be termed a non-natural, or inappropriate, use of its land. Therefore, MotorCo is prima facie answerable for all the natural consequences of its activity.

(C) Trespass is the direct and immediate application of force to the person or property of the plaintiff. Because the occurrence which damaged Potter's vehicle did not occur as the direct result of any action on the part of MotorCo, Potter can recover, if at all, only upon a showing of negligence.

(D) Potter did not take upon himself any risk of harm from these dangerous activities, and if MotorCo's experimental cars are likely to do harm if they escape its land, Potter should recover even in the absence of negligence on MotorCo's part.

118. Same facts as above. Assume Potter's strict liability action against MotorCo is brought on an "abnormally dangerous activity" theory under *Restatement (Second) of Torts* §§ 519–520. Which of the following statements is most likely correct?

    (A) Because MotorCo's activity caused harm to a person outside the property, MotorCo is strictly liable.

    (B) If the social benefit that might be gained from MotorCo's efforts outweigh the risk created by the activity, MotorCo cannot be held strictly liable.

    (C) Because the feature of the experimental car that made it dangerous was the explosiveness of the type of fuel being used, MotorCo cannot be held strictly liable.

    (D) If MotorCo could have prevented the car from slipping into gear by the exercise of reasonable care, it is more likely that MotorCo will be held strictly liable.

119. OilCo stored gasoline in huge storage tanks. The tanks were kept on platforms 30 feet above the ground. One of OilCo's full tanks fell over when defective steel used to build the platform could not sustain the weight of the tank. The tank crushed a car owned by Patty, which was parked along the curb on the street next to OilCo's property. Patty brings an action against OilCo.

    Which of the following statements is most correct?

    (A) OilCo will be strictly liable to Patty.

    (B) OilCo will be liable to Patty if this type of platform was not customary in the oil storage industry.

    (C) OilCo will only be liable to Patty if its failure to discover the defect in the steel platform was the result of negligence on its OilCo's part.

    (D) OilCo will not be liable if it did not build the platform.

120. Which of the following strict liability claims would be most likely to come out differently depending on whether the jurisdiction follows the *Second* or *Third Restatement*?

    (A) An action for physical injuries following a Fourth of July fireworks display, where the plaintiff was a spectator.

    (B) An action for physical injuries following blasting in an oil field 50 miles from human settlement.

    (C) An action for emotional distress following blasting operations, where the plaintiff was recently released from a mental institution and experienced the noise as upsetting.

    (D) An action for property damage following leakage out of a truck carrying propane gas.

Products Liability

121. Tony started to boil water for instant cocoa in a brand new, inexpensive electric tea kettle. This kettle had arrived at his home the day before via an online order from the manufacturer. The kettle had a handle on one side, a spout on the other, and a lid on top. Users remove the lid, fill the kettle with cold water, replace the lid, and plug the kettle into an outlet. Tony duly complied with these tasks. As Tony tipped the kettle to pour water into a mug, the handle broke off, splashing boiling water onto his arm.

Tony, who suffered burns, prevailed in a strict products liability action against the manufacturer. Which of the conclusions about this action is most likely to be well founded?

(A) The kettle had a defective warning.

(B) The kettle was designed defectively: putting the handle on top as opposed to on the side of the kettle would have decreased the risk of the handle breaking off.

(C) The kettle was designed defectively: under normal use the handle of a brand new kettle does not break off.

(D) The kettle was manufactured defectively.

122. Bronwyn was driving on a dark road, using her high beams. When a car driven by Cliff approached, Bronwyn tried to flip the handle to dim the headlights, but due to a manufacturing defect in the handle, it broke off in her hand, and the high beams stayed on. Cliff was temporarily blinded, and as a result, lost control of the car and went off the road. Diane, a passenger in Cliff's car, was badly injured in the accident. Bronwyn purchased her car from a new car dealer several years previously.

Which of the following causes of action against the manufacturer would offer Diane the best chance of succeeding and would be easiest to prove?

(A) Negligence coupled with res ipsa loquitur.

(B) Express warranty.

(C) Strict products liability.

(D) Absolute liability.

123. Because their wheels form a single line, in-line skates work much like ice skates. In-line skates provide a fast, exciting ride, but they are also more dangerous than old-fashioned roller skates. The parents of six-year-old Joni bought her a pair of in-line skates manufactured by RollersInc. As soon as she received her skates, Joni ran to the top of a hill, put on the skates, and took off. It wasn't as easy as she expected it to be. Joni's ankles collapsed inward as she

gained speed, and she fell hard, sustaining serious injuries. She brings an action against RollersInc in a jurisdiction that follows *Restatement (Third) of Torts: Products Liability*.

Assuming RollersInc can prove any necessary facts, which of the following arguments would help RollersInc's defense?

(A) If reasonable parents had known the dangers in-line skates pose to a six-year-old skater, Joni's recovery may be reduced.

(B) Joni's conduct in skating down a hill on her first experience with in-line skates was unreasonable.

(C) RollersInc intended the skates to be used only by children over the age of 10.

(D) In-line skates are more expensive than traditional rollerskates.

124. At a birthday party hosted by Wilson, a guest named Megan gave Wilson a new Gametendo as a present. Gametendo, made by GamInc., is a hand-held gaming device that allows players to play race-car driving, sumo wrestling, and other electronic games. "It's my favorite," Megan said to Wilson. Wilson was impressed by this endorsement because Megan was the best gamer he knew. While Wilson was playing with his new Gametendo the device administered an unexpected electric shock. Wilson suffered burns along with the inability to use his thumbs for a number of weeks. Investigation later revealed a manufacturing defect in 500 Gametendo devices, including Wilson's. When Wilson filed strict products liability actions against GamInc. and Megan, both defendants filed motions to dismiss for failure to state a claim.

What should the court do?

(A) Grant both motions. Wilson has no strict products liability claim against either GamInc. or Megan.

(B) Deny both motions. Wilson might not prevail at trial, but he is entitled to proceed against both GamInc. and Megan.

(C) Grant GamInc.'s motion and deny Megan's.

(D) Grant Megan's motion and deny GamInc.'s.

125. Believing that rising auto prices made it very hard for low-income people to afford new cars, Corvair Motor Co. (CMC) decided to design and manufacture a cheaper alternative. Its Workerswagon was a very basic car that barely complied with federal safety standards, and carried a base price of just under $10,000. Shortly after the car's introduction, Millicent bought one and drove it for two years before giving it to her friend's son Danny as a college graduation present.

Six months later, Danny negligently ran a red light and was struck from the side by a car traveling through the intersection from his left. Danny's car door was displaced inward in the crash and badly injured him. He contacted an attorney, who learned that the steel beams placed in the car's doors to protect occupants were thinner than those used by all other auto manufacturers and that the design made it easier for the car's door to be pushed into the occupant when the car was struck from the side. The attorney also learned that this design feature saved CMC $200 per Workerswagon and that had CMC adopted any of the other designs then in use, Danny's injuries would have been substantially reduced.

Danny brings an action against CMC, alleging defective design. Based on the facts provided and reasonable inferences that may be drawn from those facts, which of the following arguments offers CMC the best chance of defeating Danny's action or substantially reducing his recovery? Assume the jurisdiction accepts *Restatement (Third) of Torts: Products Liability*.

(A) Consumers do not expect inexpensive cars to offer as much crashworthiness as expensive cars.

(B) CMC complied with all relevant federal safety standards.

(C) Danny was comparatively negligent.

(D) Danny assumed the risk.

126. Same facts as above. Does it matter for Danny's claim that Danny was not the purchaser of the car?

(A) Yes. The fact will make it less likely that Danny will prevail.

(B) Yes. The fact will make it more likely that Danny will prevail.

(C) No. The fact will have no effect on Danny's possible recovery.

(D) Maybe. The original bill of sale could have included reservations of rights that would bind Danny.

127. What are the major criticisms of the "reasonable alternative design" requirement as provided in *Restatement (Third) of Torts: Products Liability*?

ANSWER:

128. Explain the concept of implied warranty of fitness for a particular purpose, as codified in UCC § 2-315.

ANSWER:

129. Most products liability actions brought against manufacturers of prescription drugs allege warning defect rather than design defect because

(A) warning-defect claims have a longer statute of limitations.

(B) under the risk-utility test, warning-defect claims have criteria that are more demanding for plaintiffs.

(C) prescription drugs have been approved by the Food and Drug Administration, and thus necessarily have some utility.

(D) drug manufacturers enjoy qualified immunity for design-defect claims but not warning-defect claims.

130. Three-dimensional printing ("3-D printing") can enable an individual to make a product at home, without having to set up and operate a traditional manufacturing plant. Suppose that Stella, a law student with an engineering background, figures out how to use 3-D printing to make a product. Because Stella bought a batch of substandard plastic to build the product, the product has a manufacturing defect. Stella sells the product to Nicolette and Nicolette is injured by it. Stella has never sold a product made by her 3-D printing to anyone else. In an action by Nicolette against Stella, which of the following statements is most accurate?

    (A) The Second Restatement provision on products liability applies, but the Third Restatement provision on products liability does not.

    (B) The Third Restatement provision on products liability applies, but the Second Restatement provision on products liability does not.

    (C) Stella is not liable under either the Second or Third Restatement provisions on products liability.

    (D) Stella can be liable under both the Second and Third Restatement provisions on products liability.

131. Courts generally reject liability for failure to warn of a risk that was not known, and could not have been known, at the time of marketing. Nevertheless, some courts have held that post-sale duties can arise after the risks become known. To whom are these post-sale duties owed, and what should a manufacturer do to fulfill these duties?

    ANSWER:

132. Rodger loved chocolate-chip muffins. One evening, after he and his date Tiarra finished dinner at the Hungry Heifer, the two visited Anyushka's Desserts to pick up a dozen muffins. Rodger had paid for dinner; to reciprocate, Tiarra insisted on paying for this dessert. The couple headed back to Tiarra's apartment to enjoy the muffins. Halfway through his sixth muffin, Rodger started choking. He grabbed his throat, stood up, thrashed around, turned as blue as Tiarra's hair, and fell to the floor, hitting his head on the table as he fell. Tiarra raised Rodger to his feet and applied "the Heimlich Maneuver," which dislodged a large rusty nail from Rodger's throat. Rodger's head was bleeding profusely, and Tiarra rushed him to the hospital.

    Rodger brings an action against Anyushka's for products liability. Which of the following, if true, would hinder Rodger's chances of prevailing?

    (A) Tiarra, rather than Rodger, is considered the purchaser of this good even though she paid for the muffins to reciprocate for dinner.

    (B) Anyushka's was not the manufacturer of the muffins in question. It had bought the batch in question from Bart's, a large commercial bakery.

    (C) The nail was placed in the muffin by a disgruntled former employee of Anyushka's who sneaked into the kitchen of Anyushka's.

(D) Before he placed it in his mouth, Rodger felt something sharp in the muffin with his fingers.

133. Same facts as above and assume that choice (B) for question 132 adds a true statement. If Rodger also brings a products liability action against Bart's, the bakery that actually made the muffins, for products liability, which of the following facts, if proven, would hinder Rodger's chances of prevailing?

(A) Tiarra, rather than Rodger, is considered the purchaser of this good even though she paid for the muffins to reciprocate for dinner.

(B) The nail would have been detected by a reasonable inspection conducted by Anyushka's before selling the muffin.

(C) The nail was placed in the muffin by a disgruntled former employee of Anyushka's who sneaked into the kitchen of Anyushka's.

(D) Bart's did not sell the muffin to Tiarra but only to Anyushka's, an intermediary.

134. Sally was an experienced in-line skater who wanted to be the fastest kid on the block. To achieve even greater speeds, but knowing that this would affect her skates' stability, she decided to replace the existing wheels with a different kind. The process was very difficult because RollersInc, the manufacturer of Sally's skates, had welded the wheel brackets into place. Still, Sally managed to change the wheels. She could indeed skate faster with the new wheels, but after she'd been skating for about an hour, she lost control while at top speed and suffered a bad fall. Sally has sued RollersInc, citing the *Restatement (Third) of Torts: Products Liability*.

Which of the following potential arguments by RollersInc is weakest?

(A) The product made by RollersInc was not a cause in fact of Sally's injury.

(B) The product made by RollersInc was not the proximate cause of Sally's injury.

(C) Sally assumed the risk of her injury.

(D) The product was not defective because the plaintiff misused it in an unforeseeable manner.

135. Skatz, a manufacturer of in-line skates, has the best quality control procedures in the business. While other companies inspect each skate once, Skatz puts each skate through three inspections. This care is costly for Skatz, and any additional costs would make the skates unprofitable. Despite these procedures, the left skate in a pair purchased by Greg from a sporting goods store exited the Skatz plant with a weak wheel mount. After Greg had used the skates for a month, the weak wheel mount suddenly gave way, causing the left skate to collapse, and Greg to fall and injure himself.

If Greg brings an action against Skatz for product liability citing the *Restatement (Third) of Torts: (Products Liability)*, which of the following statements is most accurate?

(A) Because Greg was injured by a product manufactured by Skatz that deviated from its intended design and caused his injury, Greg can recover.

(B) Because Skatz cannot operate profitably with any quality control procedures beyond those it already uses, Skatz cannot be held liable.

(C) Because Skatz's quality control procedures exceeded even what would be considered reasonable care, Skatz cannot be held liable.

(D) Because Greg can recover directly from the store from which he purchased the skates, he cannot hold Skatz liable.

Defamation

136. In a defamation action based on website content, with Roberta as plaintiff and Brunhilde as defendant, which of the following points would *not* be central to Roberta's prima facie case against Brunhilde?

     (A) Brunhilde posted a story on her website falsely saying that Roberta had been convicted of embezzlement five years ago.

     (B) Roberta experienced severe emotional distress that she attributes to the publication of Brunhilde's false story on the website.

     (C) Roberta has suffered harm to her reputation that she attributes to the publication of Brunhilde's false story on the website.

     (D) Brunhilde's website, containing the false story about Roberta on its home page, is fully operative, and its history indicates that many visitors have clicked on the site.

137. Editor Edsel printed a story in a daily newspaper, the Succotash *Times*, that described state senator Burt Bumpkin as corrupt. The story relied on an extensive, tape-recorded interview with a grandfather figure of organized crime, Magoo, who recalled his illegal contributions to Bumpkin's election campaign in the last year. Everything in the story that described Bumpkin's corruption was conveyed in quotations attributed to Magoo. Investigation has now revealed that Magoo suffers from senile dementia and in the interview had confused Bumpkin with another politician, long dead, whom he had bribed in decades past. His reminiscences about Bumpkin were false.

     Bumpkin brings an action against Edsel and the Succotash *Times*. Which of the following additional facts, if substantiated, would most strengthen Bumpkin's claim?

     (A) During the interview, Magoo frequently referred to Bumpkin by the wrong name and apparently had trouble finishing his sentences.

     (B) While admitting that he is a public figure, Bumpkin has asserted his "right to privacy" when reporters were investigating rumors of his marital infidelity.

     (C) Edsel is a close friend of Bumpkin's archrival in the state senate, and actively desires the downfall of Bumpkin's career.

     (D) The Succotash *Times* employs fact-checkers and prints a "Corrections" notice in each day's edition.

138. Which statement most accurately describes the limited privilege to make a defamatory statement in a judicial proceeding?

     (A) The statement must be reasonably related to issues disputed in the proceeding.

(B) The statement must implicate a matter of common public concern.

(C) The statement must be reasonably tailored to minimize foreseeable harm to the person referenced.

(D) The statement must be made in a criminal proceeding; the privilege does not apply in civil cases.

139. Professional baseball pitcher Rooster McHew has long been suspected of resorting to "spit-balls"—baseballs that a pitcher illicitly moistens with saliva—in violation of major league baseball rules. Although by tradition the rule has not been strictly enforced, a new commissioner has cracked down on pitchers, and now those who throw spitballs can lose their jobs. McHew has always denied the spitball rumors. At a recent game, news reporters gathered around old-timer Perry Gay, who retired from baseball decades ago, and asked him what he thought of McHew's successes. Perry Gay is the most infamous spitball-thrower in baseball history. "I think he gets by with a little help from his friend," Gay replied to the question.

Can Gay's remark support a defamation action by Rooster McHew against Gay?

(A) No, because McHew has consented to Gay's expression of opinion.

(B) No, because Gay's words are innocuous and cannot harm McHew's reputation.

(C) Yes, because a reasonable person would infer that Gay was referring to spitballs.

(D) Yes, because the privilege to offer an opinion on a matter of public comment is not present under these facts.

140. Channel 7 News, based in the town of Eureka, aired a segment called "Rooted in Slavery" that looked at institutions and individuals who had lived in Eureka as slaveholders and enslaved persons in the nineteenth century. "Rooted in Slavery" took a "where are they now?" look at this history, interviewing several successors and descendants of these institutions and individuals. The program claimed that Paul Henry Shipley, the mayor of Eureka from 1851 to 1855, had owned five slaves. This statement was false. Shipley had never owned a single slave and had indeed participated in the abolitionist movement. His descendants, owners of Shipley Shipping, have suffered lost business because their customers now associate the enterprise with slavery. These descendants wish to bring an action against Channel 7 news.

Under the common law of defamation such an action by the individual descendants would fail, because

(A) the real party in interest is Shipley Shipping, and a corporation cannot be defamed.

(B) the dead cannot be defamed.

(C) the statute of limitations has run on the claim.

(D) the First Amendment to the United States Constitution offers a limited privilege to Channel 7 news that covers the facts of this case.

141. Who encounters more onerous obstacles to building her prima facie case for defamation: a public *figure* or a public *official*?

(A) A public figure, because public figures typically have more power in the media than do public officials, and can protect themselves against defamation.

(B) A public figure, because the consequences of public figures' being defamed are less severe.

(C) A public official, because of the public interest in permitting criticism of government.

(D) A public official, because public officials enjoy relative immunity from defamation liability as defendants.

142. In a jurisdiction that has not modified the common law rule, is truth a complete defense to defamation?

(A) Yes.

(B) No. Liability remains when the publication of truthful material is unjustified.

(C) No. Liability remains when the defendant is motivated by actual malice.

(D) No. Liability remains for exceptional invasions of privacy.

143. It is possible for a plaintiff to bring a successful defamation claim against a defendant for having said something literally true, provided that the statement is implicitly false and defamatory. Give an example.

ANSWER:

144. For purposes of bringing a defamation claim, a "public figure" is in a weaker position than an ordinary private citizen. The category has a few nuances. Describe the public figure in its strong form and its "limited purpose" form.

ANSWER:

145. In a debate over whether to abolish the doctrine of slander per se, which of the following rationales militates most strongly in favor of keeping it?

(A) Certain common accusations have predictable effects, and it would burden plaintiffs unduly to have to gather evidence of reputational harm when they are defamed by these accusations.

(B) Slander, unlike libel, compels a plaintiff to prove reputational harm.

(C) Technological innovation has not fully blurred the distinction between oral and written communication.

(D) It is relatively easy for a plaintiff to prove financial harm with respect to business activity, but unduly difficult to prove reputational harm with respect to his or her private life.

146. Legislator Lawrie delivered an impassioned speech in the well of the state assembly attacking "the Wall Street of Main Street," shortly before the legislature voted on a large appropriation

to businesses in the state. In the speech, Lawrie faulted several business leaders of the state for their inadequate commitment to citizen well-being. The speech included an accusation by Lawrie that local millionaire Milton employed undocumented workers to clean and serve food at his chain of hotels. This accusation was false, and Milton believes he suffered financial loss as a consequence. Furthermore, Milton finds the accusation gratuitous because his hotel, like all hotels in the state, was not in line to receive any funding from the appropriation being debated, and Milton has no other business interests in the state.

A defamation claim by Milton against Lawrie is likely to

(A) succeed, because Lawrie's remarks lacked a reasonable relation to the legislative endeavor at hand.

(B) succeed, because Milton is a public figure.

(C) fail, because Lawrie's remarks need not pertain to the legislative endeavor at hand in order to be covered by the legislator's privilege to commit prima facie defamation.

(D) fail, because of Lawrie's First Amendment privilege to engage in debate on a matter of public interest.

147. *Restatement (Second) of Torts* § 559 gives a definition of a *defamatory statement* that the courts cite frequently: it is a communication that tends to lower the plaintiff in the esteem of the community, or deter people from associating with her. Almost any statement about a person can be "defamatory," however, in the sense that someone might find the statement disgraceful. For example, calling a high schooler "an A student" might hurt her reputation at some schools.

How do courts deal with this problem in their definition of "defamatory"?

ANSWER:

Invasion of Privacy

148. Marther rents out his spare bedroom using InnTerNet, an online resource to guide searches for lodging. His guests would be surprised to learn that inside the headboard of their antique king-sized bed is a recording device. Marther enjoys sitting with headphones elsewhere in his home tuning into the conversations of guests in the spare bedroom. One day his device picked up the words of a married man named Jeff. Marther heard Jeff confess to his wife, in response to her questioning, that he, Jeff, had had homosexual experiences before their marriage. Marther repeated this gossip on Twitter, causing injury to Jeff.

Can Marther be liable to Jeff in an action for invasion of privacy?

(A) No, because the information that Marther repeated was truthful.

(B) No, because the home belongs to Marther and Marther has a privilege to enter the rooms of his property.

(C) Yes, because a reasonable person would find the disclosure of homosexual conduct repugnant.

(D) Yes, because Jeff had a reasonable expectation of privacy in his room.

149. Benita Bevilaqua, a psychotherapist, thought nobody would know that she and three friends, guests in her condominium, smoked marijuana using a water-cooled pipe that one of the guests, Jordan, had brought. As luck would have it, however, the building's smoke alarm went off and the building was evacuated. A television news crew came to the scene. Jordan was videotaped clutching the pipe. Jordan posted this video as a clip on his Bookface social media page, disclosing what the pipe was for and in whose home he had been. Some acquaintances of Benita watched this video on the evening news and others saw it on Bookface. Benita suffered damages related to professional disgrace. She is angry at Jordan, but sees no point in litigation against him because he has no money.

If Benita brings an action against the television station for invasion of privacy, what is the greatest weakness of her claim?

(A) There was no intrusion.

(B) Benita experienced no injury.

(C) The television station is not the proper defendant.

(D) The gathering and dissemination were not unreasonable.

150. Tarpala runs a "business intelligence" consulting business. Her work consists of attempting to learn her clients' competitors' trade secrets and other informational assets kept from the public. In May, posing as a United Way charities solicitor and acting on behalf of a client

named Marco, Tarpala gained entry to the factory floor of Gobble Inc., a manufacturer of children's toys, and surreptitiously took pictures of the top-secret Christmas line. Marco used this information for competitive advantage against Gobble, Inc.

Gobble, Inc. seeks your advice about whether it has a sound basis to bring an action against Tarpala for invasion of privacy. How would you advise Gobble, Inc. on this question?

(A) Gobble, Inc. is likely to prevail because Tarpala engaged in fraud.

(B) Gobble, Inc. is likely to prevail because Tarpala's entry to the factory floor was not privileged.

(C) Gobble, Inc. will not prevail because a corporation cannot bring an action for invasion of privacy.

(D) Gobble, Inc. will not prevail even assuming Tarpala has fulfilled the elements of invasion of privacy, because Gobble, Inc. cannot prove that Tarpala's actions caused its losses.

151. A Hollywood actress, Hilda-May, earns $30 million per movie. Despite her wealth and fame, not to mention a busy schedule, Hilda-May has time and leisure to consider litigation against some of the many people who offend her.

Which of the following behaviors would give Hilda-May her strongest claim for "appropriation of the plaintiff's name or likeness"? Assume that Hilda-May has consented to none of them.

(A) A struggling entrepreneur uses the name and photo of Hilda-May on the packaging of his new line of squash rackets.

(B) A start-up entertainment magazine prints a photograph of Hilda-May storming away from her boyfriend in a restaurant, and captions it "Hilda-May Flying Low!"

(C) A starving novelist names one of his characters Hilda-May. The character, a waitress with ambitions to sell a screenplay she has written, is manipulative and dishonest.

(D) A disgruntled ex-lover of Hilda-May's gives a long interview to Infotainment Tonite, a television show, describing their defunct relationship in painful detail. He is not paid by Infotainment Tonite, but he uses his appearance on the show to promote self-recorded music on his BoobTube channel.

152. Super model Cassandra Philandra, standing nearly six feet tall, weighs 150 pounds. Although she appears slender, she has won praise in the media for being "sensible" and "reasonable" in her size, in contrast to other models deemed "too thin." Journalist Elmer uncovered a bit of dirt about the "sensible" Cassandra: Ten years ago, as a teenager, Cassandra had weighed 105 pounds and was hospitalized for eating disorders. Cassandra has just learned that six months ago, Elmer repeated this truthful story about her to a circle of journalists. No media announcements have emerged. Cassandra has asked you to advise her about a possible action against Elmer alleging invasion of privacy.

How would you advise Cassandra's about the validity of her potential claim, and why?

(A) She is likely to prevail because the matter is not of legitimate public concern.

(B) She is likely to prevail because this disclosure is highly offensive to a reasonable person.

(C) She is unlikely to prevail because she is a public figure.

(D) She is unlikely to prevail because there has been no publication to the public at large.

153. Why does tort law bother with privacy—that is, what value does privacy serve, and why is tort law needed to achieve this value?

ANSWER:

154. One small city remembers well the case of John Septuagenarian, an elderly man who lived alone at the edge of town. Years ago, a teenage girl arrived at the police station and claimed she had escaped from Septuagenarian's house, where she had been kept in a basement dungeon. She showed the police the house. When they entered, they found six other girls, ages 12 to 16, in the basement. Septuagenarian had kidnapped and sexually abused them. On the testimony of the girls, whose names were kept from the public, Septuagenarian was convicted and sent to prison, where he died. The town still talks about the trial. Last week the local newspaper ran a story about television actress Gina Mulcahy, age 22. According to the news story, Mulcahy had been one of the "Dungeon Seven," one of Septuagenarian's victims. The story is true. The newspaper learned the information from civil court records; two years ago Mulcahy filed a quiet, low-profile civil suit against the estate of Septuagenarian, and received a (relatively small) settlement from his limited assets. Mulcahy is embarrassed and distressed by the newspaper story.

Mulcahy has brought an invasion of privacy claim against the newspaper. How would you characterize the strength of Mulcahy's case, and why?

(A) The case is strong because Mulcahy was a minor at the time of the kidnapping.

(B) The case is weak because the information the newspaper revealed was a matter of public record.

(C) The case is strong because the news disclosed is not a matter of public significance.

(D) The case is weak because Mulcahy consented to the publication.

155. Suppose you are a state supreme court judge considering whether to abandon your state's recognition of a tort claim for invasion of privacy. Which of the following considerations is *least* relevant to that project?

(A) The availability of other remedies for wrongful conduct, such as trespass and deceit.

(B) The distinction between true and false disclosures.

(C) Individuals' interest in keeping their private lives to themselves.

(D) The public interest in defining "newsworthiness" broadly.

156. Gothika, a famous recording artist, has consulted you about bringing an action against FanRagZine, an online magazine that had been struggling for two years and was about to shut down for lack of cash when it stumbled on a news story about Gothika: she had entered drug rehabilitation and was becoming a born-again Christian. FanRagZine published many pho-

tographs of Gothika and ran several stories about her transformation, all without her consent. Gothika can prove that FanRagZine gained thousands of dollars in new advertising revenue by exploiting her story. She seeks a share of these profits on a theory of "appropriation," the subcategory within invasion of privacy.

Why would her claim be unlikely to succeed? Advise her.

ANSWER:

Emotional Distress

157. District Attorney Doyle was irked by divorced persons who failed to make court-ordered child support payments. To crack down on these "deadbeat parents," Doyle constructed a large billboard in a prominent location. Each month, the billboard featured a photo of the "Deadbeat Parent of the Month," and a statement of how much the person owed for child support. For April, and as an April Fool's joke on her old friend Giles Crane, Doyle posted Crane's photo and a statement that Crane owed more than $20,000 in child support. When Crane learned of the poster, he suffered serious emotional distress, eventually leading to the breakup of his marriage. He became a shut-in, refusing to leave his luxury condo. He brings an action against Doyle for intentional infliction of emotional distress. Assume Doyle is not immune from tort liability.

    Which of the following statements best predicts the outcome of Crane's action and the primary reason for that outcome?

    (A) Crane will not prevail because Doyle did not intend to cause serious emotional distress.

    (B) Crane will not prevail because Doyle did not act maliciously.

    (C) Crane will not prevail because he did not suffer bodily harm.

    (D) Crane will likely prevail because he can satisfy all elements of the prima facie case and Doyle does not appear to have a valid defense.

158. Parker and Dawn, both seventh graders, liked to kid around with each other. One day, as Parker was placing her lunch tray on the table and starting to sit down, Dawn pulled the chair out from under her. Parker noticed this too late, lost her balance trying to avoid falling, and spilled the entire tray of food onto her clothes. Dawn and the others at the table began to laugh loudly, and soon the entire cafeteria was looking at Parker and laughing. Parker began to cry and ran from the room to the school nurse, who called her parents to pick her up. For several weeks, Parker felt so humiliated that she refused to return to school. In addition, she became physically ill, stopped eating, and needed to be placed on medication to improve her appetite.

    If Parker brings an action against Dawn for intentional infliction of emotional distress, which of the following statements is most likely correct?

    (A) Parker's claim will probably fail because Dawn's behavior was not extreme and outrageous.

    (B) Parker's claim will probably fail because Dawn did not mean to injure her.

    (C) Parker's claim will probably fail because she assumed the risk.

(D) Parker has a strong claim.

159. Under what conditions might it be proper for a court to hold a defendant liable for negligent infliction of emotional distress as experienced by a "hypersensitive" plaintiff—that is, when the defendant's behavior would not have caused a normal, ordinary person to suffer emotional distress?

ANSWER:

160. Celebrities Kim and Kanye had been together for several years, and although their relationship had become more serious since the birth of a daughter, Kanye decided he no longer wished to stay with Kim. He sent Kim a text message informing her of his decision at a time he knew Kim would be on the set of her reality TV show: "Yo, Kim, I'm really happy for you, and I'mma let you finish but Taylor is one of the greatest women of all time! I feel we would be better off not seeing each other anymore. I wish you all the best." Kim, not willing to believe the news, called Kanye to find out if the message was a cruel joke, but he did not pick up the phone. She left him numerous texts and voicemails, which he did not respond to, either. After not hearing from Kanye for days, Kim fell into a deep depression, got little sleep, and lost her appetite. She also went into intensive therapy for several months and had serious suicidal thoughts.

Kim is contemplating an action against Kanye for intentional infliction of emotional distress. Of the following, which poses the greatest potential difficulty with Kim's claim?

(A) The outrage element.

(B) The severe distress element.

(C) The fact that Kanye did not intentionally cause severe distress; his intentions were benign.

(D) The failure of Kim to experience physical manifestations of her distress.

161. "Negligent infliction of emotional distress" includes a range of emotional consequences under one doctrinal label. What sort of adverse emotions may be compensable injuries?

ANSWER:

162. Some decisional law on intentional infliction of emotional distress involves a scenario that also includes battery or assault claims that are time-barred, while the intentional infliction of emotional distress claim is still available under the statute of limitations. Why would a state legislature provide a longer limitation period for intentional infliction of emotional distress than for assault or battery?

(A) With intentional infliction of emotional distress, the injury is more subjective.

(B) With intentional infliction of emotional distress, the injury may take more time to develop.

(C) With assault or battery, the injury is linked more closely with the defendant's conduct.

(D) With assault or battery, the limitation period relates more closely to that of negligence.

163. Park, who is Asian-American, worked as an assistant to Smith at BigCorp, a large corporation. Over a period of several months, Smith repeatedly derided Park's ethnicity in front of other workers. He uttered crude, disparaging remarks about Asian-Americans and spoke with what he might have thought was an Asian accent when Park was in the room. Smith thought he was being funny and building camaraderie among the staff. Unamused and upset, Park complained to Smith's supervisor. When the supervisor failed to do anything about Smith's behavior, Park quit her job and brought an action against BigCorp for intentional infliction of emotional distress.

Which of the following statements about this claim is most accurate?

(A) BigCorp cannot be liable because Smith's actions were outside the scope of employment.

(B) Park can recover only if she suffered physical illness as a result of Smith's behavior.

(C) Park cannot recover because Smith did not intend to cause emotional distress.

(D) Park has a good claim for intentional infliction of emotional distress.

164. Laureen agreed to undergo surgery performed by Dan. Dan was HIV-positive, but did not inform Laureen of this fact because he genuinely believed it to be a private matter that posed no risk to her. Dan carefully avoided cutting himself during surgery, and the surgery was successful. Six months after the surgery, however, Laureen learned of Dan's HIV status. She became extremely apprehensive, and took an HIV test that came back negative. Nevertheless, the anxiety she suffered was extremely severe, and led to significant weight loss and other physical illness. Laureen has consulted an attorney, who is considering filing a claim for intentional infliction of emotional distress on Laureen's behalf against Dan.

Of the following arguments, which gives Dan the greatest chance of avoiding liability?

(A) Because Dan did not act maliciously, he did not satisfy the intent requirement, and Laureen cannot recover.

(B) Because Dan's conduct was not "extreme and outrageous," Laureen cannot recover.

(C) Because there was no contact between Dan's blood and Laureen's body, Laureen cannot recover.

(D) Because claims of severe emotional distress can be faked to easily, Laureen cannot recover.

165. Risa was eating lunch with Paddy in the company cafeteria when Diego, a co-worker, solemnly approached Risa and said "HR just got a call from County General. Wendy [Risa's wife] is admitted. Car accident. Bad. They don't think she's going to make it." Neither Paddy nor Risa asked why Risa was receiving bad news this way. Risa ran from the room and headed for County General hospital. As she drove, her phone rang. It was Wendy, asking Risa to pick up milk on the way home — indicating that she was fine; there had been no accident. Diego had been "just kidding," as he later said. Meanwhile Paddy, who, unknown to Diego, was a close friend of Risa and Wendy, suffered severe emotional distress. Though Paddy learned

later in the day that the statement was a prank, his anxiety was severe, and he required psychiatric care.

If Paddy brings an action against Diego for intentional infliction of emotional distress in a jurisdiction that accepts § 46 of the *Restatement (Second) of Torts*, which of the following statements is most correct?

(A) Paddy has a strong claim.

(B) Paddy will lose because Diego's conduct was not "extreme and outrageous."

(C) Paddy will lose because he did not suffer bodily harm.

(D) Paddy will lose because it was not reasonably foreseeable to one in Diego's position that Paddy would suffer severe emotional distress.

166. (Returning here to Question 52 in the duty chapter, you need not return to it yourself.) On board a commercial airline flight, things were going fine until the captain accidentally played for the passengers a pre-recorded announcement stating that the plane was about to crash into the sea. There was no actual emergency, and after a short time, the captain realized the error and announced that all was well and that the first announcement had been a mistake. Daphne, an elderly passenger, suffered a serious anxiety attack as a result of the erroneous announcement. Daphne brings an action against the airline for intentional infliction of emotional distress.

Of the following, which constitutes the airline's strongest argument against liability?

(A) Daphne was extra sensitive.

(B) There was no intent.

(C) The conduct was not extreme and outrageous.

(D) Daphne did not suffer physical injury.

167. Peter, his wife Pauline, and their son Padua drove together to the Sparkle Car, a car wash. Sparkle Car was a drive-through place, and customers were permitted to remain in the car while it rolled through the washing and drying areas. Peter and Padua remained in the car, while Pauline got out, intending to watch the car through thick windows along the way. When the car was part way through, one of Sparkle Car's employees negligently handled a piece of equipment, causing it to crash through the passenger-side window and impale Padua. Peter was looking the other way when this happened, but Pauline saw the whole thing and immediately fainted from emotional distress. Peter also became extremely upset when he noticed what had happened a few moments later.

If Pauline brings an action against Sparkle Car for negligent infliction of emotional distress, which of the following statements is correct?

(A) If the court applies the most common test, Pauline's case will fail.

(B) If the court applies the "impact" rule, Pauline will prevail.

(C) Regardless of the test used, Pauline's case will fail because Pauline was not in the zone of danger caused by the employee's negligence.

(D) Regardless of the test used, Pauline will prevail.

168. Same facts as above. Assume that when the piece of equipment broke the car window, flying glass also injured Peter, who was sitting in the driver's seat. Peter brings an action against Sparkle Car. Which of the following statements is most correct?

(A) Peter will not recover any damages because he did not witness the injury occurring to Padua.

(B) Peter will recover for his bodily injury, but will not recover for emotional distress if that kind of harm was not a reasonably foreseeable consequence of improperly handling the equipment.

(C) Peter will recover both for his bodily injury and for the emotional distress he suffered on observing his son's injuries.

(D) Peter will recover for his bodily injury, but whether he will recover his emotional distress damages depends on the test used in that jurisdiction for the tort of negligent infliction of emotional distress.

169. Same facts as above, except assume that Peter was not physically injured in the accident. Peter brings an action against Sparkle Car for negligent infliction of emotional distress. Which of the following statements is correct?

(A) Peter will not recover under either the "impact" or "zone of danger" rules.

(B) Peter will not recover under the "impact" rule, but will recover under the "zone of danger" rule.

(C) Because Peter did not witness his son's impaling, but only saw the consequences a few moments later, he may not recover under the more lenient test of cases such as *Dillon v. Legg*, but may recover under the "zone of danger" test.

(D) Peter will recover under any test for negligent infliction of emotional distress.

170. Which of the following doctrines that can relate to a claim of negligent infliction of emotional distress does *not* have the effect of keeping distressed persons out of court?

(A) The impact rule.

(B) The physical consequences rule.

(C) Zone of danger.

(D) Consortium.

Harm to Economic Interests

171. Which of the following is *not* an element of the tort of intentional misrepresentation?

    (A) Knowledge of the consequences of falsity.

    (B) Knowledge that the statement made was false.

    (C) Intent to induce reliance.

    (D) Materiality of the statement.

172. In order to obtain financing to buy an ongoing business, Dolly asked her husband, Madison, to hire an accounting firm and have that firm prepare an audited statement of Dolly's and Madison's joint net worth. Unknown to Dolly, Madison was engaged in various ongoing frauds. Dolly thought she and Madison were worth about $10 million, but actually they had less than $1 million in assets. Madison produced for Dolly an "audited financial statement," actually a document prepared by a crony of his, which grossly overstated the couple's assets. Dolly appended this "audited financial statement" to her loan application. The lending bank scheduled an interview with Dolly to evaluate the loan application. An official of the bank asked Dolly whether she personally had chosen the accounting firm that prepared the financial statement. Dolly said yes. She received the loan. Sometime later, Dolly defaulted on the loan. Assume the bank wants to recover from Dolly (but not Madison).

    Which claims would be plausible under these facts?

    (A) Intentional misrepresentation only.

    (B) Negligent misrepresentation only.

    (C) Both intentional and negligent misrepresentation.

    (D) Neither intentional nor negligent misrepresentation.

173. Partners of the law firm of Hoof & Mouth knew that the managers of its corporate client, Regiment, were given to making false representations. When Regiment sought to apply for a loan from Metrobank, its managers gave Hoof & Mouth documentation about its ownership of various assets. The Hoof & Mouth partners knew that Regiment managers had made material and false statements in the documentation. Nevertheless, Hoof & Mouth helped redraft the documents to make them look more convincing, and submitted these papers in the loan application to Metrobank. Metrobank made the loan. Regiment later defaulted and is now insolvent.

    In a lawsuit by Metrobank against the Hoof & Mouth partners, which of the following states the primary reason Metrobank should prevail?

(A) Although the true wrongdoer is Regiment, as between Metrobank and Hoof & Mouth, Hoof & Mouth should bear this loss.

(B) Hoof & Mouth partners knowingly assisted in the commission of tortious fraud.

(C) Hoof & Mouth partners were the agents of Regiment.

(D) The representations of Regiment were unlawful, and harms to Metrobank flowed proximately from this wrong.

174. Gargle, a celebrated bass-baritone singer, entered into an agreement with the Liberace Opera House to perform the title role in Mozart's "Don Giovanni" in September, one year after the contract was signed. Unfortunately, over Labor Day weekend, shortly before the scheduled opening night, Gargle's favorite bartender served him a platter of antipasti that the bartender should have known had gone bad. After consuming the platter of bad food, Gargle ended up stricken with nausea and vomiting. Resulting harm to his voice caused Gargle to have to cancel his appearance, which in turn forced the Liberace Opera House to spend thousands of dollars refunding advance tickets. In addition, the Liberace Opera House had to hire a substitute singer and pay him a salary. The Liberace Opera House brings a negligence action against the errant bartender and her employer, Da Ponte Lounge.

Which of the following statements is correct?

(A) The Liberace Opera House should prevail because a reasonable server would have known not to serve the food in question and Da Ponte Lounge is liable under respondeat superior.

(B) The Liberace Opera House should prevail because the expenditures it incurred in response to Gargle's harm were foreseeable.

(C) The Liberace Opera House should not prevail because there is no tort liability for negligent interference with contractual relations.

(D) The Liberace Opera House should not prevail because the contract between Gargle and Liberace Opera House covered this contingency.

175. Louisa and Bonnie Blue were business partners who habitually made real estate purchases together. They submitted a written offer to purchase a country estate. This offer ran several pages long and was signed on the final page by both Louisa and Bonnie Blue. Unknown to Bonnie Blue, Louisa removed the front page of the offer, the one that named and described the property, substituted a new front page describing both that property and a second property, and submitted this new document as an offer to a different seller, with both signatures on the final page. Louisa was hoping, on behalf of herself and Bonnie Blue, to buy both properties quickly and sell them quickly. Louisa's tampering was discovered before the prospective sellers signed the contracts; both sellers decided that Louisa and Bonnie Blue were shady operators, and refused to deal with them. Consequently, the Louisa-and-Bonnie-Blue partnership lost money.

Which claims by Bonnie Blue against Louisa are plausible?

(A) Misrepresentation.

(B) Tortious interference with contractual relations.

(C) Both misrepresentation and tortious interference with contractual relations.

(D) Neither misrepresentation nor tortious interference with contractual relations.

176. What is the difference between tortious interference with contract and tortious interference with economic opportunity (or tortious interference with prospective economic advantage)?

ANSWER:

177. Nemo worked as a forklift operator for Rayon, Inc. One day he was injured while using the forklift. He received workers' compensation payments and also filed a products liability claim against Forko, the manufacturer of the forklift, alleging manufacturing defects. Several months later, while Nemo's claim was pending, Rayon Inc. hired an outside company, Timeshare Inc., to perform maintenance and cleanups at various worksites. Misunderstanding its work orders from Rayon Inc., Timeshare Inc. disassembled the forklift that had injured Nemo and had since been put into storage. This disassembly caused pieces of the forklift to be lost. With no forklift to examine, Nemo's products liability claim became unprovable and he had to withdraw it.

Nemo has asked you to advise him about whether he could bring a successful negligence action against Timeshare, Inc. Of the following, which best states the advice you should give?

(A) Nemo should prevail because Timeshare assumed a duty of care, breached it, and caused financial loss to Nemo.

(B) Nemo should prevail because Timeshare exceeded the terms of its employment and caused financial loss to Nemo.

(C) Nemo should not prevail unless Nemo can prove aggravation of physical injuries.

(D) Nemo should not prevail unless Nemo can prove an undertaking.

178. Which of the following illustrates a claim of strict liability for misrepresentation that could succeed?

(A) Genevieve showed Barton a surveyor's map of her land and told him that according to this map that she had commissioned, the land had unobstructed access to a lake. Barton inferred that the land had access to the lake and bought it from Genevieve. It turned out that the surveyor had surveyed the land inaccurately: the land did not have access to the lake. Barton suffered a financial loss. Barton brought an action against Genevieve.

(B) A state statute requires that all fruits and vegetables treated with the pesticide CREECH must disclose this condition on a label. Alfred, a grocer, bought vegetables from a reputable organic grower and inspected them for pesticide residue. The vegetables appeared to be free of pesticides. Alfred sold them unlabeled. It turned out that a carrier had switched some boxes and the vegetables were indeed treated with CREECH. A customer suffered a reaction to CREECH after eating the vegetables, and brought an action against Alfred.

(C) Dalma hired Enron Auditors to prepare financial statements about her business when she was offering it for sale. Enron Auditors prepared statements that significantly over-stated the value of the business, causing injury to the buyer, an investor who lived out of state. When Dalma hired Enron Auditors, she knew the company had a reputation for producing inflated, "rosy scenario" financial statements. This reputation was not widely known beyond Dalma's community. The buyer brought an action against Dalma.

(D) Robin sincerely believed that the prize heifer she was selling had no diseases. A reason-able person experienced in dealing with heifers would have realized that the appearance of Robin's heifer indicated a congenital defect. Emma bought Robin's heifer, and like Robin took no notice of the telltale appearance of the heifer. The heifer turned out to have a disease related to the congenital defect and Emma suffered financial loss. Emma brought an action against Robin.

179. Q and W are parties to a contract. S induces Q to breach the contract with W, causing finan-cial loss to W. W brings an action of tortious interference with contract against S. S contends that W must bring an action against Q for breach of contract, either before or during the suit against S, before any judgment can be entered against S.

Is S wrong?

ANSWER:

180. Lawyer Llewellyn represented client Carmen in her attempts to collect on a succession of ill-fated loans. He filed lawsuits against the debtors, with only partial success. One of Carmen's debtors, Dravath, agreed to pay a reduced amount in settlement of Carmen's claim. Llewellyn prepared a settlement agreement, to be signed by Carmen and Dravath. In this settlement agreement, which Llewellyn himself typed in haste, the amount that Dravath agreed to pay, which should have been $820,000, was recorded as $280,000. Llewellyn gave the document to Carmen to review; Carmen, also hurrying, did not notice the error, and signed it. (Dravath signed it too, although what he knew or noticed at the time is unknown.) Llewellyn had sev-eral occasions to catch the error before filing the agreement, but did not proofread the doc-ument at any time before filing it. Relying on the erroneous rendering of the settlement amount, the court in which the agreement was filed determined that Carmen could receive only $280,000 instead of $820,000 from Dravath. In an action for legal malpractice by Car-men against Llewellyn for the difference between the two sums, a judge would note Carmen's failure to spot the error before signing the agreement.

Which of the following statements best describes the proper judicial response to this failure of Carmen's?

(A) The error should have no effect on Carmen's claim for legal malpractice.

(B) The error may be considered contributory or comparative negligence.

(C) The error may be considered contributory or comparative negligence if Llewellyn can establish that Carmen would have otherwise been able to collect the full amount of the settlement.

(D) Because Carmen had the last clear chance to avoid harmful consequences, the error should defeat Carmen's claim against Llewellyn.

181. Which of the following arguments provides the *weakest* support for making tort liability available to remedy consequential economic loss caused by negligence when plaintiff and defendant are not united by a contract?

(A) The extent of liability expands in nearly infinite chain reactions of economic harm.

(B) The defendant is by hypothesis negligent and its negligence has caused economic harm.

(C) Absent such liability, the defendant will frequently be underdeterred from negligent behavior.

(D) The plaintiff will frequently lack adequate alternative sources of compensation for injury that it cannot prevent through reasonable care.

182. In a claim for tortious interference with contract, can a plaintiff recover for his emotional and reputational harm as well as his financial loss? What is the contrary argument?

ANSWER:

Damages

183. Unlike many U.S. states, the state of Lympet has enacted no change to the collateral source rule. In a personal injury action filed against Celeste in a Lympet court, Vincent attributed $15,000 in lost income and $40,000 in medical expenses to the tortious conduct of Celeste. Vincent sought recovery for these losses only, making no claim for any nonpecuniary damages. The court entered judgment in favor of Vincent and against Celeste. Of Vincent's medical expenses that resulted from Celeste's tortious conduct, $35,000 was paid before trial by Vincent's private health insurance: Vincent himself paid out only $5,000 to medical providers.

    Lympet law on the collateral source rule provides that Celeste must pay Vincent

    (A) $20,000.

    (B) $40,000.

    (C) $55,000.

    (D) Nothing.

184. Should plaintiffs get to keep punitive damages awards, or should these awards be allotted to some defined public purpose? If you favor the latter choice, what is the most appropriate public purpose? Discuss.

    ANSWER:

185. Some courts and jurisdictions, though not all, recognize a tort of "wrongful formation" (or "wrongful pregnancy") where the defendant performed a sterilization operation without due care and a pregnancy resulted. Courts that recognize the claim face the issue of which losses to permit. Which of the following categories of damages is most likely to be awarded by a court with a conservative, or narrow, view of the wrongful formation tort?

    (A) Emotional distress experienced by the reluctant parent.

    (B) Expenses of "confinement," i.e., the cost of a hospital delivery of the baby.

    (C) Child-rearing expenses.

    (D) Offsets for the pleasure and happiness that the baby generates.

186. Which of the following types of damages will generally be discounted to present value?

    (A) Damages recoverable under the collateral source rule.

    (B) Damages for past pain and suffering.

(C) Lost future earnings damages.

(D) Punitive damages.

187. For most tort claims, a plaintiff has a duty to mitigate damages. To which of the following claims does this rule *not* apply?

(A) "Wrongful formation" of a child, due to negligence in sterilization surgery.

(B) A "second injury" claim where a plaintiff has been injured due to the negligence of two defendants acting separately.

(C) Tortious interference with contract.

(D) Negligent failure to diagnose a life-threatening condition.

188. For cases involving permanent disabling injury, give arguments for and against allowing a plaintiff's lawyer to argue to jurors that they should fix the future pain and suffering award based on something like "Calculate the dollar value of the amount of pain [name of plaintiff] suffers each day, then multiply it by the number of days [the plaintiff] is expected to live."

ANSWER:

189. Which of the following social problems is *least* relevant to the tort reform endeavor of reducing the amount of damages plaintiffs can seek in court?

(A) The refusal of insurance companies to write or renew malpractice insurance policies for physicians.

(B) The prosecution of marginal personal injury claims.

(C) The reluctance of manufacturing businesses to market useful products.

(D) The difficulty of identifying the optimal percentage of a judgment or settlement for the purpose of fixing a contingency fee.

190. Jessamyn purchased a Tootlin' TX model sport utility vehicle from a retail dealer. Within a year of the sale, the entire body of the Tootlin' TX was covered in rust. She brought an action against the manufacturer, TTX Inc. It emerged in discovery that TTX Inc. had used on 500 of its Tootlin' TXs an inferior grade of paint that it had bought very cheaply from a disreputable supplier. An internal document revealed that TTX Inc. had recommended to dealers that these inferior vehicles be sold "whenever possible" to women, minorities, and customers likely not to qualify for favorable financing, because "they're too intimidated to complain and they don't know the [state] lemon laws." A jury awarded Jessamyn $30,000 in compensatory damages and $80,000 in punitive damages.

Is the punitive damages portion of the award proper under the Supreme Court standard expressed in *BMW of North America, Inc. v. Gore*?

(A) Yes, because a jury could reasonably find that TTX Inc. acted with actual malice.

(B) Yes, because TTX Inc.'s behavior is reprehensible, the ratio of punitive to compensatory damages is not too high, and potential sanctions for comparable misconduct are likely to be similar.

(C) No, because this standard pertains only to personal injury damages, not the property damage experienced here.

(D) No, because punitive damages claims are preempted by deceptive trade practices statutes like "lemon laws."

191. Thousands of residents of Wilkaukee, a city, became severely ill with diarrhea and other intestinal problems over a period of several days. A city investigation revealed that the drinking water had become contaminated with a bacterium. Almost everyone who became ill recovered fully within a few days, but for people with weak immune systems, the problem was much more serious. One such person was Arni, a person with AIDS and severe organ damage, whose immune system was extremely weak. Arni died from the bacterial infection brought on by the drinking water. Arni's estate has sued the city of Wilkaukee for negligence. Assume Wilkaukee is not immune.

Which of the following arguments is most plausible for Wilkaukee to raise?

(A) Because Arni was extra sensitive, the action should fail.

(B) The water contamination was not the cause in fact of Arni's death.

(C) Because illness almost certainly would have shortened Arni's life, he suffered no damage.

(D) Because illness almost certainly would have shortened Arni's life, his damages should be reduced.

192. In which of the following cases would a court be most likely to award nominal damages, relieving the plaintiff from the burden of showing actual loss or injury?

(A) *Estevez v. New York Empire.* The plaintiff is the vice president of the United States and the defendant is a New York newspaper. Estevez objects to an Empire news story claiming that he had been treated for depression with electroshock therapy. The story is false: Estevez had been treated for depression with a combination of tranquilizers and muscle relaxants that are frequently used in conjunction with electroshock treatment. A psychiatrist reviewing files for the Empire story had inferred that Estevez must have been receiving electroshock therapy, and told the Empire reporter that Estevez had indeed received such treatment.

(B) *Susquehanna v. Lackawanna.* The parties' own adjacent lands. Lackawanna installed a tool shed at the edge of her property that protruded into Susquehanna's land. After receiving two threatening letters from Susquehanna, Lackawanna took down the tool shed.

(C) *Grossnickel v. Wilcox.* The parties reside in separate, adjacent condominium units in the Waterhole, a fashionable high-rise. Wilcox enjoys a hobby of attempting to make perfume at home. The resulting odors sicken Grossnickel and have caused him to work less well in his Waterhole home office, causing lost income.

(D) *Dumm v. Bummer*. Dumm, the plaintiff, suffered severe emotional distress when she saw the defendant, Bummer, ride his motorcycle negligently over the foot of her husband. Dumm heard what she described as "the crunch of bone." She has suffered sleep disturbances, but no physical injury.

193. Caps on damages for non-economic losses have been criticized as making it harder for elderly plaintiffs in the U.S. to receive any compensation for tortuously caused injury, not just money for non-economic damages. What is the connection between being elderly, caps on non-economic damages, and being at risk to receive no compensation for an injury?

ANSWER:

Multiple Defendants and Vicarious Liability

194. Which of the following is *not* an example of vicarious liability recognized in tort law?

    (A) Superseding cause.

    (B) Aiding and abetting.

    (C) Respondeat superior.

    (D) The liability that a driver who participated in a drag race but did not hit anyone can have in an action brought by a pedestrian who was hit by a car driven by someone else.

195. Barry was a passenger in a boat owned and rowed by Vlad. The two were headed to a meeting of geopolitical significance located on an island. Vlad negligently caused the rowboat to turn over and then swam away without helping Barry, a non-swimmer. Fortunately, a passing motorboat arrived in only a few minutes and transported Barry to shore. Barry and the rescuer agreed that although Barry felt well, it might be a good idea for Barry to go to an emergency room. An ambulance drove Barry to the hospital. Unfortunately, Dr. Medvedev, the emergency room doctor, negligently injured Barry's back while attempting to move him onto a hospital bed.

    If Barry brings negligence actions against both Medvedev and Vlad for the back injury, which of the following statements is most accurate?

    (A) Only Vlad will be held liable.

    (B) Only Dr. Medvedev will be held liable.

    (C) Both Vlad and Dr. Medvedev will be held liable.

    (D) Neither Vlad nor Dr. Medvedev will be held liable because it is impossible to apportion the injury between the two defendants.

196. In claims of respondeat superior, who decides the question of whether an employee's act falls within the scope of employment: the judge or the jury?

    ANSWER:

197. Ermintrude brings an action against Needlenose and Link for negligence. Ermintrude's case goes to the jury, and the jury determines that Ermintrude suffered $10,000 in damages but that all three parties failed to exercise reasonable care. The jury assesses Link's causal contribution as 50 percent of the total, Needlenose's as 15 percent of the total, and Ermintrude's as 35 percent of the total. The judge is about to enter judgment accordingly.

If the jurisdiction has adopted a "pure" form of comparative negligence, and has not abolished the common law rule concerning joint and several liability, which of the following statements is correct?

(A) Ermintrude will receive a judgment for $6500 against both Link and Needlenose, and may recover all or part of that sum from either or both defendant.

(B) Ermintrude will receive a judgment for $5000 against Link and $1500 against Needlenose.

(C) Ermintrude will receive a judgment of $10,000 against both Link and Needlenose, and may recover all or part of that sum from either or both defendants.

(D) Ermintrude will receive a judgment of $5000 against Link, but nothing against Needlenose because her negligence exceeded his.

198. Describe the most significant type of vicarious liability recognized by tort law.

ANSWER:

199. What is the difference between "contribution" and "indemnity"? Give an example of each.

ANSWER:

200. How does *respondeat superior* resemble strict products liability?

ANSWER:

201. Which of the following is *not* a plausible argument in support of the choice made by some states to abolish joint and several liability?

(A) Joint and several liability is inconsistent with the modern adoption of comparative fault.

(B) Joint and several liability assigns liability out of proportion to a defendant's degree of relative culpability.

(C) Joint and several liability compels solvent defendants to supply what insolvent or immune defendants do not contribute to an award of damages.

(D) Joint and several liability is imposed whether or not the plaintiff's fault contributed to the injury.

202. Parents are not generally liable for the torts of their children. What are the exceptions to this rule?

ANSWER:

203. In a state which has retained joint liability while accepting percentage-based apportionment, a court awarded Mike a judgment of $1,000,000 against four defendants: Bradley, Ed, Zach, and Justin. The jury apportioned responsibility among the four defendants as follows: Bradley 30 percent, Justin 20 percent, Zach 40 percent, and Ed 10 percent.

Justin is insolvent and cannot pay any portion of the judgment.

How much should Mike collect from each defendant?

(A) $400,000 from Zach, $300,000 from Bradley, $200,000 from Justin, and $100,000 from Ed.

(B) $500,000 from Zach, $375,000 from Bradley, and $125,000 from Ed.

(C) $400,000 from Zach, $300,000 from Bradley, and $100,000 from Ed.

(D) $480,000 from Zach, $360,000 from Bradley, and $120,000 from Ed.

204. Lorelei, a second-year law student, worked an hourly-wage job on a flexible basis at her cousin's landscaping business, Scudder Gardens. The work consisted of data entry and billing, but one Friday when two workers failed to show up, the cousin asked Lorelei if she could join a team on a garden site. Lorelei agreed. The site supervisor, Willis, instructed Lorelei to drag large bags filled with weeds and branches to a shredder and then throw in the contents. The shredder was half full when Lorelei started work. She was nearly done with the job when her classmate Trish unexpectedly walked by. Unknown to Lorelei, Trish's parents owned the garden site. Trish made an unkind, bigoted remark implying that as a sub-gardener, Lorelei did not belong in law school. Lorelei challenged Trish to a fistfight.

In the scuffle, the shredder tipped over, emptying its contents onto Trish and Lorelei. Lorelei and Trish both suffered skin reactions requiring hospital treatment. Investigation later showed that due to carelessness by Willis, a large quantity of poison ivy had been tossed into the shredder before Lorelei started work there. A reasonably careful gardener/site supervisor can identify poison ivy and does not put it into a shredder.

Is the careless behavior of Willis that contributed to Trish's and Lorelei's injuries attributable to Willis's employer, Scudder Gardens?

(A) Yes, because a landscape business can foresee the danger of poison ivy to human skin.

(B) Yes, because Willis supervised the sorting of weeds as part of his work for Scudder Gardens.

(C) No, because the fistfight between Lorelei and Trish was a superseding cause of Trish's injury.

(D) No, because Lorelei participated voluntarily in the fistfight.

205. Same facts as above. Lorelei, who attends your school and admits she slept through Torts, has asked you whether she has a claim of negligence against Scudder Gardens for her poison ivy injury. She has a vague idea that workers' compensation might be an issue.

Which of the following statements about workers' compensation is most correct?

(A) If Lorelei is deemed an employee of Scudder Gardens, she will be eligible for workers' compensation and her negligence claim will be barred.

(B) If Lorelei is deemed an employee of Scudder Gardens, she can elect either workers' compensation or a negligence action but not both.

(C) Because Lorelei is primarily a law student and only a casual employee of Scudder Gardens, she faces no workers' compensation bar and may bring a negligence action.

(D) Because workers' compensation covers traumatic injury rather than toxic exposure, Lorelei is ineligible for workers' compensation. An action for negligence against Scudder Gardens is not necessarily precluded, however.

206. What is the difference between "contribution" and "indemnity" in the context of multiple parties and financial responsibilities for tortious conduct?

(A) Contribution considers whether a second tortfeasor played a role in causing the harm; indemnity does not.

(B) Contribution is available in intentional tort claims as well as claims of negligence; indemnity is available only for negligence.

(C) Indemnity obliges a second person or entity to pay the first person or party for damages paid out; contribution provides for sharing of this expense.

(D) Indemnity provides that a second person or entity will not be liable for tortious conduct; contribution makes this immunity discretionary rather than mandatory.

207. Darren owns First Step, a board and care facility for mental patients who have been deemed ready for partial independence. (We met Darren and his First Step business in Question 115, which need not be referenced to answer this question.) One night Endora, a resident of First Step, climbed out through a second-story window and attacked Jade, a pedestrian who was walking past the facility. Jade suffered cuts and bruises.

If Jade brings an action against Darren, which of the following statements is most accurate?

(A) Unless Darren was negligent in supervising the residents at night, Jade will not be able to recover.

(B) Because Darren is vicariously responsible for Endora's tortious conduct that is a foreseeable consequence of her residency at First Step, Darren will be liable.

(C) Because Endora's criminal conduct superseded any negligence on Darren's part, Jade will not be able to recover.

(D) Because Darren negligently permitted Endora to escape, Darren will be liable.

Practice Final Exam

208. In *Larry and Arthur v. Rugby Board of the United States*, two players, ages 19 and 21, brought actions against the unincorporated entity that writes rules for amateur rugby. Larry and Arthur, who played on weekends in the same community league, were injured in separate games two years ago. Both were playing "nabber," the middle position in the front row of the scrum. In the years before their injury, evidence had mounted to show that nabbers were endangered by the way opposing teams come together in a rugby game. Larry and Arthur noted that a year after they were injured, Rugby Board of the United States (RBUS) had modified the game rules so that players in the front row must first crouch, then pause, and then engage slowly. Their complaint alleged that RBUS injured them through negligent failure to amend the rugby rules at the time that danger to nabbers became known. RBUS now contends that it cannot be liable because it owed Larry and Arthur no duty of care.

Which analogy best supports RBUS's position?

(A) Choreographers are not liable to dancers for torn ligaments caused by inadequate pre-rehearsal stretching.

(B) Legislators are not liable to factory workers for failing to have enacted workplace safety legislation.

(C) Football linemen cannot recover for battery when they are tackled by opposing players.

(D) Employees who suffer fatigue from overwork cannot collect workers compensation when they become unable to continue their jobs.

209. Same facts as above. Which of the following points, if correct, is *least* relevant to Larry and Arthur's cause of action?

(A) In community league play, referees seldom enforce RBUS rules.

(B) RBUS rules are optional for community leagues; some have declined to adopt them.

(C) High school athletes who sign up for school rugby are sometimes compelled to play under RBUS rules.

(D) Because of supermajority voting rules and notice requirements, RBUS rules are almost impossible to revise.

210. As Doug was driving along Main Street, he became distracted by his ringing cell phone and crossed the center line, colliding with a car driven by Pearl. Pearl was uninjured, but her car's steering mechanism was damaged. Pearl tried to drive the car to a safe spot at the side of the road, but lost control along the way and ran directly into a utility pole, injuring herself. Pearl brings a negligence action against Doug.

If Doug claims he is not responsible for Pearl's injury, which of the following statements is most likely correct?

(A) If a reasonable person in Pearl's position, taking into account the emergency, would have been able to maneuver the car safely to the side of the road, Pearl's conduct will be treated as a superseding cause that absolves Doug of responsibility for her injury.

(B) If a reasonable person in Pearl's position, *not* taking into account the emergency, would have been able to maneuver the car safely to the side of the road, Pearl's conduct will be treated as a superseding cause that absolves Doug of responsibility for her injury.

(C) Because Pearl was acting to avoid the consequences of Doug's negligence, her conduct will not affect Doug's liability for her injury.

(D) Because Pearl was acting to avoid the consequences of Doug's negligence, her conduct will not absolve Doug of responsibility for her injury, but Pearl's recovery may be reduced if the jury finds her to have been contributorily negligent under the circumstances.

211. Whatsamatta U negligently maintained the electrical system in its building. One day, a fire broke out, destroying the building as well as an adjacent house owned by Winkle. The next day, a raging forest fire swept out of the hills behind the campus and took a path directly through the place where Winkle's house had stood. The forest fire was started by Rocky, a smoker who discarded a lit cigarette carelessly. Whatsamatta U is insolvent. Winkle has brought an action against Rocky for negligence, seeking to recover the value of his burned house.

Which of the following statements is most accurate?

(A) Because the house was not destroyed by the fire Rocky started, Rocky will prevail.

(B) Because Winkle cannot prove that Rocky's fire would have destroyed the house, Rocky will prevail.

(C) Because Rocky is a negligent party, the law will not permit him to shield himself behind the fortuitous fact that his fire came after the one caused by Whatsamatta U. Therefore, Winkle will prevail.

(D) Because Whatsamatta U is insolvent and Winkle is an innocent party, Rocky will be held liable.

212. Myringotomy is one of the most common types of surgery in the United States. Usually performed on young children who suffer from chronic ear infections that can cause permanent ear damage, the surgery involves placing tiny tubes in the eardrums to allow fluid to escape, preventing the onset of ear infections. Because the ear is delicate, surgeons customarily use a light general anesthetic on children who might move around too much if they are awake during the procedure. Aside from risks normally associated with general anesthesia, a rare risk of the surgery is that the tubes will permanently damage the eardrums.

Cara, age 4, had already had many serious ear infections and did not respond well to antibiotics. Her pediatrician recommended that she see Gary, an ear specialist, to determine whether she should undergo a myringotomy. After examining Cara and consulting with her parents, Gary recommended the surgery. He told Cara's parents exactly what the surgery entailed, as well as its risks and benefits and the risks and benefits of the other alternatives. In keeping with medical custom, however, he did not tell Cara herself that the surgery involved puncturing her eardrums to insert tiny tubes. The parents approved the surgery.

Just before the surgery was to begin, Cara became very frightened when she overheard some nurses discussing the nature of the surgery. Before Cara could say she didn't want to go through with it, a mask was placed over her face and she was off to dreamland. During the surgery Gary used a larger tube than is customarily used for children of Cara's size, and when he inserted it in her right ear, the large hole it made permanently impaired Cara's hearing in that ear.

If Cara wishes to bring an action against Gary, which of the following theories has the greatest chance of success?

(A) Battery, for performing surgery against her wishes.

(B) Negligence, for using a tube larger than that customarily used in the profession.

(C) Assault, for causing Cara's apprehension of suffering imminent harmful or offensive contact.

(D) Strict liability, based on the abnormally dangerous nature of the procedure.

213. Wynona Law School was building a new parking garage. The land was cleared and work began on shoring the perimeter with concrete columns sunk 30 feet into the ground. Much heavy equipment was needed, including a number of special concrete mixers, one of which was very valuable. Each night, workers would suspend that mixer about 15 feet in the air on a cable attached to a construction crane. Late one night, prankster law students Adam and Eve (whom we met in Questions 41 and 42; those questions need not be reread here) painted the words "FRAT MIXER" on a large piece of cardboard, climbed over the six-foot fence separating the construction site from the rest of the property, and hoisted the sign onto the mixer. As they were leaving, a sudden and powerful wind gust caused the mixer to swing wildly on the cable from which it was suspended. Adam was injured when a metal part broke off the mixer and struck him in the head. Adam has brought a negligence action against Wynona Law School to recover for his injury.

Assume the state in which the action is filed adheres to traditional rules regarding the liability of land owners and occupiers. Which of the following states the most likely outcome of Adam's action?

(A) Wynona will be liable for negligence because it is unreasonable to leave equipment where it could swing in a wind and injure someone on or off the property.

(B) Wynona will not be liable for negligence because its negligent act was not the cause in fact of Adam's injury.

(C) Wynona will not be liable for negligence because it had no duty to protect Adam from the harm that occurred.

(D) Wynona will be liable for negligence because as a law student, Adam is an invitee.

214. Same facts as above, but this time assume that the state in which the action is filed has abolished the common law rules governing the liability of landowners and occupiers. Which of the following states the most likely outcome of Adam's action?

    (A) Wynona will be liable for negligence if the court determines that Adam retained his status as an invitee when entering the garage site.

    (B) Wynona will not be liable for negligence because its negligent act was not the cause in fact of Adam's injury.

    (C) Wynona will not be liable for negligence because it had no duty to protect Adam from the harm that occurred.

    (D) Wynona will be liable for negligence if a factfinder determines that it is unreasonable to leave equipment where it could swing in a wind and injure someone on or off the property.

215. District Attorney Drucilla, like District Attorney Doyle of Question 157, was sick and tired of divorced parents falling behind on court-ordered child support payments. To crack down on these "deadbeat parents," Drucilla also rented a large billboard in a prominent location. Each month, the billboard featured a photo of the "Deadbeat Parent of the Month" and a statement of how much the person owed for child support. For April, Drucilla chose Walden, a businessperson who owed more than $20,000 in child support. Unfortunately, the Walden whose photograph was used on the billboard was not the Walden who owed the money. The photo, instead, depicted a prominent psychiatrist. When psychiatrist Dr. Walden learned of the poster, he suffered serious emotional distress, eventually leading to the breakup of his marriage. He became a shut-in, refusing to leave his home. He has sued Drucilla in her official capacity as D.A. Assume Drucilla failed to exercise reasonable care to ensure that the correct photograph was selected, and that she is not immune from suit.

    Assuming that negligent infliction of emotional distress is not limited to "zone of danger" circumstances, how would it be applied to these facts? Would intentional infliction of emotional distress work better?

    ANSWER:

216. Shakira and Shamrock were high school classmates 13 years ago and still get together occasionally. Today Shakira holds steady employment as a paralegal and stays out of trouble, but she had been a very reckless teenager. Shamrock, well behaved in high school, went on to become an orthopedic surgeon. Shakira recently went to Shamrock's office and complained about pain in her wrist. Shamrock diagnosed carpal tunnel syndrome and recommended surgery on her hand. "No," said Shakira, "I don't cut myself anymore." "This isn't cutting yourself, goofball, I'm cutting," Shamrock replied. "Not interested," said Shakira.

    Puzzled by Shakira's new conservatism and unwilling to accept it, Shamrock asked Shakira if she would agree to "twilight sleep," a light anesthetic, and vigorous massage of her wrist when she was semi-conscious. "Okay," Shakira said. Shamrock gave Shakira the anesthesia and while Shakira was semi-unconscious, eyes closed, proceeded with the surgery he had recommended. Shakira's wrist never bothered her again, but she wants to bring a tort action against Shamrock.

Under which tort may Shakira prevail?

(A) Negligence.

(B) Battery.

(C) Conversion.

(D) Assault.

217. Which of the following is a difference between Second Restatement and Third Restatement provisions on intentional infliction of emotional distress?

(A) The Third Restatement eliminates the "extreme and outrageous" criterion for intentional infliction of emotional distress.

(B) The Third Restatement introduces "serious emotional harm," a phrase not present in the Second Restatement.

(C) The Second Restatement required that the plaintiff experience physical manifestations of intentionally inflicted emotional distress; the Third Restatement does not.

(D) The Third Restatement permits liability for recklessly as well as intentionally inflicted emotional distress; the Second Restatement did not.

218. Demetria witnessed a homicide, and told Detective Richards that Frank was the killer. Richards told Demetria about a witness protection program and said that whenever a witness is threatened she is relocated. Frank was arrested, charged with murder, and jailed. Soon, an anonymous caller told Demetria that if she testified, her home would be blown up. Demetria told Richards about the call, and Richards advised Demetria to contact him if the threats continued. Though Richards believed the threat was coming from the jailed Frank or Frank's family or friends, and though Richards believed Frank to be dangerous, he did not tell Demetria that Frank was a suspect in other murders or that he had threatened witnesses in those other cases. Just before she was to testify at Frank's trial, associates of Frank killed Demetria while she was waiting for a bus. Though Frank was still in jail, he had ordered the killing.

Demetria's estate has brought a negligence action against the city based on the actions of Detective Richards. The city might claim it had no duty to warn Demetria or act to prevent her murder. Dispute this contention about no duty.

ANSWER:

219. Same facts as above. If the city agrees that it owed Demetria a duty of care, but claims it satisfied its duty by confining Frank, which of the following statements is most accurate?

(A) Because Frank was jailed at the relevant times, the city satisfied its duty as a matter of law.

(B) Because Demetria was killed despite the fact that Frank was jailed at the relevant times, the city breached its duty as a matter of law.

(C) The court should allow the jury to determine whether the city breached its duty.

(D) The court will shift to the city the burden of demonstrating that it did not breach its duty.

220. Same facts as above. Assume duty and breach are present. The city claims that Demetria assumed the risk by riding public transportation after receiving a death threat and shortly before she was scheduled to testify against a person charged with murder. Which of the following statements is most accurate?

(A) It would be reasonable for a jury to decide that Demetria assumed the risk in the primary sense, eliminating any duty the city owed to her.

(B) It would be reasonable for a jury to decide that Demetria assumed the risk in the secondary sense, thereby reducing any possible recovery.

(C) Because Demetria's decision to ride public transportation was unreasonable and was a causal factor in her death, any discussion of assumption of risk is unnecessary.

(D) The court should rule as a matter of law that Demetria did not assume the risk.

221. The concert was sold out, but Diva went to the stadium hoping to buy a ticket from a scalper just before the show. Scalpers' prices were higher than Diva could afford, and Diva began to walk back to her car, dejected. Suddenly, Diva had an idea. She ran toward Pluto, who was holding his ticket, waiting to enter the arena, and let out a blood-curdling scream. As Pluto turned to check out the noise, he saw Diva rushing toward him. Diva reached him within a couple of seconds, grabbed his ticket and ran toward the entrance. Pluto started after her, but could not catch up.

If Pluto brings an action against Diva for assault, which of the following statements is most accurate?

(A) Because Diva touched an object closely connected with Pluto's person (the ticket), Pluto's proper cause of action would be for battery. Therefore, Pluto's assault action will not succeed.

(B) Because Pluto was not frightened by Diva, Pluto's assault action will not succeed.

(C) By holding his ticket in a manner that would allow someone to grab it, Pluto assumed the risk. Therefore, his assault action will not succeed.

(D) Pluto's assault action will probably succeed.

222. Same facts as above. Suppose Pluto had reacted very quickly to Diva's rapid approach, and had struck her with his fist just as she reached him, knocking her down and bruising her. If Diva brings an action against Pluto for battery, and the case is tried to a jury, which of the following statements is most accurate?

(A) If the judge finds that Pluto reasonably believed Diva was going to batter him, and that Pluto did not use excessive force in repelling Diva, then she should enter judgment for Pluto.

(B) If the jury finds that Pluto reasonably believed Diva was going to batter him, and that Pluto did not use excessive force in repelling Diva, then it should render a verdict for Pluto.

(C) If the judge finds that Diva did not intend to touch Pluto, she should hold Pluto liable.

(D) If the jury finds that Diva did not intend to touch Pluto, it should hold Pluto liable.

223. Gamblers' Express (GE) runs package tours for senior citizens from River City to Lost Wages, a gambling resort. GE is *not* a common carrier. Eliot, age 79, signed up for an excursion and boarded the bus one Tuesday morning. A few minutes before the bus was scheduled for a rest stop, James, a 75-year-old passenger sitting just behind Eliot, got up to remove an item from the overhead bin. An hour out of River City, the bus' air conditioning system failed. While James was still standing, Marny, the driver, pulled the bus to the side of the road so she could open an overhead air vent. Unfortunately, Marny did not tell the passengers at the beginning of the trip to stay seated at all times, and she failed to check her mirror to see if anybody was standing in the aisle before she pulled over. As the bus came to a stop, James lost his balance and fell into Eliot, injuring Eliot's shoulder.

Eliot wishes to bring an action against James. Which of the following theories is most viable on the law and supported by the facts?

(A) Battery, based on the theory that James should have recognized he was substantially certain to lose his balance and fall into another passenger.

(B) Battery, based on the theory that James knew his age made him more prone to falling than a younger person.

(C) Negligence, based on the theory that a reasonable person in George's position, taking account of his age and health, would not have stood up while the bus was moving.

(D) Negligence, based on the theory that a reasonable person of average age and health would not have stood up while the bus was moving.

224. Augustine owned August Summer Bakery Inc., a small business. Her cousin Kermit, who had worked in the bakery as a child, was interested in buying it from Augustine when she retired. Kermit and Augustine had chatted off and on for 10 years about how the bakery would transfer eventually from Augustine to Kermit, although they never reduced their conversations to writing. The two were never close, despite their familial relationship. While Augustine operated the bakery, her neighbor Jon decided he wanted to buy it. He worried that Augustine would favor Kermit over him as a buyer. To induce Augustine to sell the bakery to him instead, Jon told Augustine a true story she did not know: Kermit had pleaded guilty to charges related to child abuse 15 years earlier. Augustine was horrified and decided to sell the bakery to Jon instead of Kermit.

These facts might give rise to a claim by Kermit against Jon for

(A) tortious interference with prospective economic opportunity.

(B) tortious interference with contract.

(C) defamation.

(D) invasion of privacy.

225. Huckleberry was a passenger on a tour bus owned and operated by Bus Co. (not a common carrier). At one point, the driver pulled over to the side of the road so she could fix something on her uniform, which had become uncomfortable. While the bus was stopped, it was struck from the rear by another vehicle. Huckleberry was injured when the collision caused him to hit his head on a metal bar. Huckleberry brings an action against Bus Co. for negligence, alleging that the driver had a duty not to stop the bus except at designated rest stops and that she breached her duty by stopping when she did. Bus Co. regulations provide that drivers must stop only at designated rest stops.

Which of the following statements is accurate?

(A) Because the driver's conduct violated company regulations, her actions were a superseding cause of Huckleberry's harm, defeating Huckleberry's claim.

(B) If the jurisdiction follows a "scope of risk" theory, the driver's conduct, if negligent, would be viewed as a superseding cause, defeating Huckleberry's claim.

(C) Because the driver's conduct constituted an intentional tort, Bus Co. may not be held vicariously liable.

(D) If the driver's conduct was unreasonable, Huckleberry can recover against Bus Co.

226. In the last few seconds of a professional hockey game, Gilles, a player whose team trailed by one point, hit a hard shot toward the goal from a great distance. A long shot in every sense of the word, this play was a desperate effort to tie the game. The puck missed the goal and flew into the stands, striking Fred, whose seat was several rows up from the ice. Fred brings an action against Gilles.

Which of the following statements is most accurate?

(A) Because Gilles knew with substantial certainty that the puck would strike somebody if it did not go into the goal, he can be liable for battery.

(B) Because Gilles should have known with substantial certainty that the puck would strike somebody if it did not go into the goal, he can be liable for battery.

(C) Because Gilles negligently hit the puck, he can be liable for negligence.

(D) Gilles ought to prevail.

227. Vorch knew nothing about hockey, had never attended a game, and had no idea that pucks can fly off the ice and into the stands. Some friends persuaded Vorch to join them at a professional game at a stadium owned and operated by HockeyCo. Vorch spent his time playing with his smartphone and paid little attention to the game. At one point, a puck flew off the ice and struck Vorch, injuring him. Vorch brings a negligence action against HockeyCo, alleging that HockeyCo should have constructed a higher barrier that would protect him from flying pucks. The barrier used by HockeyCo was the same height as barriers used in all other hockey stadiums at which professional teams play.

Which of the following statements is most accurate?

(A) Vorch should not recover because HockeyCo did not owe him a duty with respect to this kind of injury.

(B) Vorch's recovery should be reduced because, even though HockeyCo was negligent, he confronted a danger of which most people are aware.

(C) Vorch's recovery should be reduced because he was comparatively negligent for choosing a seat that was not protected by the barrier.

(D) Vorch should recover fully for his injuries.

228. Which of the following scenarios illustrates negligent (as compared with intentional) defamation?

(A) Libby, desiring to injure the reputation of her sorority sister Sondra, posted on her social network page a statement alleging that Sondra was sexually promiscuous.

(B) Morticia, editor of a small neighborhood weekly newspaper, ran a story without editing it, because she was too busy that day with personal matters to do her job. The story reported an accusation of sexual assault. Contrary to the newspaper's policy, and much to the dismay of Morticia, the story included the name of the accuser.

(C) Real estate broker Sheraton sends a monthly letter to clients and potential clients describing his recent closings. In his last letter, Sheraton forgot to mention having sold Gabriel's house. Gabriel infers that Sheraton wishes to dissociate himself from the sale, thereby impugning Gabriel and his house.

(D) Because of an intern's shakiness with numbers and tendency to transpose by mistake, a newspaper published a story saying that Wimpy's restaurant scored 49 on a health inspection. The restaurant actually scored 94. A score below 70 is considered failing.

229. Shamarina Hall, a remodeled 18th century house, can be rented for elaborate parties like wedding receptions. Large glass doors in the back of Shamarina Hall open to a terraced garden. In good weather, the doors are typically kept open so that guests can easily walk in and out; in bad weather, the doors are locked and covered with heavy curtains. The glass, installed 40 years ago, is thin and vulnerable to shattering. Glass doors manufactured in the last 30 years are much more shatterproof.

Unfortunately for Brenda, the weather at the wedding she attended at Shamarina Hall was neither good nor bad; the hosts kept the glass doors closed but not locked or covered. A bit tipsy during the cocktail hour, mistakenly thinking the doors were solid, Brenda tried to steady herself against the glass and crashed into it, suffering injury.

If Brenda brings an action for negligence against the owner of Shamarina Hall and the owner seeks judgment as a matter of law, the court should

(A) grant judgment in favor of the owner, because no reasonable jury could find that the condition of the glass evinced negligence.

(B) grant judgment in favor of the owner, because the owner did not owe Brenda a duty of care; the hosts of the wedding were in possession of the premises when she was injured.

(C) refuse to grant judgment in favor of the owner, because Brenda was only partially responsible for the injury she suffered.

(D) refuse to grant judgment in favor of the owner, because the owner owed her a duty of care and may have breached its duty.

230. Same facts as above. Assuming that Brenda may bring an action for negligence concerning the nature of the glass, which statement about its non-shatterproof condition is most correct?

(A) The condition may be unreasonably dangerous, and the plaintiff should be permitted to show the jury that for the last 30 years, glass doors have been safer.

(B) The condition may be unreasonably dangerous, but the plaintiff must demonstrate its danger without reference to contemporary glass, because the condition of contemporary glass does not pertain to Brenda's injury and would be prejudicial.

(C) The condition is not unreasonably dangerous as a matter of law because it comports with the standard of care for glass installation that prevailed at the time of manufacture and installation.

(D) The condition is unreasonably dangerous as a matter of law because it does not comport with the standard of care for glass installation that prevailed at the time of injury.

231. Steve and Rose were playing tag in the park. Steve spotted Rose, and moved slowly toward her to tag her. Rose moved backward to avoid Steve. Steve knew Rose was nearing the edge of a sidewalk and a rather high curb, and he sensed that Rose was not aware of these facts. Nevertheless, he continued to advance. Rose stumbled over the curb and fell into the street, suffering several cuts on her arms and head. Rose brings an action against Steve for assault to recover for the fear she suffered as Steve slowly advanced toward her, just before she fell into the street.

Which of the following statements is most accurate?

(A) Because Steve acted with intent to cause apprehension of imminent contact, and because Rose suffered such apprehension, Steve is liable.

(B) If Rose knew she could avoid Steve's touch by simply running around him, Steve will not be liable.

(C) Because Steve was privileged to commit the touch that his actions threatened, he did not possess actionable intent and will not be liable.

(D) Without more facts, it is not possible to determine whether Steve is likely to be liable to Rose for assault.

232. Norm was driving near a park. Though the speed limit was 25 mph, he was driving 45 mph. Just after he rounded a corner, a child named Ronnie, who had been playing in the park, fell into the street. Norm did not see Ronnie in time to stop, and struck her. Had Norm been traveling 25 mph or less, he would have been able to stop in time. Ronnie brings a battery action against Norm.

Which of the following statements is most accurate?

(A) Because Norm was intentionally driving the car at the time and place and in the manner he was driving, and because he struck Ronnie, Norm will be liable.

(B) Because Norm should have known the grave risk of striking a child if he drove at such a high speed near a park, Norm will be liable.

(C) Because Norm violated a statute designed to protect a class of persons that included Ronnie, Norm will be liable.

(D) Because Norm did not act with the necessary intent, Norm will not be liable.

233. Which of the following statements best expresses a deterrence rationale for the doctrine of respondeat superior?

(A) Employers can obtain liability insurance more easily than employees for work-related conduct.

(B) Employers profit from the actions of employees done in the scope of employment.

(C) Many employees cannot pay for the cost of the injuries they negligently inflict.

(D) Some employees would commit torts in the scope of their employment even if their employers took every possible precaution to guard against this risk.

234. Elinor was mentally ill and had been institutionalized in a series of facilities over the years. Often she would walk away from the facilities, become disoriented, and would have to be located and returned. If the facility was an unlocked one, she would simply leave; if it was a locked one, she would walk away when left unattended in an insecure place. At one point, Elinor's guardian decided that Elinor needed to be in a locked facility, but the one chosen refused to accept her. Thus, she was placed in Serene Chateau, an unlocked facility operated by Jackson. Neither the guardian nor Farr, Elinor's social worker, told Jackson that Elinor had a habit of leaving facilities or that she would become disoriented when she did so. A day after entering Serene Chateau, Elinor stole a car and left. She was arrested and returned. A few days later, at a meeting attended by Elinor, her parents, Jackson, Farr, and the guardian, Elinor was told she had to stop walking out if she wanted to be allowed to stay at Serene Chateau.

Elinor was told to ask permission if she wanted to leave. She agreed to their conditions. A few days later, Elinor was granted permission to leave Serene Chateau to go shopping, and was told to be back by 5:30 for dinner. She failed to return. Two days later, she appeared on the driveway of a home that adjoined the busy coast highway. The resident noticed that Elinor seemed "kind of wobbly," but refused to help her when she sought food. A few minutes later, Elinor walked onto the highway, where she was struck and gravely injured by an automobile.

Elinor has sued Farr (the social worker) and the state (Farr's employer), alleging that they were negligent for failing adequately to advise Serene Chateau of Elinor's tendency to walk away and become disoriented when she would do so. Assume defendants are not immune. (In the actual case on which this question is based, *Brookhauser v. State*, 10 Cal. App. 4th 1665 (1992), the court held that the defendants were immune.)

Which of the following arguments on behalf of defendants is most plausible?

(A) Defendants did not have a duty to inform Serene Chateau of Elinor's tendencies.

   (B) Even if they had a duty to warn Serene Chateau of Elinor's tendencies, defendants did not breach their duty.

   (C) Defendants' conduct was not a "but-for" cause in fact of Elinor's harm.

   (D) Elinor's own fault should reduce her recovery.

235. Same facts as above. Assume the defendants argue that, even if they should have provided the information to Serene Chateau, and even if their negligence was a cause in fact of the harm, they should not be held liable. If the jurisdiction in which the action is being tried has adopted a "directness" theory of proximate cause, which of the following statements best represents what the court is most likely to say?

   (A) Because a reasonable person in the defendants' position would foresee harm resulting from the failure to provide the information, the defendants were negligent. They are then liable for the full extent of the harm because the harm that occurred was precisely what one might expect to occur.

   (B) Because a reasonable person in the defendants' position would foresee harm resulting from the failure to provide the information, the defendants were negligent. They are then liable for the full extent of the harm if the consequences that actually occurred followed directly from the negligence.

   (C) Because a reasonable person in the defendants' position would foresee harm resulting from the failure to provide the information, the defendants were negligent. However, because the harm came about as an immediate consequence of Elinor's own carelessness, the harm was indirect and the defendants cannot be held liable.

   (D) Because the zone of risk created by the defendants' carelessness included personal injury to Elinor, and because the manner in which Elinor was injured was precisely what one might reasonably foresee, the defendants are responsible for the full extent of the harm.

236. Same facts as above. Suppose the defendants wish to argue that, even if they should have provided the information to Serene Chateau, and even if their negligence was a cause in fact of the harm, they should not be held liable.

If the jurisdiction in which the action is being tried has adopted a "risk rule" approach to proximate cause, which of the following statements best represents what the court is most likely to say?

   (A) The test of liability for injury by highway accident is the foreseeability of injury by highway accident. Unless a reasonable person in the defendants' position could have foreseen injury of this kind to Elinor, she cannot recover.

   (B) The test of liability for injury by highway accident is the foreseeability of injury by highway accident. Because no reasonable person in the defendants' position could have foreseen the chain of events that led to Elinor's injury, Elinor cannot recover.

   (C) It would not be consonant with current ideas of justice or morality to hold a party responsible unless the harm occurred as a direct and natural consequence of its carelessness. Because the accident occurred through the intervention of both the driver of the car and of Elinor herself, the chain of causation was broken and Elinor cannot recover.

(D) It is not the hindsight of a fool but the foresight of a reasonable person that guides the determination of this question. Unless a reasonable person in the defendants' position could imagine that Elinor would suffer injury of this extent by virtue of the failure to provide the information to Serene Chateau, the defendants cannot be held responsible.

237. The state of Rhubarb has retained the common law categories of trespasser, licensee, and invitee. Muskrat, a wealthy resident of Rhubarb, decided to excavate a large stretch of his property in the back of his house in preparation for adding a new outbuilding on the land. He did not illuminate the excavated site of his land or post a warning sign. Muskrat's land is not fenced and, although he has not noticed any trespassers on his property, he has also done nothing to keep them away. One night, teenage trespasser Tommy took a shortcut through Muskrat's land to hurry home after breaking curfew. Tommy fell into the excavation and was injured.

An action by Tommy against Muskrat should

(A) fail, because Tommy assumed the risk.

(B) fail, because Tommy was not a known trespasser.

(C) succeed, because it was negligent for Muskrat not to illuminate his property or warn visitors.

(D) succeed, because Tommy's trespassing was foreseeable.

238. Louise was on a walk when she noticed a very young child lying face down and completely still in the yard in front of Walter's house. Believing the child was injured, Louise climbed the short fence separating the sidewalk from the yard and approached him. When she touched his shoulder and asked if he was okay, the child turned over and said he was fine. Walter, the child's father, observed this activity from his front window and became extremely frightened because he believed Louise was accosting the child. Subsequently, he brought an action against Louise for trespass.

Which of the following statements is most likely correct?

(A) The action will fail because Louise's entry onto Walter's property was not voluntary.

(B) The action will fail because Louise's trespass did not damage Walter's property.

(C) The action will fail because, under the circumstances, Louise was entitled to be on the property.

(D) The action will succeed.

239. Which subcategory of invasion of privacy has the greatest overlap with defamation? Explain.

ANSWER:

240. Dr. McAllister, a sinus specialist, recommended surgery to correct Kevin's deviated septum (the cartilage separating the nose into two segments), and to clear blocked passages. McAllister told Kevin the surgery would improve his breathing and help prevent lingering infections. Kevin asked McAllister what was involved in the surgery, and McAllister explained that the surgery was a very common, "endoscopic" procedure performed under general anesthesia, and that "few patients suffer any significant problems." Kevin asked what problems had arisen. McAllister said there were very rare cases in which surgeons punctured the patient's eye socket or caused brain damage by puncturing the brain cavity. He said he had performed the procedure hundreds of times without such mishaps. Kevin decided to go forward with the procedure.

McAllister did not disclose several possible side effects. Unfortunately, Kevin had some of them, including temporarily blocked sinuses, "adhesions" (tissue stuck together), numbness in his teeth, and severe pain. For a month, Kevin was in pain and couldn't concentrate at work. McAllister did what he could to relieve the side effects, but they did not disappear entirely for several months. Eventually, Kevin recovered completely, and he can breathe better than ever.

If Kevin brings a negligence action against Dr. McAllister, which of the following arguments would give McAllister's his best chance of defeating the claim?

(A) Kevin cannot recover because the undisclosed information did not relate to the surgery itself, only to the side effects.

(B) Kevin cannot recover because, even though he suffered pain from various side effects of the surgery, the pain was more than offset by the beneficial effects of the procedures.

(C) Kevin cannot recover if a reasonable patient in his position would not have considered the undisclosed information material to a decision whether to have the surgery.

(D) Kevin cannot recover if physicians in McAllister's position customarily do not disclose the information about the side effects that affected Kevin.

241. Same facts as above. If Kevin brings a negligence action against Dr. McAllister, and McAllister wishes to testify that he decided not to reveal the information in question to Kevin because he feared Kevin might make the irrational decision not to have the surgery, which of the following statements is most likely correct?

(A) The court should not allow McAllister to present this testimony because his views are irrelevant to the determination of negligence.

(B) The court should not allow McAllister to present this testimony because the patient's right to self-determination overrides the physician's views of the patient's best interests.

(C) McAllister should be permitted to present this testimony to show he believed Kevin would have foregone the procedure if informed of the side effects.

(D) McAllister should be permitted to present this testimony if it represents a sound medical judgment that providing the information would have presented a threat to Kevin's well-being.

242. Same facts as above. Assume Kevin proceeds on a negligence theory. McAllister claims that, even if he had a duty to disclose the side effects and breached it by failing to disclose them, Kevin cannot prove the breach was a cause in fact of the harm. Which of the following statements is most accurate?

    (A) Kevin can prove causation if he persuades the jury that he would not have undergone the surgery if McAllister had disclosed the side effects.

    (B) Kevin can prove causation only if he persuades the jury that neither he nor a reasonable person would have undergone the surgery if McAllister had disclosed the side effects.

    (C) Kevin can prove causation only if a reasonable person in McAllister's position would have foreseen harm resulting from failure to disclose the side effects.

    (D) Kevin has shown causation once he demonstrates that McAllister breached his duty to disclose the side effects.

243. Crowbar was walking towards a bus terminal at the Port Authority, a government-owned facility. On his way to the terminal, he walked by a row of benches with a sign overhead declaring them a Designated Lunch Area. Three minutes earlier, Muriel had been eating an apple on the bench. When Muriel was finished eating the apple, she carelessly threw the core on the terminal walkway. Subsequently Crowbar tripped over the apple core and broke his collarbone.

    If Crowbar brings a negligence action against the Port Authority, which of the following statements is most accurate?

    (A) He will be compensated for his damages because he is an invitee, and the Port Authority had a duty to protect him from the injury he experienced.

    (B) Though the Port Authority has a duty to keep the walkway clean and clear of litter, Crowbar's case will fail because picking up every piece of trash on the ground at all times is beyond the scope of the Port Authority's duty.

    (C) Because the Port Authority is a government-owned public facility, it is immune from suit, and therefore Crowbar's claim will fail.

    (D) The Port Authority owed a duty to keep the walkway clean and clear of litter, but Crowbar assumed the risk of walking in a busy terminal where people are known to eat lunch, and therefore his claim will fail.

244. A sudden downpour soaked a ground already saturated from days of steady rain, threatening Wingnut City with serious flooding as the river began to rise. At the same time, the dam protecting the town began to crack from the pressure of water backed up in the lake behind it. Finally, the river overflowed its banks, and water began spreading through the town. At almost the same time, the dam burst, sending a torrent of water toward the town. A few blocks from Abel's art gallery, water from the river mixed with the water from the burst dam, and the flood bore down on the gallery, destroying all of Abel's valuable art. Later an investigation showed that the dam burst because of improper maintenance. Had the dam been maintained properly, it would have held the water back. Abel brings an action against Wingnut City, which was responsible for maintaining the dam, for negligence. Assume either force standing

alone (water from the river or the dam) would have been sufficient to destroy Abel's art collection. Assume also that Wingnut City is not immune.

Which of the following statements is most accurate?

(A) Because Abel's art gallery would have been flooded even without the city's negligence in maintaining the dam, Wingnut City's failure to maintain the dam was not a cause in fact of Abel's damage and is not liable.

(B) Wingnut City's failure to maintain the dam will be considered a cause in fact of the damage only if Abel can show that the volume of water from the dam that reached his gallery was greater than the volume of water from the river that reached his gallery.

(C) Wingnut City is liable only for the portion of the harm that corresponds to the percentage of water flooding Abel's gallery that came from the dam.

(D) Wingnut City's failure to maintain the dam was a cause in fact of the harm and the City is liable for all of the harm Abel suffered.

245. Same facts as above, except assume that water from the dam reached Abel's gallery and destroyed Abel's artwork about an hour before the river water inundated the property. If the dam had held, Abel would have had time to remove some of his goods from the gallery before the river water inundated it.

For which losses might Wingnut City might be liable?

ANSWER:

246. ChemCo negligently allowed a tank of chemicals to leak. Platt lived two miles from the ChemCo plant. Six months later, Platt became ill with a rare form of cancer.

If Platt wishes to recover from ChemCo, and ChemCo claims it was not the cause in fact of Platt's harm, what must Platt prove in order to overcome this contention?

ANSWER:

247. As Pecan City grew, farmland on the eastern edge of the city was converted to other uses. Clavin Enterprises (CE) purchased a parcel of east side land and built a complex to serve as its headquarters and main plant. CE manufactured computer chips, and its plant employed several hundred workers. Like most chipmakers, CE used toxic chemicals in its manufacturing process. CE workers were carefully trained in the proper use and storage of the chemicals, and CE followed and often exceeded all of the industry's customary safety guidelines for the use of toxics. One day, a CE worker was using a forklift to move a drum of toxic chemicals. The worker's route took him close to the edge of CE's property. Due to factors of which CE had no reason to be aware, one of the hydraulic lifts holding up the drum snapped, and the drum rolled off the forklift, and crashed through the fence separating CE's property from that of Diane, a soybean farmer. The drum split open, and the chemicals spilled out. Diane

was not present at the time. CE immediately sent a crew to Diane's land to clean up the toxic liquid, but much of the liquid had already seeped into the soil, contaminating Diane's ground water and killing many of the crops. In addition, the heavy equipment CE used in the clean-up destroyed some of Diane's crops, some of which would not have been harmed by the chemicals.

Diane brings an action against CE for negligence, claiming its worker negligently handled the drum of chemicals. Which of the following statements is most accurate?

(A) CE had a duty to handle the drum with reasonable care, and because harm occurred when it was handling the drum, CE will be liable.

(B) Because CE was experienced in handling chemicals, it had a higher duty than a less experienced company, and its failure to handle the drum in a manner that would prevent an accidental spill will make it liable.

(C) CE had a duty to handle the chemicals with reasonable care, but because its procedures met or exceeded the industry's standards, CE will not be liable.

(D) Because CE had no reason to anticipate the breakdown of the hydraulic lift, it will not be liable even though its conduct led to significant harm.

248. Does "the economic loss rule," the position taken by most courts in the United States that a plaintiff cannot recover damages for financial loss in a negligence action unless she has suffered physical injury or damage to physical property, apply to legal malpractice?

(A) Yes. Legal malpractice requires either a physical injury or damage to physical property.

(B) Yes. An attorney owes a duty to avoid imposing economic loss on a client.

(C) Partially. Clients need not attribute economic loss to legal malpractice, but nonclient plaintiffs must do so.

(D) No. Financial losses alone, with no physical or property damages required, are recoverable in legal malpractice.

249. Give an example of overlap between invasion of privacy and intentional infliction of emotional distress.

ANSWER:

250. By ordinance, the town of Horsefeather prohibits residents from keeping a chinchilla. Lawmakers believe that chinchillas are vicious and aggressive, therefore hazardous. Gretchen, a resident of Horsefeather, decided to keep a chinchilla as a pet. She named the animal Dragon. She figured that as long as she kept Dragon in her cage, nothing would go wrong. One day Gretchen's friend Maureen came to visit. Maureen asked if she could play with Dragon. Gretchen said no. While Gretchen went to prepare a snack, Maureen took the opportunity to remove Dragon from her cage in order to pet her. Dragon then bit Maureen, requiring Maureen to be rushed to the hospital for stitches.

Which of the following statements is most correct?

(A) Gretchen cannot be liable for Maureen's bite because the contact was not consensual; she never gave Maureen permission to handle Dragon.

(B) Gretchen may be liable for Maureen's bite if the court finds that her leaving Maureen alone with Dragon constituted negligence.

(C) Gretchen is liable for Maureen's bites because her keeping a chinchilla was negligent.

(D) Gretchen is liable for Maureen's bites under the doctrine of negligence per se.

251. Which of the following is a difference between Second Restatement and Third Restatement provisions on infliction of emotional distress?

(A) The Third Restatement eliminates the "extreme and outrageous" criterion for intentional infliction of emotional distress.

(B) The Third Restatement introduces "serious emotional harm," a phrase not present in the Second Restatement.

(C) The Second Restatement required that the plaintiff experience physical manifestations of intentionally inflicted emotional distress; the Third Restatement does not.

(D) The Third Restatement permits liability for recklessly as well as intentionally inflicted emotional distress; the Second Restatement did not.

252. Some critics of contemporary products liability law say that courts are too eager to hold defendants liable for failure to warn. When an unfortunate accident has injured the plaintiff, it is too tempting — and wrong, say the critics — to conclude that a warning would have prevented the injury.

Give arguments in support of this criticism, and then critique the criticism with counterarguments.

ANSWER:

Essay Issue-Spotter Questions

These six problems, all involving fictitious accounts of harm to persons, are laid out to approximate a range of different testing patterns that you may encounter. They omit strict liability and advanced topics like defamation, privacy, and products liability: their focus on intentional torts and negligence approximates what turns up more often in issue-spotter essay questions. Answers, which are rendered in outline form, use "actual cause" and "cause in fact" interchangeably. Most questions give you a little information up front about what will be covered; one of them intentionally withholds this disclosure.

253. **Intentional torts only**

At the Urban Cowboy bar, owned by Latham, patrons challenge one another to ride "Bucko," the wooden horse attached to the floor near a jukebox. Bucko runs on an electric current that propels it up and down, side to side, back and forth. For the first few minutes many riders can hang on to Bucko, but the speed of the movement increases, and usually everyone falls off, landing on a square of foam padding. Latham charges $5 per ride.

While enjoying a couple of beers, Travolta and Winger, who were not drunk, watched the riders as they mounted Bucko, clung to it for a few moments, and then fell off. "Bet you $10 you can't stay on," said Winger, after there had been seven riders fall and only one stay on for the entire ride. Travolta, accepting the challenge, began to walk toward Bucko. While his back was turned, Winger slipped into the basement of the Urban Cowboy and pulled a control lever, doubling the amount of current flowing into Bucko's mechanism. Neither Latham nor anyone else saw Winger enter the basement. Travolta, riding Bucko, was flung up to the ceiling, well forward of the foam padding. Dexterously, he grabbed for a beam and held on. Winger came up to the basement door.

Latham spotted Travolta near the ceiling, and called, "Hey! Get off that beam! It's four hundred years old, it was salvaged off a Spanish galleon, it's valuable." Travolta said, "Are you crazy? I'm here until you get a ladder!" The beam began to splinter. Seconds later, Travolta and the beam fell. Because he had been able to break his fall by holding on, Travolta landed on the floor with only a broken ankle; doctors later told him that being propelled from Bucko to the floor would have crushed his pelvis and broken both legs. The beam, which was damaged beyond repair, turned out not really 400 years old — Latham had been misinformed — but it was an antique and worth about $1,800.

"Say, Winger," said Redford, who had just walked him into the bar and missed the crash. "I'd like to play a song and dedicate it to you." Redford patted Winger on the head and kissed her cheek. "Oh, thanks, Redford," Winger replied. Redford approached the jukebox, snickering, and chose "Rabbit," the song Winger's husband had left playing repeatedly on his iSnooz when he killed himself five years ago. Redford knew that Winger had checked into an expensive mental institution for three months after that suicide, in part because she had felt responsible for it.

Meanwhile, lying on the floor, Travolta saw Winger near the basement door, 15 feet away. "Hi," said Winger. Travolta tried to get up, but couldn't. He reached into his pocket, slipped on a set of brass knuckles, and waved his fist toward Winger. "I'll smash your face in, you rotten little creep," he said.

"You owe me ten dollars on the bet," said Winger. "You fell off Bucko, which is what you should have expected to do." Just then, "Rabbit" came on over the loudspeakers. Winger wanted to sob, but she kept stoic.

Identify the intentional torts claims that are presented in this scenario, along with any defenses.

ANSWER:

254. **Negligence only**

Studies appear to confirm that using a mobile phone while driving is dangerous. Canadian researchers concluded that the risk of having an automobile collision while using a phone was approximately four times greater than when the driver was not using the phone, and that hand-free devices did nothing to alleviate this risk. A United States Department of Transportation study concluded that people who use cell phones while driving have a 34 percent greater chance of involvement in a collision than people who do not. A number of countries ban drivers' use of mobile phones, but efforts in the United States to pass similar laws have not been very successful so far.

Corporate executive Steverino hated to waste time, and in his mind, time behind the wheel was wasted if he couldn't get work done. So before leaving the office one day, he arranged to participate in an important conference call from his car. He then left the office and began driving along Main Street.

Meanwhile, Lois, another driver, was driving her friend Chris to the hospital. The two had been enjoying a picnic at a local park when Chris began experiencing chest pains. Because he had a history of heart trouble, Chris thought he should go to the hospital, and they were traveling along Main Street just behind and to the right of Steverino.

As the cars approached an intersection with marked crosswalks but no traffic lights or stop signs, two things happened almost simultaneously. Bobby stepped off the sidewalk into a crosswalk and began to cross Main Street, and Steverino's cell phone rang: it was the conference call he'd arranged. Steverino looked down for a moment to pick up the phone, and failed to notice Bobby in the crosswalk. When Steverino looked up and saw Bobby in front of him, he realized that he could not stop in time to avoid a collision, so he swerved to the right. At the same time, Bobby jumped out of the way, suffering a leg injury when he tumbled to the pavement. Steverino missed Bobby, but his maneuver sent him directly into the path of Lois's car. The two cars collided violently, knocking Steverino, Lois, and Chris unconscious.

Steverino's car continued out of control through the intersection, up onto the sidewalk, and through the plate glass window of Peggy's Café, where it severed a water line. Water immediately began flooding the restaurant, causing significant damage to the café and its contents.

Chris's instincts had been correct. The chest pains he felt were the first stages of a massive heart attack. Though a kind passerby transported Chris to the nearby hospital and doctors performed admirably, Chris died. Had Chris reached the hospital without the delay caused by the accident, he would have had a much better chance of surviving.

Discuss the actions listed below, and ONLY the actions listed below, in the order given. If there is more than one plausible basis on which any of the suits might be brought, discuss each one separately. If you discuss intentional torts, analyze both the prima facie case and any plausible defenses. Do not analyze defenses to negligence. The actions to discuss are as follows:

(A) Bobby v. Steverino;

(B) Lois v. Steverino;

(C) Chris's estate v. Steverino (assume the estate stands in Chris's shoes); and

(D) Peggy (owner of Peggy's Café) v. Steverino

ANSWER:

255. Intentional torts mixed with negligence

Gang member Danny left a store one evening when he was spotted by Ron, a member of a rival gang who had just pulled up in front of the store. Because Ron's gang considered the neighborhood part of its territory, Danny knew he was in trouble and ran for his life. Ron threw his car into gear and took off after Danny. For several blocks, Danny tried to shake Ron, but to no avail. Danny then stopped, turned toward Ron's car, pulled a gun, aimed at Ron's windshield, and fired. The shot missed Ron's car and struck the leg of Pixie, who was riding a bicycle and who was unaware that anyone had fired a weapon until she was hit. Pixie suffered serious injuries.

Danny took off again, this time down an alley, over a fence, and into the back yard of Bumble, where he took refuge in some bushes. He lay there for a while, hoping that Ron had lost his trail. While waiting, a feeling of fatigue overcame Danny and he fell asleep. He did not awaken until several hours later, when he felt a slight kick and looked up to see Bumble, the homeowner. Bumble was furious because he didn't want Danny on his property and because while Danny slept, he had rolled over onto Bumble's valuable flowers and harmed them. Bumble ordered Danny to leave, but Danny pleaded with Bumble to let him stay a while longer because he was afraid he'd be killed if he emerged from hiding. (In fact, Ron had given up the search just minutes after Danny took refuge in Bumble's yard.) Bumble rejected Danny's excuse and threatened to kill Danny himself if he did not leave.

Frightened to leave but frightened to remain, Danny saw no real choice, so he got up to leave. He climbed back over the same fence he'd used before, walked back up the alley, and peeked around the corner. Seeing nothing threatening, Danny started to walk home along the sidewalk. On the way, he heard a crash and turned in time to see a car heading right for him. Before Danny could get out of the way, the car struck and injured him. The car that hit Danny was driven by Fran. Fran had become distracted trying to program her navigation system and failed to notice that another car, driven by Corey, had crossed the center line and was heading directly toward her. Fran looked up just in time to swerve to the right, causing her to jump the sidewalk and hit Danny. She did not see Danny before striking him.

Discuss the actions listed below, and ONLY the actions listed below, in the order given. If there is more than one plausible basis for any suit, discuss each basis separately. If you discuss intentional tort claims, be sure to analyze both the prima facie case and any plausible defenses. If you discuss any negligence claims, do not consider issues of proximate cause or defenses.

The actions to discuss are as follows:

(A) Danny v. Ron (consider only intentional torts; the answer will include discussion of weak ones);

(B) Pixie v. Danny;

(C) Bumble v. Danny; and

(D) Danny v. Fran & Corey.

ANSWER:

256. **Essay with little information about which types of tort claims are included**

It was a beautiful spring weekend in Ocean City. The sun was out, the air was warm, and residents young and old were enjoying the outdoors. Among them were Abe and Bee, 10-year-old friends who met to try out their new skateboards. Along the sidewalks they rode, unsteadily at first but gradually getting the hang of it as the minutes and hours passed. Abe and Bee raced along the sidewalk on what they had come to call their "battle boards." At one point, Bee rode ahead and hid in some bushes when Abe stopped to tie his shoe. Her plan was to frighten Abe when he rode by. A few moments later, Bee heard the sound of wheels approaching and jumped out of the bushes, yelling "Boo, Dude!" But it wasn't Abe. Instead, it was Dirk, a middle-aged man trying to skateboard for the first time. The sound of Bee's voice and her sudden appearance on the sidewalk ahead of him caused Dirk to lose control and fall. Though uninjured, Dirk was very angry and demanded to know Bee's name and phone number so he could call her parents. Instead of complying, Bee fled the scene.

Meanwhile Carol, a college professor who lived in the same neighborhood as Abe and Bee, was strolling along the sidewalk about 20 feet from a street intersection when Abe rounded the corner on his battle board and headed at warp 5 (very fast) in Carol's direction. Carol did nothing at first, but when Abe was just a few feet away, Carol dove into the green strip that separated the sidewalk from the street. An unfortunate choice: she landed directly on top of a wooden box on which the words "Danger High Voltage" were printed. The box was four-sided and designed a bit like a pyramid, though it did not come to a point at the top. It was about 3 feet high, 2 feet on a side at the base, and about half as wide at the top. One side of the box was touching the curb, and the box was both sufficiently visible and far enough away from the sidewalk that people using the sidewalk were unlikely to trip over it. Employees of Ocean City Power Co. (OCPC) had loosely placed the box over exposed high voltage lines on which they had been working. (Because this was a Sunday, company employees had the day off.)

Carol's fall broke the box, though she narrowly missed the exposed power lines. When the box broke, several long nails that had held it together became exposed, and one of them punctured Carol's chest and nearly struck her heart. Carol collapsed in a heap, barely conscious and in great pain. Abe went over to Carol to see if she was okay. Crouching next to her, Abe accidentally touched the exposed high voltage line. The electrical shock caused him significant injury.

Discuss the actions listed below, and ONLY the actions listed below, in the order given. If there is more than one plausible basis for any suit, discuss each basis separately. If you discuss intentional torts, analyze both the prima facie case and any plausible defenses. If you discuss negligence, do not consider defenses. The actions to discuss are as follows:

(A) Dirk v. Bee (consider only intentional torts in Dirk's action);

(B) Carol v. Abe;

(C) Carol v. Ocean City Power Co.; and

(D) Abe v. Ocean City Power Co.

ANSWER:

257. **Intentional torts, negligence, and** *respondeat superior*

Lindsay attended the University of Edgemo School of Law. Her first semester grades were average, but she failed the fall half of Civil Procedure, a year-long course with more than 100 students. At the beginning of the spring semester Lindsay complained to her roommate, Angela, that her Civil Procedure professor, Madding, needed "to be taken care of."

In late January Madding called on Lindsay in class to ask about the summary judgment standard. After Lindsay tried her best to respond, Madding said, "Your logic is creative. Creative like a kindergartener with her first can of finger paint. Try again."

Lindsay came home and, weeping, told Angela, "I can't stand that good-for-nothing wannabe anymore! He needs to die." Angela was concerned that Lindsay might actually take action, so she called campus security and told the story to young security lieutenant Carl Jugala. Jugala called psychiatrist Dr. Bigbrain, who told Jugala that that this story did not seem sufficiently serious to warrant detention. Dr. Bigbrain suggested that campus police follow Lindsay for a few days to monitor her conversations and behavior. Jugala and Dr. Bigbrain decided that Jugala would dress like a student and carry books so as to blend in with student life.

A year earlier, following the passage of a new state statute authorizing school security guards to carry firearms, the University of Edgemo had issued revolvers to some members of its security force, including Jugala. Jugala kept his loaded revolver out of sight at all times. One afternoon, Jugala followed Lindsay into her Civil Procedure class and took a seat eight rows behind Lindsay. Madding stood at the podium and lectured.

Forty minutes into the lecture, Jillian, a student sitting next to Lindsay, felt desperately bored. Although Madding had a forbidding demeanor that intimidated students into staying put until he dismissed them, Jillian dared to get up to leave the room. Jugala, believing that Jillian was Lindsay and about to shoot Madding, removed his revolver and fired twice. The first shot hit Jillian. The second shot hit Madding. After the classroom was evacuated and the injured parties were taken to the nearby hospital, Lindsay was identified and searched. She had no gun or any other weapon. She expressed no regrets that Madding was seriously injured.

Madding and Jillian brought separate actions against the university for the conduct of Jugala. If Jugala is liable, the University is legally responsible. The same parties are also considering bringing an action against Dr. Bigbrain. Several psychiatrists have been consulted and have taken the position that Dr. Bigbrain should have suggested that Lindsay be temporarily committed to determine the seriousness of her mental condition.

You are a summer intern at the firm representing one of the plaintiffs, assigned to research this case as your first task. Discuss the possible claims that could be brought up between

(A) Jillian v. the university/Jugala;

(B) Madding v. the university/Jugala; and

(C) Madding and Jillian v. Dr. Bigbrain.

ANSWER:

258. **Essay including theory**

In the west coast city of Metropolis no radio personality was as famous as Daniel "the Dragon" McDermott, who held the coveted "drive time" morning slot on the KDDD station. McDermott made the following statement over the air, in a loud voice:

> The Dragon is dashin'. I am all over Metropolis in my lime-green VW Bug [an automobile model]. The car with a big KDDD painted on the side. You can't miss me. But can you catch me? That's what I want to know, and I've got TEN THOUSAND DOLLARS riding on the answer. When you see me, overtake me on the road. I don't pull over easy, I warn you. But if you can give me a tap on the rear bumper I AM YOURS! And TEN THOUSAND DOLLARS is yours! Quit draggin' and catch the Dragon. If you can.

For weeks the Dragon eluded his pursuers as he drove through Metropolis in the afternoons and evenings. He told gleeful stories on the radio of his escapes. His ratings soared. The Dragon was, indeed, never caught, and KDDD never paid the promotional $10,000.

Unfortunately, however, a young driver named Eddie who had listened to the Dragon's broadcasts caused an injury to a pedestrian, Flora, while seeking the elusive VW Bug. Eddie had spied the Bug in one of its rare stops, when the Dragon was about to pull out of a curbside parking space. Knowing that he had to tap the bumper, Eddie accelerated through a green light, not looking at anything but the Bug fender. Just then Flora began to cross the street, out of the crosswalk. Eddie's car hit Flora. After colliding with Flora, Eddie's car also hit the left side of the Bug, missing the bumper. Flora's ribs and leg were broken, and Eddie suffered a head injury and damage to his car. The Dragon was unhurt; the Bug, however, which belonged to the Dragon and not his employer KDDD, was damaged.

Flora brought an action against Eddie, the Dragon, and KDDD. Eddie brought an action against the Dragon and KDDD. The Dragon thought about suing Eddie, but his lawyer advised him not to. The presiding judge, Gloria, did not dismiss Eddie's and Flora's actions against the Dragon and KDDD. For allowing these charges to proceed to trial, Gloria was ridiculed by some members of the press. The jury found that Eddie was liable to Flora, but the Dragon and KDDD were *not* liable to Flora. The jury also found that the Dragon and KDDD were *not* liable to Eddie. Flora was compensated for about 80 percent of her injury by Eddie's liability insurance; Eddie had no assets of his own to satisfy the judgment. The state in which Metropolis is located takes a modern approach to apportionment of responsibility between plaintiff and defendants (i.e., it does not apply contributory negligence).

Discuss the following:

(A) As you know, Gloria ruled that the claims of Eddie and Flora against the Dragon and KDDD were not precluded as a matter of law. How could the Dragon and KDDD be liable to Flora? To Eddie? Explain the theory of liability in full detail.

(B) Why do you think Gloria was ridiculed for allowing the claims of Flora and Eddie against the Dragon and KDDD to proceed?

(C) Why might the jury have reasoned as it did?

(D) On what basis could the Dragon bring an action against Eddie? Why did the lawyer advise him not to?

(E) Why was KDDD a defendant in the lawsuits?

(F) What would a corrective justice theorist say about Flora's experience as a plaintiff?

ANSWER:

Answers

Intentional Torts: Battery and Assault

1. **Answer (B) is correct.** Intentional, offensive touching can suffice for battery liability, and unconsented-to operations have been held to satisfy the contact requirement. Because Sharon did not apprehend the touching before it happened, she would have no claim for assault.

    Answer (A) is incorrect because Dr. Doolittle's touching of Letitia is privileged as emergency medical treatment.

    Answer (C) illustrates an assault without a battery. Patrick was able to avoid harmful contact. Dr. Proctor's behavior satisfies the elements of assault.

    Answer (D) is incorrect because Cankersore was aware of the touchings as they became imminent. If the battery claim is good, then the assault claim is equally good.

2. **Answer (A) is correct.** You may recognize the facts from the venerable *Mohr v. Williams*, 104 N.W. 12 (Minn. 1905), the only change being eyes instead of ears. *Mohr* comes from an era when a physician generally would not testify that another physician violated a medical standard of care; back then, it was pretty much battery or nothing for victims of medical error. But the holding is good law more than a century later when negligence is available. Unauthorized touching that offends dignity and autonomy, a medical procedure included, is actionable under battery.

    Answer (B) is incorrect because the facts suggest that the defendant's choice was arguably reasonable. Here, in a chapter about assault and battery, moreover, negligence language like "unreasonable" telegraphs a wrong answer.

    Answer (C) is incorrect because pain is not required for a battery (or a negligence) claim.

    Answer (D) is incorrect when the wrong is understood as a boundary crossing rather than the intentional infliction of harm. The defendant had the mental state of purpose; he operated on the unauthorized eye intentionally.

3. **Answer (D) is correct.** Bill intended to cause harm to Kevin by throwing a helmet at his head. Kevin did not consent to any physical contact of that kind, because they were not engaged in a contact sport at the time.

    Answer (A) is incorrect. A claim for battery requires intent. Jorge did not intend to hit Pedro.

    Answer (B) is incorrect for the reason just given.

    Answer (C) is incorrect. Joe purposely engaged in a game of football and therefore consented to be tackled. Although consent can be understood as an affirmative defense, courts interpret it as precluding a prima facie claim of battery when the plaintiff was injured in a game.

4. **Answer (C) is correct** because of the law of transferred intent. Although the Hulk did not intend to punch Superman, he did intend to punch someone and this intent transferred to the ultimate victim.

    Answer (A) is incorrect for the reason just given.

    Answer (B) is incorrect. Battery does not require the victim to apprehend the contact.

    Answer (D) is incorrect. This answer combines consent, a defense available only for intentional torts, with a risk of harm rather than a (certain) intentional contact. In order for consent to be present, the jury must be able to find that Superman knew the Hulk was going to try to punch Superman on that occasion and it was substantially certain that he, Superman, would suffer harmful contact.

5. At age five, a person can fulfill the basic elements of battery: intent, act, and the causation of harmful contact. A young child will sometimes choose to bite or hit another person to express anger. Imposing responsibility on a young child for harmful intentional contact makes sense. By contrast, imposing responsibility for imprudence or carelessness—deficiencies that can be overcome only developmentally, with the tutelage of experience—probably asks more of young children than they can deliver.

    A realistic, practical approach to the answer: Most young children lack wealth; few young children can inflict costly harmful contact on purpose; liability insurance held by parents does not cover intentional torts that children in the household commit; and the common law does not impose vicarious liability on parents for the torts of their children. Thus few persons injured by children who acted intentionally will file battery claims. The stance permitting liability for battery will rarely arise in real life, and therefore will not do much harm.

6. **Answer (A) is correct.** Although Jane did not threaten immediate harm, her threat was accompanied by physical intimidation with a deadly weapon, which caused Narcissa to apprehend that she was in imminent danger.

    Answer (B) is incorrect. Ian did not intentionally throw the ball at Meghan.

    Answer (C) is incorrect. Damon's threat to cause harm in the future did not cause the bouncer to apprehend imminent harm. Although a threat of harm in five minutes might be seen as "imminent" in some contexts, it is not imminent in this scenario because it gave the bouncer adequate time to summon aid and thus avoid infliction of the threatened harm.

    Answer (D) is incorrect. Edgar never apprehends that he is in danger, and Jed did not have the requisite intent.

7. **Answer (D) is correct.** The claim might fail for other reasons, but (D) is the better of the two No answers. Some courts have accepted the touching of cigarette smoke as sufficient to constitute harmful contact, but intent requires either purpose or substantial certainty that the smoke will reach a person's body. Because Elise thought she was alone, she could not have believed that the smoke would inflict harmful contact upon Johanna.

    Answer (A), though true as far as it goes, is incorrect because it neglects the lack of intent on Elise's part.

Answer (B) is incorrect because it is not true: Elise thought she was alone and so lacked intent to inflict harmful contact on anyone.

Answer (C) is incorrect because an actor can be liable for battery if the elements of battery are met, even if the actor failed to accomplish what he or she wanted to achieve.

8. **Answer (A) is correct.** This question asks you to distinguish intent from motive. (If you have covered privileges, you can also think of the question as involving a mistake about a privilege.) Kerys meant well, but acted intentionally to inflict harmful contact on the tall woman.

    Answer (B) is incorrect because no facts in the question support any claim for any tort against Channel 7 News.

    Answer (C) is incorrect because landing on the ground and breaking one's wrist is always harmful contact, as far as tort law is concerned. A person who inflicts this contact might not be liable for it, but traumatic fracture fulfills the injury element of any tort claim.

    Answer (D) is incorrect because Kerys wanted the woman to fall. Desire fulfills the intent requirement. "Substantial certainty" is present here too, because grabbing a runner's leg unexpectedly likely will generate a fall. Although Kerys's belief about the woman's identity was mistaken, the inflicting of harmful contact was intentional. What happened here was no accident.

9. **Answer (A) is correct.** There are two ways for an actor to fulfill the intent requirement of battery: either purpose (or motive, or desire) or substantial certainty. If the element of purpose is present, substantial certainty need not be present.

    Answer (B) is incorrect because Siobhan did not act with substantial certainty. She was doubtful of her ability to carry out her plan.

    Answer (C) is incorrect because although substantial certainty was not present, purpose was present, and that suffices.

    Answer (D) is incorrect because even though the contact took place somewhat indirectly, Siobhan's actions set in motion a force that resulted in harmful contact.

10. Yes, she can. Liability for assault turns on the (reasonable) understandings and perceptions of a plaintiff. If the defendant has acted in a way that indicates her capacity for inflicting imminent harmful contact, then the plaintiff who apprehends this contact can bring a claim for assault. For example, pointing an unloaded pistol at the plaintiff and pulling the trigger will typically suffice for assault liability, even if the pistol is unloaded. Lunging at the plaintiff while shouting a threat will also suffice, even if the defendant knows that she is weak and will collapse before she can reach the plaintiff's body.

11. **Answer (C) is correct.** "Apprehension" has sowed confusion for a long time; "anticipation" may have an unfortunate positive connotation, but it provides a better contrast to fear, which is not required for an assault claim.

    Answer (A) is incorrect because assault does not require physical harm in any edition of the Restatement.

    Answer (B) is incorrect because although law reformers have argued for decades that a rigidly enforced "imminence" requirement has had bad consequences for victims of domestic violence, the Third Restatement does not permit assault liability for the threat of battery in the future.

Answer (D) is incorrect because the standard for perception of an imminent battery remains subjective in the sense that the plaintiff herself or himself must have experienced it. Courts will sometimes demand that apprehension or anticipation be reasonable, but here the Third Restatement has made no change of what came before.

12. **Answer (C) is correct.** A person who forms the intent to contact and carries out the contact is liable for battery, if the contact is unlawful. Even if the person suffers from an illness that makes her delusional or affects her ability to recognize the impropriety of her conduct, she is liable. Here, Zebbia intended to strike Brion. Zebbia is liable for battery.

    Answer (A) is incorrect because it provides only a policy reason for holding a person suffering from mental illness liable for battery. Zebbia cannot be held liable, however, unless she harbors the necessary intent.

    Answer (B) is incorrect because a person must commit an "act," which in tort law means a volitional movement. If she did not control her arm's movement, Zebbia did not commit an act. (On the facts here, she did "act.")

    Answer (D) is incorrect because the law of intentional torts does not base liability on the defendant's moral shortcomings if she intended to commit a contact that is sufficient (assuming the contact occurred and it is one that society deems unlawful).

13. Both fear and apprehension take place from the perspective of the target, or plaintiff. Apprehension refers to anticipation: the plaintiff expects harmful contact. Fear refers to the way he feels about such contact. Fear is narrower than apprehension; in assault cases every feared contact is an apprehended contact, but not every apprehended contact is a feared contact. A plaintiff might apprehend, but not fear, an instance of imminent harmful contact for several reasons. He might be strong enough to withstand pain or laugh it off; he might have faith that no harm can befall him; he might rate himself as stronger or more dangerous than the assailant.

14. **Answer (B) is correct.** A jury is likely to find that, although Sam impliedly consented to being "tagged" in the game, he did not consent to being slugged. True, Rebecca did not mean to hurt Sam, but most courts do not require this in order to make out a battery claim.

    Answer (A) is incorrect because Rebecca was not exercising her right of self-defense. That is not the way the game of "tag" works. One seeks to avoid any contact with the person who is "it."

    Answer (C) is incorrect because, as indicated above, a jury is likely to find that Sam consented to light touches, not being slugged.

    Answer (D) is incorrect because most courts hold that a defendant in a battery case need not intend injury; it is sufficient if she intended a contact that the law deems inappropriate under the circumstances.

Intentional Torts: Invasions into Land, Harm to Property, and False Imprisonment

15. **Answer (A) is correct.** Although Klutzmonkey's behavior might be the basis of liability using another tort theory—strict liability or nuisance, perhaps—trespass to land usually requires that something tangible or visible enter the other's land. Sound waves do not fulfill this criterion.

    Answer (B) is incorrect because Yodel has fulfilled the elements of trespass to land. He has acted intentionally with the desire to create an invasion, and the neighbor's land was invaded.

    Answer (C) is incorrect because invasions just above the lateral surface of the earth are sufficiently low to constitute trespass. (Jet airplanes flying thousands of feet in the air are not low enough.)

    Answer (D) is incorrect because the failure to remove a physical object once privileged to be there, but no longer privileged, constitutes a trespass.

16. The tort of conversion applies to tangible physical property that can be moved, as well as to documents in which title to a chattel is merged, such as a bill of lading, and documents that convey the value of a tangible chattel, such as a promissory note. The tort is intended to cover that which can be quickly alienated and has a visible aspect. Real property is not included. Neither is intellectual property. Intangible assets, such as the goodwill or trade secrets of a business, are also not included.

17. **Answer (C) is correct.** In order to establish a claim of false imprisonment, the defendant must intentionally act in such a way that causes the plaintiff to be confined. Olivia had no way of knowing that slamming the door would result in John's confinement, and did not intend for him to be confined.

    Answer (A) is incorrect. Although Olivia's action did result in John's confinement, the element of intent is lacking.

    Answer (B) is incorrect. Negligence is not at issue here. This question only asks whether Olivia is liable for the intentional tort of false imprisonment.

    Answer (D) is incorrect. Although John may have been able to make it to his presentation in time had he checked his door sooner, his failure to check does not constitute consent to being imprisoned.

18. **Answer (D) is correct.** Since Agathon invited Phaedrus to his home, he had the ability to revoke his consent once the party was over. Phaedrus' insistence on remaining after his invitation had been revoked constituted a trespass. It does not matter that Agathon's father owned the

land. The facts suggest that Agathon, a member of the owner's family, was a lawful land oc-
cupier. A person with that status has the right to exclusive possession and thus to consent to
entry by others and to revoke that consent.

Answer (A) is incorrect. Although Phaedrus was invited, his invitation expired once Agathon
informed him he was no longer welcome.

Answer (B) is incorrect. Although Agathon's father is the true owner of the home, it was
Agathon, not his father, who originally invited Phaedrus. Therefore, Agathon was authorized
to revoke this invitation.

Answer (C) is incorrect. It can be assumed that Agathon was authorized to invite friends to
his home since he himself lived there. The court would require more information in order to
find that anyone not personally invited by Agathon's father is a trespasser.

19. Subsurface entry differs from entry by aviation in a few ways. It almost always touches ground
possessed by the plaintiff, whereas an airplane can enter someone's land at 37,000 feet, invisible
and impalpable. Thus, it is more likely to disrupt the plaintiff's life. Subsurface entry also can
involve extraction—that is, removal by the defendant of valuable materials below the surface
of the plaintiff's land—in contrast to air entry, which typically takes nothing away.

A classic case touching on both these themes, *Edwards v. Sims*, 24 S.W. 2d 619 (Ky. 1929),
raises the problem in pure form. The defendant extracted nothing and did his entry from the
outside rather than by setting foot on the plaintiff's land. His motive for entering was to ex-
plore a beautiful cave, of which the plaintiff had been ignorant, in the hope of creating a ticket-
selling attraction. Should he be kept out through a strict application of the *cujus est solum*
maxim? *Edwards v. Sims* invites an economic analysis of the rule that land possessors can pro-
hibit or discourage wealth-generating entry below the surface of their land.

20. **Answer (A) is correct.** Denny put Potter in the position of choosing between leaving without
his wallet and staying in the car. He had no right to impose this no-win option. Potter was
not truly free to leave, as doing so would have required him to give up both his car and his
wallet. Thus, he was, in a real sense, confined.

Answer (B) is incorrect for the reason just given. Potter did not really have a free choice.

Answers (C) and (D) are incorrect because the existence of other possible causes of action
does not deny access to the false imprisonment claim. The same facts can give rise to several
claims.

21. In most jurisdictions, through statutes or case law, Escamillo has a limited privilege to protect
the store against shoplifting using reasonable detention. The facts suggest that the privilege
would have force here. Escamillo may intercept Angie on her way out the door and detain
her—that is, tell her that she may not leave for a limited period of time while he investigates.
The privilege has requirements. First, Escamillo must have a reasonable belief that Angie is in
the middle of committing theft. This requirement appears to be fulfilled. Second, the detention must take place in a reasonable manner. If Angie resists detention, Escamillo may not use
deadly force to detain her. Third, the detention must take place for only a reasonable period
of time, and this time must be used for investigation.

22. **Answer (A) is correct.** Although an omission can sometimes be the basis of liability for false imprisonment—for example, when a jailer refuses to release a prison inmate after getting lawful orders to do so, the jailer might be liable to the inmate—the defendant must have owed the plaintiff a duty. Pia and Rhonda were strangers and the facts give no basis for imposing a duty to rescue on this passerby. Thus, Pia did not imprison Rhonda.

    Answer (B) is incorrect because more than one individual can be liable in tort for the same consequences. Tort law does not recognize the concept of one solitary "proper defendant" for each injury.

    Answer (C) is incorrect because voluntary entry into a space does not preclude liability for false imprisonment thereafter.

    Answer (D) is incorrect because the facts do not establish that Rhonda was a trespasser; and, in any event, the condition of being a trespasser does not, of itself, defeat a claim for false imprisonment.

23. **Answer (C) is correct.** Frank bought a ticket to a particular destination, as did the other passengers. Though one can understand Frank's anxiety after the engine blowout and his desire to land at a closer airport, there was, in fact, no need to divert the plane. Thus, the airline's refusal, which kept Frank confined for longer than he wanted to be, was not unlawful.

    Answer (A) is incorrect because there *was* confinement. As explained above, it was not unlawful, but Frank was certainly confined.

    Answer (B) is incorrect because it makes no sense. The other passengers would not be falsely imprisoned by landing at a closer airport. In fact, their confinement on the plane would end sooner than if they proceeded to the original destination.

    Answer (D) is incorrect because physical harm is not an element of false imprisonment, as long as the victim knows of the confinement (and Frank is well aware of it in this situation).

24. **Answer (B) is correct.** False imprisonment is one of the intentional torts that are covered by the doctrine of transferred intent. Under transferred intent, a defendant may be liable for the consequences of one intentional tort when he acted intentionally to fulfill the elements of another tort. Hommyside intended to kill Hurley (consequence: battery) and his behavior caused her to be confined (consequence: false imprisonment).

    Answer (A) is incorrect because "physical barrier" usually refers to a more direct physical obstacle, such as a locked door. Answer (A) also omits reference to Hommyside's mental state, a crucial element of any intentional tort.

    Answer (C) is incorrect because under the doctrine of transferred intent, an actor can intend one set of consequences and be liable for another.

    Answer (D) is incorrect because voluntary entry into a space does not preclude liability for false imprisonment thereafter. Moreover, assumption of risk typically applies to accidental harms, not intentional ones.

25. **Answer (B) is correct.** Conversion is an intentional tort, based on the defendant's intent to perform an act that interferes with a plaintiff's right of possession. Intentional alteration of a

chattel—for example, spray-painting it with graffiti—could constitute conversion. Negligent alteration is merely negligence.

Answer (A) is incorrect because wrongful transfer—for example, using someone else's chattel as collateral for a loan and then causing the chattel to be seized by the creditor—can constitute conversion.

Answer (C) is incorrect because *theft*—the crime of taking something that isn't yours with the intent of depriving the owner of possession—fulfills the elements of conversion.

Answer (D) is incorrect because even a good-faith purchaser can fulfill the elements of conversion when the chattel was stolen from the true owner.

26. **Answer (C) is correct.** Trespass to chattels, unlike trespass to land, requires actual damages. There are two kinds of trespass to chattels: intermeddling, where the defendant does harm to the chattel, and dispossession, where the defendant does something to interfere with the plaintiff's right of possession. Howard's behavior would fall within the intermeddling category. Were there no "World's Greatest Clunker" competition, Sheldon would probably have no remedy against Howard. But because the computer might well have been a prizewinner in its original state, Howard has harmed the chattel.

    Answer (A) is incorrect because Leonard is not a possessor of the chattel and so his consent to the intermeddling is of no significance.

    Answer (B) is incorrect because under the facts Sheldon experienced detriment as well as benefit from the intermeddling.

    Answer (D) is incorrect because Leonard had authority to admit a visitor to his dormitory room. The injury is to a chattel, not to the possession of land.

27. **Answer (C) is correct.** When a person is unaware of his confinement during the time he is confined, he may only recover for false imprisonment if he suffered physical injury as a result of the confinement. Because Peter did not learn of his confinement until after it had ended, and because he was not physically injured by the confinement, he may not recover for false imprisonment.

    Answer (A) is incorrect because actual confinement is not sufficient.

    Answer (B) is incorrect because, even if the emotional effects of learning of the confinement are severe, the plaintiff who was unaware of the confinement while it was occurring may not recover for false imprisonment unless the plaintiff was physically injured.

    Answer (D) is incorrect because false imprisonment is a "trespassory tort," and intent to confine one person will "transfer" to the person actually confined. Thus, it does not matter that the manager intended to confine a different person.

28. The rise of commercial aviation made it desirable to supersede the trespass claims of land possessors. Air travel would come to a halt if land-holding plaintiffs could collect damages for the use of flight paths. Congress in effect has nationalized the nation's airspace, restricting trespass claims to intrusions low enough to interfere with normal use of land. In this respect, trespass law moved closer to nuisance.

29. **Answer (C) is correct.** An action for false imprisonment requires intentional confinement. Although a defendant often takes more direct measures to confine the plaintiff, wrongful withholding of property can fulfill the element of confinement. Because Grudgepudge would forfeit his laptop if he left Sparky's office without it, and because Sparky had no good reason to take Grudgepudge's laptop, Sparky has fulfilled the elements of this intentional tort.

Answer (A) is incorrect because Sparky had no privilege to possess the laptop.

Answer (B) is incorrect because, as was stated above, the wrongful withholding of property can amount to confinement.

Answer (D) is the least incorrect of the three incorrect choices, but it does not explain the outcome in terms of Sparky's intentional behavior; moreover, "reasonable compulsion to remain" is not an element of false imprisonment.

Defenses to Intentional Torts

30. **Answer (B) is correct.** Jean expressly "invites," or challenges, Ralph to commit what would otherwise be a battery (the intentional infliction of harmful bodily contact).

    Answer (A) is incorrect because Victor did not consent to harmful bodily contact. Under these facts, he might have consented to false imprisonment.

    Answer (C) is incorrect because Dilbert's raising of his arm constitutes at most implied consent, not express consent.

    Answer (D) is incorrect because, as is the case with answer (C), there is no express consent, merely acquiescence in a longstanding trespass.

31. **Answer (A) is correct.** A key problem with spring guns and other indiscriminate property-protecting devices is that they do not know whom they injure. Some intruders are present for innocent reasons. A related problem with these devices is that they can hurt not only intruders but inhabitants. Accordingly, a "good" place to use a spring gun, if there is such a place, is a remote location where inhabitants won't get hurt and where protection by human beings (police officers, private security personnel) is unavailing for some reason. Answer (A) best fits this description.

    Answer (B) is incorrect because the spring gun is likely to hurt the inhabitants.

    Answer (C) is incorrect because security personnel are much less indiscriminate than spring guns, and can keep unnecessary wounding (or killing) to a minimum.

    Answer (D) is incorrect for an array of reasons. One of them is that setting up a spring gun presumes a sharp distinction between intruders and inhabitants—but in this house they are more or less the same people. Shooting heedlessly at drug sellers, users, or customers is a bad solution to the social problems that these persons manifest and cause.

32. As a general rule, yes. A defendant should not be allowed to escape liability simply because he or she successfully defrauded the plaintiff. Courts do, however, distinguish between "fraud in fact" or "fraud as to an essential matter" on the one hand, and "fraud as to a collateral matter" on the other. For example, if the plaintiff agreed to what would otherwise have been a battery in exchange for a payment of money, and the payment turns out to be counterfeit money or a bad check, then the consent to the harmful contact is valid. The plaintiff cannot recover for the harmful contact and will have to try to get paid by some other means, such as a contract action or a private right of action based on violation of the criminal law or consumer law.

33. **Answer (A) is correct.** Most courts would hold that a person is entitled to use self-defense if she reasonably believes she is under attack by another. Thus, even a mistaken belief can justify self-defense.

Answer (B) is incorrect because the facts do not suggest temporary insanity, a concept that tort law does not recognize as a defense. Moreover, even if Norris was temporarily insane, a court would still query whether his reaction was reasonable under the circumstances.

Answer (C) is incorrect because Norris's reaction was volitional. The facts make clear that he meant to do what he did.

Answer (D) is incorrect because the facts show that Norris was not deprived of the ability to control his movements. On the contrary, he meant to do exactly what he did.

34. **Answer (C) is correct.** Public necessity is a defense that arises when property is destroyed or harmed to benefit a large number of people, typically towns or neighborhoods. In the classic *Mouse's Case* (1608), this privilege supported the destruction of heavy objects to help save a ferry whose four dozen passengers were at risk of drowning. Private necessity is available for individuals or, as suggested in the famous *Ploof v. Putnam*, 71 A. 188 (Vt. 1908), small families.

   Answer (A) is incorrect because although Fifth Amendment takings claims are sometimes available when property is destroyed pursuant to public necessity, they may be unavailable.

   Answer (C) has it backward. Public necessity is an absolute privilege; private necessity is a qualified privilege, meaning that the defendant has to pay for what is destroyed.

   Answer (D) is incorrect because neither public nor private necessity applies to the destruction of human life. This action might be governed by self-defense or defense or others, but never necessity.

35. **Answer (B) is correct.** The privilege to inflict deadly force on another arises when a person reasonably believes that such deadly force is necessary in order to fend off an attack. When it appears that a burglar is holding a firearm, a homeowner or other person in possession of a home is privileged to defend himself or herself through deadly force. This person has no duty to retreat inside the home.

   Answer (A) is incorrect because Joplin had no duty to retreat.

   Answer (C) is incorrect because Joplin had the mental state to sustain a prima facie claim of battery by Rugrat. The claim is defeated by Joplin's privilege of self-defense.

   Answer (D) is incorrect because there is no such status in tort law as a "criminal trespasser." Moreover, Rugrat's entering another person's home in order to commit a crime is not the reason that his battery claim fails. The privilege turns on Joplin's reasonable beliefs, not Rugrat's reasons for being there.

36. **Answer (C) is correct.** Horace had a good reason to enter Dr. Yertle's land and that reason gave him a privilege to enter, but he has to pay for the damage his entry caused. It matters not that Horace may have thought his entry did Dr. Yertle a favor under the circumstances.

   Answer (A) is incorrect because the facts eliminate harm to the garden.

   Answer (B) is incorrect because Horace had a qualified privilege to act as he did. Under the facts as described, the flower garden (vulnerable to damage by Tangyfangy) appears more valuable than the decrepit fence.

Answer (D) is incorrect because an intentional entry into another's land does fulfill the prima facie elements of trespass.

37. **Answer (A) is correct.** "Had no choice" as a statement by the defendant = a necessity defense. (Note that tort law generally regards both dogs and chickens as property.) Under necessity, an actor is privileged to inflict lesser harm to prevent a greater loss.

    Necessity is analyzed as a snapshot; courts look at the circumstances the moment the defendant acted. Answer (B), (C), and (D) all talk about the past.

    Answer (B) is incorrect because an animal's reputation or propensity for aggression is considered only in a separate realm of torts—actions for harms by the animal, like biting or other attacks.

    Answer (C) is incorrect because this prior effort does not affect the necessity defense, although presumably it would make the plaintiff appear more sympathetic to a jury.

    Answer (D) is incorrect because the dog's history also does not affect a necessity defense when the actor, to prevent the destruction of more valuable property, has killed a dog in the act of killing other animals.

38. Rupert has a claim against Hannah, and Hannah has a claim against Rupert, for battery. Battery is the intentional infliction of harmful contact. Each of these two individuals "pounded at" the other in this fistfight that began as a discussion of professional sports, indicating that the blows were intentional acts. Hannah and Rupert both desired to inflict harmful contact on the other, and harmful contact resulted from their actions. Jurisdictions differ on whether their consent to the blows will bar their claims. The fistfight appears to have been consensual. The majority rule is that consent to an illegal act is ineffective. The *Restatement (Second) of Torts* and some jurisdictions disagree, holding that consent to a criminal act is a valid defense in an action for an intentional tort. If the jurisdiction follows the majority rule, the status of the fistfight as a criminal breach of the peace would make the consent ineffective, and so Rupert and Hannah would each have a battery claim against the other.

39. You could be wrong, but it looks as if the person about to drink has been given a dangerous substance without her consent. Your privilege to use force in her defense extends to what is reasonable under the circumstances. Knocking the drink out of her hand onto the floor would be reasonable, and you'd have a privilege in an action by the person about to drink, should she bring a claim for battery, or by the bar, for trespass to their chattel. Brawling with the maybe-assailant would go beyond the needs of defense because the person has already poured the vial of liquid into the other person's drink.

40. **Answer (D) is correct.** "Consent implied by law" is a kind of implied consent where the plaintiff did not, in fact, imply that he or she consented to an action. Instead the law infers that a reasonable person would in that circumstance have accepted the challenged behavior. The doctrine is used where a plaintiff is unable to give or withhold consent. Here, it seems fair to infer that Dauphine needed some kind of touching in order to be rescued; she could not say yes or no at the time, and Pallowag's touching does not exceed these bounds.

Answer (A) is incorrect because to the extent any consent is implied, it is implied in fact—or, in other words, by Axel himself—rather than by law.

Answer (B) is incorrect for similar reasons. Belinda consented in fact. (She may not have given "informed consent," but that is another matter.)

Answer (C) is incorrect because the doctrine of consent implied by law, in the medical context, applies only to emergencies or other unusual circumstances where the plaintiff cannot be asked what he or she wishes. This scenario depicts a physician who deviates from a patient's consent.

Negligence: The Duty of Care

41. **Answer (C) is correct.** This question involves an issue of affirmative duty. In the absence of such a duty, Eve cannot be held liable to Adam. Friends do not fit within a traditional "special relationship" but case law, notably *Farwell v. Keaton*, 240 N.W.2d 217 (Mich. 1976), suggests that friends on a joint social venture have an affirmative duty to protect one another. Adam's best argument here would be to assert that he and Eve were on such a venture.

    Answer (A) is incorrect because, although it was improper for Adam and Eve to scale the fence on the construction site (they were trespassers), it was not the act of going there that in itself caused harm to Adam and for which he seeks to hold Eve responsible. It was her failure to render assistance to him after he was injured.

    Answer (B) is incorrect because vicarious liability does not apply to this situation. Adam was not Eve's agent. To be held liable, Eve must have been negligent, meaning that she either committed an act of misfeasance or failed unreasonably to help Adam when she had a duty to do so.

    Answer (D) is incorrect because it is not enough to say that failure to assist was the cause in fact and proximate cause of harm. The traditional no-duty-to-rescue rule is not based on considerations of causation or proximate cause. It is a policy-based rule that applies even when a party is the cause in fact and proximate cause of another party's harm.

42. **Answer (B) is correct.** Sara had no duty to assist Adam, but if she chose to do so, she was obligated to exercise reasonable care in her undertaking. It will be a jury question whether, under the circumstances, it was unreasonable for Sara to attempt to convey Adam to the hospital if her vehicle was very low on gasoline.

    Answer (A) is incorrect because it assumes Sara would be strictly liable once she undertook to assist Adam. Her duty, once assumed by Sara, is only that of a reasonable person.

    Answer (C) is incorrect because it assumes one may not be found negligent when acting under emergency circumstances. The law provides that the jury may take the emergency into account as one factor in determining whether the party acted reasonably. It is possible to act unreasonably even under emergency circumstances.

    Answer (D) is incorrect because it assumes "Good Samaritan" statutes protect all rescuers except those whose conduct constitutes intentional wrongdoing. In fact, the protections of these statutes are narrower; they tend only to protect rescuers whose conduct is merely negligent. Rescuers whose conduct constitutes something worse than negligence, such as recklessness, "willful or wanton" misconduct, or intentional misconduct, are typically excluded from the protection of the statutes. In addition, some statutes only protect medical professionals.

43. **Answer (A) is correct.** Jojo acted carelessly and caused harm, but he did not owe a duty of care to Alma. The facts fall within the center of the "no duty for consequential economic loss" rule.

    Answer (B) is incorrect because the professional standard of care relates to breach, not duty.

    Answer (C) may be true under the facts but doesn't matter. When a person gives unsound financial advice, reliance is not sufficient to create a duty of care.

    Answer (D) is incorrect because the "undertaking" exception to a no-duty category involves an overt, explicit statement or gesture where the defendant agrees to look out for the welfare of the plaintiff. It is not applied to economic loss claims like this one.

44. Imposing a general duty to exercise reasonable care through both affirmative conduct and failure to act, or eliminating "duty" from the prima facie case, would make many more claims actionable, with unfortunate results. Claims alleging economic and emotional injury would be much harder to dispose of before trial. Liability for omissions would expand: without limited duty, an obligation to prevent harm by others or to eliminate suffering unrelated to tortious conduct would foster new claims.

45. **Answer (B) is correct.** The problem asks you to come up with a correct label for Natalia as land visitor and then identify the duty owed to a visitor so labeled. As a social guest, Natalia was a licensee. Licensees are not owed reasonable care. The land possessor must warn them of hidden dangers, but the danger on Marie's property was not hidden.

    Answer (A) is incorrect because Natalia, made welcome by Marie, was not a trespasser.

    Answer (C) is incorrect because as a licensee, Natalia was not owed reasonable care. That level of care is owed only to invitees.

    Answer (D) is incorrect because Natalia was not an invitee. The start-up business point would have mattered if Natalia was on the land to advance Marie's business interests. Moreover, alone among the choices, this one does not focus on duty and can be easily rejected for that reason.

46. **Answer (B) is correct.** This duty question falls in the category of physical injury + misfeasance, derived from the old English case of *Heaven v. Pender*. When your activity poses a foreseeable risk of physically injuring a person, you have a duty of reasonable care.

    Answer (A) is incorrect because it focuses on the status of the plaintiffs on the premises. We don't know whether we are in a jurisdiction that cares about the status of visitors to land.

    Answer (C) is incorrect because it rests on an obsolete use of privity. Ever since the landmark *MacPherson v. Buick Motor Co.*, a contractual relation between the defendant and the plaintiff is not needed to establish a duty of care with respect to physical injuries.

    Answer (D) is incorrect because it is incorrect to suppose that only performers and stagehands will stand on a stage. Other uses of a stage are foreseeable—e.g., school graduation ceremonies, trade shows, political debates.

47. **Answer (A) is correct** because of all the choices it is most pertinent to the central concept of Archie's duty, and most helpful to him as a litigant. If Archie undertook to build a stage that could support 800 pounds, and the total weight of persons and objects on the stage was 1500

pounds at the time of the collapse, then it becomes less correct to blame Archie for the injuries. He did what he was hired to do.

Answer (B) is incorrect because it helps Archie only a little—it reduces the amount of damages he has to pay—whereas a finding of no breach of duty would be maximally helpful to him.

Answer (C) is incorrect because it is redundant: we know from the fact summary that Archie is "a licensed and qualified architect."

Answer (D) is incorrect because it too is redundant: we know that "Archie's plans were followed exactly."

48. **Answer (D) is correct.** Pure economic loss is no more likely than any other type of damage to involve plaintiffs responsible for their own injury. The other answers enjoy support among torts scholars.

Answer (A) is incorrect because the argument makes sense. It is probably the most often invoked rationale for the current rule.

Answer (B) is incorrect for the same reason as (A)—open-ended liability risks disproportionate liability.

Answer (C) is the leading law and economics rationale for the current rule.

49. An unforeseeable plaintiff is a plaintiff whose claim arises based on the negligence of a defendant with respect to a *different* plaintiff. The famous *Palsgraf v. Long Island R.R. Co.* provides an illustration. According to the Cardozo opinion, railroad employees negligently pushed and pulled a passenger onto a departing train, causing the passenger's package (which did not appear dangerous) to fall from his arms and explode. This negligence, Cardozo held, created liability only to a small set of potential plaintiffs who were close to the place where the railroad's employees carelessly pushed and pulled the passenger onto the train. Palsgraf was standing at some distance from the push and suffered injury from the explosion. According to the Cardozo rationale, Palsgraf was an unforeseeable plaintiff. The risk of injury to her was outside of what a reasonable person in the position of defendant's employees would have foreseen.

50. **Answer (B) is correct.** Though Bobby was not in the store to conduct any business, he was accompanying Hank, who was there for such a purpose and was therefore an invitee. Under the circumstances, it is unlikely that Hank could have done his shopping without taking the kid along, so in a sense, his presence in the store was necessary to Hank's doing business there. Thus, Bobby was also an invitee, to whom a duty of reasonable care was owed. Because a question of material fact remains about whether Arlene's exercised reasonable care in maintaining its display of power saws, summary judgment is not appropriate.

Answer (A) is incorrect because, as explained above, Bobby was an invitee.

Answer (C) is incorrect because Bobby was not a licensee.

Answer (D) is incorrect because even if Hank negligently supervised Bobby, his negligence would not be imputed to Bobby so as to defeat Bobby's claim against Arlene's. (Once again, duty is not implicated in this choice.)

51. **Answer (B) is correct.** The firefighter's rule provides that a public employee who suffers an injury caused by a kind of hazard that she confronts as a normal part of her job does not have a negligence claim against the person who created the hazard. Pursuing suspects is part of Krumpke's job as a police officer. He may not sue Willie for negligence.

    Answer (A) is incorrect because it fails to take account of the firefighter's rule.

    Answer (C) is incorrect because Willie had no duty to protect Krumpke from this hazard.

    Answer (D) is incorrect because the facts do not make clear that Krumpke actually failed to exercise reasonable care. The opposite is probably true; the facts state that Krumpke could tell that the stairway was rotted, but tried to avoid the weak spots. Under the emergency circumstances in which he found himself, Krumpke probably exercised reasonable care. In addition, the court will not need to reach this issue because, as discussed above, the firefighter's rule will prevent Krumpke from recovering for Willie's negligence. (Once again we have a choice that does not implicate duty.)

52. **Answer (D) is correct.** A physician has an ethical duty to assist a person in need of medical attention, but does not have a legal duty to assist unless the physician caused the need for medical attention or has a special relationship with the person. Neither is true here. The physician's failure to act may be reprehensible but it is not tortious.

    Answer (A) is incorrect because merely having the ability to assist does not impose an obligation to do so.

    Answer (B) is incorrect because sharing the status of passengers on a commercial flight does not create a special relationship among them. In some sense, they are all "in it together," but this is more a matter of coincidence than any voluntary association. Perhaps if the plane had made a hard landing and the survivors were stranded while awaiting assistance, a court would find that their relationship was one of dependence on each other. But that is not the case here.

    Answer (C) is incorrect because, as explained above, the passengers were not in a special relationship with each other. In addition, as also explained above, the physician's ability to assist does not impose a legal obligation to assist.

53. **Answer (C) is correct** under both the Second and Third Restatements, although the Second classifies the analysis under duty (in its § 316) and the Third under breach. Comment d to § 41 of the Third Restatement says that "there is no threshold number, type, or similarity of activities that are required for foreseeability to exist," but there must be a reasonably foreseeable risk of harm.

    Answer (A) is incorrect because although negligence law provides no general duty to rescue, there are exceptions, and responsibility of a parent for the harms caused by a minor child is among them.

    Answer (B) is incorrect because it errs in the other direction. Just because reasonable care would avoid a risk does not mean that a duty exists.

    Answer (D) is incorrect because although undertaking is a separate exception to the rule of no duty, that exception does not apply to these facts.

54. The driver could argue that she had a duty only to "persons" in the vehicle, and the fetus is not a person because its existence depends on the wishes of its mother; "persons" do not have this kind of dependent, contingent existence. Courts reject this reasoning. They see a fetus (but in some states, only a viable fetus) as a holder of rights against tortfeasors, the abortion rights of pregnant women notwithstanding. The prerogative of a woman to end her pregnancy does not mean that strangers can also end it, or do harm to a fetus, without legal consequences.

Negligence: Breach of Duty

55. **Answer (C) is correct.** The railing was under the control of the boat's owner and the owner has a duty to maintain the premises in a reasonably safe condition. The most probable explanation for a railing giving way is negligent maintenance by the boat's owner.

    Answer (A) is incorrect. The steps were not under the control of the restaurant. Any number of people could have left the glass on the step. Even if the restaurant should have checked the stairs from time to time to make sure there were no hazards to customers, the facts do not suggest that the restaurant might have breached that duty; the wineglass might have been placed on the stairs just moments before Danielle tripped on it.

    Answer (B) is incorrect. It is unknown what caused the damage to Cop's car. Therefore, it is not more probable than not that Patch is responsible.

    Answer (D) is incorrect. Since Murray suffered no similar symptoms, the food that Melissa and Murray ate at the restaurant is not reasonably certain to have been the cause of Melissa's injury. Therefore, it is not certain that the restaurant had exclusive control of the instrument causing her injury.

56. The child is held to the standard of a child of similar age, intelligence, and experience. This treatment is unavailable to most adult defendants, for whom individual age, intelligence and experience usually are not taken into account. An exception arises when the child engages in an activity that is usually limited to adults. In this situation, the child is held to the reasonable person standard, with personal characteristics omitted from analysis.

57. **Answer (B) is correct.** In the Hand Formula, B ("burden") is the money that may be spent to reduce the risk of injury. PL is the expected cost of that injury. It expresses the product of P, the probability of harm, and L, the magnitude of the harm (or "loss") should it occur.

    Answer (A) is incorrect because what it expresses has nothing to do with the Hand Formula. It simply compares the cost for Rob of doing something with the cost to him of doing nothing.

    Answer (C) is incorrect because what it says about B is true about P, not B.

    Answer (D) is written as a snare for the unwary. It invites the reader to think of PL as a reference to plaintiffs, which is wrong, and although it is correct to note that B stands for burden, the burden of B is an investment in safety, not the price of being held liable.

58. **Answer (C) is correct.** Earl violated a statute the purpose of which was to reduce the risk of fires. He had no cognizable excuse for his violation. His act was a cause in fact and proximate cause of the fire, and the fire brought about physical harm to Vanessa's property.

Answer (A) is incorrect. Regardless of the wind, a reasonable person in Earl's position would know that it was unduly risky to neighbors to toss cigarettes off the balcony, especially on a windy day. Even though the wind was a natural event beyond human control (an "act of God"), the wind was a natural, everyday event of insufficient significance to relieve Earl of liability.

Answer (B) is incorrect. Although Vanessa was aware Earl threw his cigarette butts on her balcony, the facts do not indicate that she was or should have been aware they were lit at the time. Therefore, she had no reason to believe that the trash she left on her balcony would ignite if it came in contact with one of Earl's cigarettes. Vanessa is therefore not contributory negligent. (Even if Vanessa were contributory negligent, her recovery would only be reduced according to the jurisdiction's rules for comparative negligence; she probably would still recover something.)

Answer (D) is incorrect. The mere fact that a fire occurred is not sufficient to establish negligence under res ipsa loquitur. To apply that doctrine, Vanessa would have to demonstrate that this was the sort of accident that is usually caused by negligence. That showing might be difficult to make. In addition, Vanessa would have to demonstrate that the fire was caused by Earl's cigarette and not by some other instrumentality.

59. In furnishing medical services, the physician is held to exercise the care that would be exercised by a member of the medical profession in good standing. She is not held to the unmodified "reasonable person" standard, which would be too low. Jurisdictions divide over whether to compare the physician to a "national," "local," or "similar community" standard.

60. **Answer (A) is correct.** The statute prohibiting headphones on cyclists was almost certainly designed to reduce the risk of injuries that could be avoided by cyclists who can hear what's going on around them. Headphone music prevented Shimen from hearing a warning that could have avoided the collision with Phreddie.

   Answer (B) is incorrect because it is almost certain that this was the type of injury the statute was designed to prevent. It is difficult to imagine what other type of injury the statute might have been aimed at preventing.

   Answer (C) is incorrect because, under the traditional negligence per se doctrine, violation of a statute that meets the requirements set forth above does *not* present *some evidence* of negligence for the jury to consider. It *establishes* negligence (at least in the absence of a recognized excuse, none of which apply here).

   Answer (D) is incorrect because, as long as safety is one purpose of the statute, it can qualify for application of the negligence per se doctrine.

61. The emergency standard of care gives actors an extra measure of leniency when their behavior is assessed in a negligence claim. They are held to the standard of a reasonable person under the same emergency. This standard is not applied when the actor's own wrongful conduct caused the emergency to occur. Yarble should be liable.

62. **Answer (A) is correct.** Regardless of whether you agree that the plaintiff should be allowed to recover from the defendant, you should be able to see that Answer (A) engages most closely with the question asked. The other choices miss the point.

Answer (B) is incorrect because the plaintiff is objecting to the placement of the sign, not the depth of the water.

Answer (C) is incorrect because even if a DEEP WATER sign reduces the risk of drowning—which is far from clear here, given that the water was in fact shallow—the risk in this case was a head injury.

Answer (D) is incorrect for the same reason as Answer (B): the plaintiff is not objecting to the depth of the water.

63. The difference lies in how much freedom the factfinder (jury or judge) has to deem the defendant to have been *not* negligent. Under "negligence per se," violation of a relevant statute establishes duty and breach as a matter of law. The defendant is deemed negligent for having violated the statute and caused injury to the plaintiff. Under the "evidence of negligence" approach, violation of the statute is relevant to establish negligence, but not dispositive. The factfinder can reject this evidence and deem the defendant not negligent

64. **Answer (A) is correct.** The question tests the "adult activity" exception to the child standard of care. For no particularly logical reason, courts tend to limit this exception to the operation of motor vehicles.

    Answer (B) is incorrect because courts that hear negligence claims simply do not seem to think using a firearm is an adult activity. There are a few exceptions to this rule, but the motor vehicles category of Answer A is much more accepted.

    Answer (C) is incorrect because setting a fire is not an adult activity; children do it fairly often.

    Answer (D) is incorrect because riding a bicycle is an unexceptional activity for a 15-year-old.

65. **Answer (B) is correct.** Dr. Seuss is asking to be held to the standard of a small-town doctor in the same community rather than a national standard, which is higher.

    Answer (A) is incorrect because res ipsa loquitur, "the thing speaks for itself," is not present in these facts. The choice of which contraceptive to prescribe requires learning, and res ipsa loquitur is a layperson standard.

    Answer (C) is incorrect because the Hand formula compares the cost of a precaution to the expected cost of not taking that precaution.

    Answer (D) is incorrect because "customs as either probative or dispositive" refers to the issue of what a jury, or judge acting as factfinder, is permitted or required to conclude.

66. **Answer (C) is correct.** Courts have ruled that a patient is entitled to be informed by a physician not only about risks and benefits of undergoing a particular medical intervention, but also information about risks and benefits of *not* undergoing that intervention. Some patients know what a Pap smear is for but many do not, and relaying this information can make a difference.

    Answer (A) is incorrect because even though what it says is accurate, Dr. Seuss was obliged to provide information about the Pap smear.

    Answer (B) is incorrect because although it appears Dr. Seuss performed the examination with due care, it does not consider the additional possibility of an informed consent claim.

Answer (D) is incorrect because Dr. Seuss did not fail to perform the Pap smear with ordinary skill and care; Dr. Seuss failed to perform the Pap smear altogether.

67. **Answer (B) is correct.** Under this standard, the decision to become intoxicated can itself be negligence—particularly if the defendant does something risky, such as drive a car.

   Answer (A) is incorrect because courts deem it too lenient: having become intoxicated as a matter of choice, Druze should not benefit from a lower standard of care.

   Answer (C) is incorrect because negligence law does not recognize "the reasonable person with a mental deficiency" as a standard of care for defendants.

   Answer (D) is incorrect although it may look attractive for deterrence purposes. Courts do not impose it unless the combination of intoxication and conduct violates a statute, as in the case of drunk driving. There it is the violation of a statute, not voluntary intoxication, that takes the question from the jury.

68. **Answer (B) is correct.** The defendant's negligence is very doubtful, given the difficulty of eliminating the risk in question. Of all the choices, **Answer (B)** focuses most closely on the reasonableness of the defendant's conduct.

   Answer (A) is incorrect because the plaintiffs' susceptibilities are not at issue here. The problem states that E. Coli causes Hepatitis A. Some people may be more or less likely to develop the disease after exposure, but this point does not affect the question of liability for exposure.

   Answer (C) is incorrect because from the facts it appears that W&C has no control over stormwater drains "in the region."

   Answer (D) is incorrect because if correct it would, at most, permit W&C to dispute causation for a subset of plaintiffs. Because the problem states that "investigators determined that the cause of this outbreak of Hepatitis A was the consumption of contaminated W&C oysters," Answer (D) does not much affect W&C's liability.

69. **Answer (D) is correct.** This question tests your understanding of the breach element in terms of its effects: What could the defendant have done differently to avoid the risk of injury? This understanding of breach is necessary to support your understanding of cause in fact. **Answer (D)** offers the most useless suggestion: The problem states that no test exists to determine the levels of E. Coli in the defendant's oyster waters. Looking for "contamination" might have found something but it is hard to say what, or why anyone would care.

   Answer (A) is incorrect because, according to the facts, declining to sell oysters until flesh tests indicated the oysters were safe would have had a strong effect on the injury rate.

   Answer (B) is incorrect because, although it would have accomplished less than declining to sell the oysters, it does offer a risk-reducing strategy. One may infer that a warning of contamination would have reduced consumption and thus reduced the incidence of Hepatitis A.

   Answer (C) is incorrect because, as the most radical alternative, it would have done the most to prevent injury.

70. **Answer (C) is correct.** All the variables increase. A busy harbor is more likely to experience collisions than a quiet one; ships become more valuable and expensive in wartime; and wage labor becomes more expensive during wartime (able-bodied workers become occupied as soldiers).

Answers (A), (B), and (D) are incorrect for the reasons stated.

71. **Answer (D) is correct.** Circumstantial evidence asks for inferences from physical conditions. Grimy, gritty spilled shampoo was probably lying on the floor for a while, suggesting an unreasonable delay on the part of the defendant. Reasonable care would mean mopping it up promptly.

    Answer (A) is incorrect. This answer addresses an issue separate from circumstantial evidence, the standard of care for a blind person.

    Answer (B) is incorrect. Eyewitness testimony about behavior is not circumstantial evidence.

    Answer (C) is incorrect. It is possible that the plaintiff was injured because of carelessness at the hotel, but this answer does not give enough information to suggest that such negligence occurred.

72. **Answer (D) is correct.** Res ipsa loquitur applies when (1) this is the type of accident that is usually caused by negligence; (2) the instrumentality that caused the accident was in the exclusive control of the defendant; and (3) the plaintiff did not contribute meaningfully to the accident. Here, requirement (3) (which is somewhat redundant of the second requirement) is clearly satisfied; Naomi had nothing to do with the accident's occurrence. The real issues are whether there was probably negligence and whether any negligence was probably that of AmuseCo (whether the instrumentality was in AmuseCo's possession at the time of any negligence). It seems reasonable to infer as a matter of common sense and experience that a carousel does not normally accelerate too much unless there is negligence in its operation or maintenance. Though it would be better for Naomi to offer expert testimony to establish this fact, most courts would probably hold that an expert is not absolutely required to get the case to the jury. (At the very least, an appellate court is unlikely to hold that the trial court erred in denying a motion for directed verdict even though Naomi did not offer expert testimony.) And because the carousel was owned and operated by AmuseCo, it is highly likely that any negligent operation or maintenance was AmuseCo's responsibility.

    Answer (A) is incorrect because a negligence case may be established purely through circumstantial evidence. Res ipsa loquitur does not operate only if there is direct evidence of negligence.

    Answer (B) is incorrect because, as noted above, this is not a situation in which expert testimony is required to establish the first element of the res ipsa loquitur test.

    Answer (C) is incorrect because a plaintiff is not required to eliminate all other possibilities in order to get a case to the jury based on circumstantial evidence. The court need only find that a reasonable jury could believe that, more likely than not, that there was negligence, and that defendant was the negligent party.

73. **Answer (C) is correct.** If the court decides that res ipsa loquitur applies, that only means that plaintiff has a strong enough case to reach the jury. It does *not* mean that plaintiff's claim must prevail in the absence of contrary evidence offered by defendant. Thus, application of the doctrine here means only that the court should deny Naomi's motion and let the jury decide the case. (Note that in some unusual circumstances, plaintiff's circumstantial evidence might be

so strong that it entitles plaintiff to a directed verdict in the absence of contrary evidence on the negligence issue. But that clearly is not the case here.)

Answer (A) is incorrect because, as suggested above, defendant is not obligated to offer evidence of non-negligence. Though defendant might well want to do so, it need not do so.

Answer (B) is incorrect because the evidence is not so strong as to mandate a verdict for Angela; it merely gets her to the jury.

Answer (C) is incorrect because AmuseCo has no better access to information concerning the cause of the accident, the court should deny Naomi's motion.

74. **Answer (D) is correct.** The court should deny both motions because there is evidence to support both positions on the question of negligence.

Answer (A) is incorrect for the reason just given. It is not so clear that AmuseCo was not negligent that the court should take the matter out of the jury's hands.

Answer (B) is incorrect for similar reasons. The case is not so strong for Naomi as to require a directed verdict in her favor. Though the evidence presented here can cut either way, its greater force is probably to make AmuseCo's negligence *harder*, not easier, to infer. Thus, a directed verdict for Naomi is clearly not in order.

Answer (C) is incorrect because in a jury trial, gauging the credibility of a witness is a task for the jury.

75. **Answer B is correct.** The breach element asks whether someone acted reasonably in a particular instance. What is reasonable or unreasonable conduct fits well with the diversity of life experiences that juries bring to a complaint about negligently inflicted injury.

Answer A is incorrect because if it were true, then "expert resolution" should decide breach, and juries are not experts.

Answer C is incorrect because juries do need some education in the law to decide the question of breach. They receive this education in the form of instructions from the judge.

Answer C is incorrect because persons who serve on juries do not necessarily know anything about matters of fact.

Negligence: Causation— Actual and Proximate

76. **Answer (D) is correct.** Economic analysis emphasizes deterrence. Each element of the prima facie case functions to give the defendant a chance to not pay damages. Thus the causation element, considered only after the plaintiff has proved breach, permits a defendant to avoid liability after the plaintiff proves that it engaged in conduct that society condemns as wasteful and destructive. Lack of liability = less deterrence.

    Answer (A) is incorrect. In general, economic analysis is not interested in fairness.

    Answer (B) is incorrect for the same reason.

    Answer (C) is incorrect. Discovery is costly, but causation is not different from breach in this respect, a point that Answer (C) denies.

77. **Answer (A) is correct.** What made the storage negligent was the presence of unmarked rat poison that looked like cooking salt in a restaurant kitchen. What occurred was not within the scope of this risk.

    Answer (B) is incorrect because there is no reason to suppose that the placement of a thermometer on a restaurant counter by a health inspector was unforeseeable.

    Answer (C) is incorrect because it considers breach, and proximate cause is a separate element of the prima facie case.

    Answer (D) is incorrect because it considers the possibility of contributory or comparative negligence, not breach.

78. **Answer (B) is correct.** With respect to the food poisoning, the facts identify breach of duty that caused an injury. Causation of the infection by Gordon's conduct is more remote, but courts have agreed that defendants who inflict injury through their tortious conduct are responsible for a second injury that results from negligently furnished medical care.

    Answer (A) is incorrect for the reasons stated above.

    Answer (C) is incorrect because actual cause is present.

    Answer (D) is incorrect because proximate cause is present for the infection under the "second injury" rule. There is no possible proximate cause question for the food poisoning.

79. The strongest case for non-liability of the initially negligent defendant would involve unforeseeable criminal misconduct or an unforeseeable intentional tort committed by another person. Imagine a parking garage that has been open for years in perfect safety, with no crimes or even accidents taking place on the scene. At the same time, it expressly disclaims taking

safety precautions. The defendant owns the garage. Its negligence consists of not inspecting the swipe-key lock that long-term customers use to gain access to their vehicles. Unknown to the defendant, over time the lock sensor weakens in such a way that any credit card will work to open the door. All other conditions in the garage are extremely safe. An intruder enters with a credit card and, acting on a fetish, kisses the feet of a customer against his will (a battery). (More serious harms might impel a court to rule against the garage in order to compensate the plaintiff.) If the intruder is captured and has enough assets to satisfy a judgment, that fact would make the case for non-liability of the garage even stronger.

80. **Answer (B) is correct.** Andy's shooting of Millard was an act outside the scope of the risk that Granger negligently created, and was thus a superseding cause.

   Answer (A) is incorrect because selling a gun has risks beyond the dangerousness of the buyer. (For example, a defective safety engages third parties.)

   Answer (C) is incorrect because it summarizes the doctrine of negligence per se, and superseding cause can cut off liability even when duty and breach are present as a matter of law.

   Answer (D) is incorrect by reasoning similar to the explanation of Answer C. Violation of a statute does not establish proximate cause as a matter of law.

81. No, it does not. The but-for test requires that the occurrence be "necessary" in order for the harm to take place. If it is merely "sufficient," then the occurrence is usually held not to have been a but-for cause of the harm. For example, suppose X shoots Q in the heart. X intends to kill Q, but unknown to X, Q died of a stroke a half hour earlier. X's conduct — "sufficient" but not "necessary" to kill — is not a but-for cause of Q's death. Of course, the but-for test is not always used. Other approaches can be more inclusive.

82. **Answer (B) is correct.** The traditional view of causation holds that a negligent party is only responsible if the jury concludes that it is more likely than not that the party caused the harm suffered by the plaintiff. In this case, Paul had only 40 percent chance of survival even if diagnosed and treated properly. Thus, under the traditional rule, it cannot be said that "but for" Doc's negligent diagnosis, it is more likely than not that Paul would have survived.

   Answer (A) is incorrect for the reasons just given.

   Answer (C) is incorrect because under the "lost chance of survival" theory, courts permit recovery of a proportional amount of the plaintiff's damages when the defendant's negligence deprived the plaintiff of a significant chance of recovery. A 40 percent chance of recovery is probably significant. Thus, in this case, a court might allow plaintiff to recover 40 percent of the total loss. (Note that there are many different "lost chance" formulations. Most allow reduced damages, but they use different kinds of calculations.)

   Answer (D) is incorrect because, as stated above, most courts adopting a "lost chance" theory award reduced damages.

83. **Answer (A) is correct.** The risk rule focuses on the aspect of what the defendant did that made her conduct negligent. It rests on what is reasonably foreseeable at the time of action.

   Answer (B) is incorrect because it describes the counterfactual or but-for test, used to determine actual rather than proximate cause.

Answer (C) is incorrect because it describes the "substantial factor" approach as promulgated in Restatement (Second) of Torts.

Answer (D) is incorrect because it describes the directness test.

84. **Answer (B) is correct.** Sometimes known as "multiple sufficient causes" or "duplicative causation," this convergence challenges the but-for test because if the but-for test is applied, neither the negligently caused fire nor the innocent fire is the cause of the plaintiff's damage, which seems wrong or at least odd. *Restatement (Second) of Torts* § 431 coined the "substantial factor" test to provide for liability of the negligent defendant, but the current *Restatement* has abandoned this term.

    Answer (A) is incorrect because superseding events or causes are different in kind from the original negligence.

    Answer (C) is incorrect because preponderance of the evidence has no relation to the problem described.

    Answer (D) is incorrect because the merged-fires scenario is about actual cause, not proximate cause, and because the second injury rule involves carelessly furnished medical treatment.

85. **Answer (C) is correct.** This products liability action features a product that is unreasonably dangerous because of foreseeable misuse by children. But for this danger, the harm would probably not have occurred.

    Answer (A) is incorrect because but for the negligence of the defendant, the outcome would probably have been the same.

    Answer (B) is incorrect for the same reason as Answer A. Negligence by the defendant was not necessary for the harm to occur.

    Answer (D) is incorrect because the defective product or negligent conduct (we can use those terms interchangeably here) was not sufficient to cause an injury.

86. **Answer (B) is correct.** Bear in mind that you are asked here only about causation and not the claim as a whole, which may face other difficulties. The facts strongly suggest that, but for Danforth's repeated striking of Hester's car, Hester would not have been seen leaving the scene of an accident, reported to the police, and charged with hit-and-run driving. And from there, Hester would not have suffered emotional distress.

    Answer (A) is incorrect because foreseeability does not pertain to the cause in fact question.

    Answer (C) is incorrect because, while it is often difficult to prove a negative — to prove what would have happened if not for defendant's conduct — there is no such problem here. The entire situation that caused Hester to suffer emotional distress was brought about by Danforth's initial act of striking Hester's car over and over.

    Answer (D) is incorrect because more than one thing can be a cause in fact of harm. Here, it's possible that other factors contributed to Hester's suffering emotional distress. But as long as Danforth's conduct was one factor, it qualifies.

87. **Answer (C) is correct.** This question helps you find one of the takeaways of the most famous case you'll cover all semester (unless your instructor is among the minority who skip it). It is

based on a real case, *Dahlstrom v. Shrum*, 84 A.2d 289 (Pa. 1951). Answer (C) presents Lee, located on the sidewalk at some distance from the collision site, as an unforeseeable plaintiff like Helen Palsgraf.

Answer (A) is incorrect because it illustrates a different problem, "the eggshell psyche."

Answer (B) is incorrect because in this scenario, Wolfe is a foreseeable plaintiff who suffered an injury closely connected to negligent driving. The fortuity here is that Wolfe's damages were unexpectedly cheap, which is not the problem of *Palsgraf.*

Answer (D) is incorrect because it illustrates a different problem, "the eggshell skull."

88. **Answer (A) is correct.** Hardy must establish that it is more likely than not that had he been able to reach a 911 operator, Hannah would have survived, at least for a meaningfully longer time. Proving a negative is, of course, difficult, but that is a problem faced by plaintiffs in many tort cases.

    Answer (B) is incorrect because the burden of proof on causation lies with the plaintiff, not the defendant. This is true of the other elements of the prima facie case for negligence as well.

    Answer (C) is incorrect because foreseeability is not part of the determination of cause in fact. Foreseeability factors into proximate cause, but not cause in fact.

    Answer (D) is incorrect because a failure to act can have a causal connection to harm. Moreover, Phone Co. (like the driver), has engaged in some action: it has operated the 911 emergency system. The problem is that it did not do a good enough job of making the system available to callers when the phone lines were very crowded. Even if this is viewed as a case of nonfeasance, however, Phone Co.'s failure to provide Hardy with a connection to 911 will be viewed as a cause in fact if, but for that failure, Hannah's life would have been extended meaningfully or saved.

Defenses to Negligence

89. **Answer (D) is correct.** The danger of the display, as described, is apparent. A reasonable person in Lina's position would either avoid it or ask an Irving's employee for help getting the jars of jam. Accordingly, the jurisdiction would apply comparative negligence as stated in Answer D.

    Answer (A) is incorrect because even if the jurisdiction had not abolished the land visitor status categories, which makes the label "invitee" obsolete there, an invitee can have her recovery reduced under apportionment principles. All that being an invitee could ever mean for Lina is that she is entitled to reasonable care.

    Answer (B) is incorrect for the reason above that explains the correct answer.

    Answer (C) is incorrect because the presence of Robespierre as a co-defendant has nothing to do with the question asked.

90. **Answer (D) is correct.** Assumption of risk is an affirmative defense that requires defendant to prove (1) that plaintiff recognized and appreciated the specific risk she was confronting; and (2) that plaintiff chose voluntarily to confront the risk. Under a system of comparative fault like the one in the jurisdiction, the defense reduces plaintiff's recovery. Here, if the jury finds that Lina knew and appreciated the risk that the stack of jars would fall, and chose voluntarily to confront it, it may reduce her award.

    Answer (A) is incorrect because it speaks to the doctrine of "primary" assumption of risk, where the defendant did not breach its duty, rather than the secondary assumption of risk at issue here: Irving's did breach its duty to Lina.

    Answer (B) is incorrect because although it could be correct in a different jurisdiction, the question states that this jurisdiction does not treat assumption of risk as an absolute defense.

    Answer (C) is incorrect because it wrongly equates assumption of risk with comparative negligence. The two defenses have different elements.

91. **Answer (D) is correct.** Assumption of risk requires both knowledge and voluntariness. Mack did not know the true strength of the dose of Zip, and nothing about the problem suggests knowledge of any danger at all.

    Answer (A) is incorrect because voluntariness is not enough to establish assumption of risk.

    Answer (B) is incorrect because even though Mack did ask for a large dose, he did not know the likely consequences of taking it.

    Answer (C) is incorrect because the problem does not indicate that Mack was addicted to anything.

92. **Answer (C) is correct.** Isolde is trying to establish that she did not act unreasonably by sitting on the sofa next to Mack. Of the four choices, this answer describes reasonable conduct most clearly.

    Answer (A) is incorrect because the standard of care for negligence, including negligence by a plaintiff, is objective. What Isolde as an individual happened to know or not know doesn't matter.

    Answer (B) is incorrect because it too, like (A), does not comport with the objective approach to negligence.

    Answer (D) is incorrect because Alice's negligence does not relate directly to Isolde's conduct (even though Alice is a defendant). The issue here is whether Isolde acted unreasonably by sitting on the sofa next to Mack.

93. **Answer (D) is correct.** The contract is probably an adhesion contract because it was drafted by one party and appears to have been placed before the other party on a take-it-or-leave-it basis. This does not mean its exculpatory clause was unenforceable, however. Such clauses are enforceable unless they violate some important public policy. For example, courts have voided exculpatory clauses purporting to absolve operators of hospital emergency rooms of liability for negligence toward patients. Emergency rooms provide essential services that any member of the public may need at any moment, and the circumstances in which one goes to the emergency room seldom leave her with many alternatives. But courts have usually enforced exculpatory agreements that pertain to purely voluntary activities, particularly sporting activities. If Pawel did not like this clause, he could have gone elsewhere. And if all other stables used similar agreements, he could have decided whether to sign or to forgo horseback riding.

    Answer (A) is incorrect for the reasons just given.

    Answer (B) is incorrect because an exculpatory clause need not be extremely specific in order to be enforceable. The language of this clause sufficiently put Pawel on notice of Ed's limited liability. Note that the list of possible accidents contained in the Release is preceded by the words "including, but not limited to." This means the list is not intended to describe all possible scenarios.

    Answer (C) is incorrect because the agreement, if otherwise enforceable, can be applied to both experienced and inexperienced riders. Put differently, there is no strong public policy forbidding stables from exculpating themselves from liability even to inexperienced riders. In fact, it is primarily from the claims of injured novices that stables will want to protect themselves most.

94. **Answer (C) is correct.** While it was careless of Philippa to ingest unlabeled pills, the rendering of medical services to treat drug addiction includes an obligation to protect the patient from the dangers of that addiction, which include unreasonable ingestion of drugs. The duty of care that people owe to themselves that informs comparative negligence does not apply in this circumstance.

    Answer (A) is incorrect because it does not acknowledge the exceptional treatment of therapeutic relationships.

Answer (B) is incorrect because negligence by a defendant is never "imputed" to a plaintiff.

Answer (D) is incorrect because even if it were true, it would not answer the question of comparative negligence.

95. **Answer (C) is correct.** The defendant need not have been aware of the plaintiff's assumption of risk at the time of the injury, and the plaintiff need not have communicated this assumption of risk to the defendant.

    Answer (A) is incorrect. Voluntariness is an element of assumption of risk.

    Answer (B) is incorrect because many jurisdictions have merged implied assumption of risk together with comparative negligence. Both doctrines reduce, but do not eliminate, the plaintiff's recovery.

    Answer (D) is incorrect. Knowledge of the risk is an element of assumption of risk.

96. **Answer (C) is correct.** Courts hold that people who attend sporting events accept the risks inherent in that activity. This is a defense that completely defeats the claim because it amounts to a finding that the defendant did not owe the plaintiff a duty with regard to that injury. Thus, if Clinton had been hit by a flying hockey puck, he would not be able to recover. But that is not what happened. Clinton was injured by a risk that is not inherent in the game: flying glass from an improperly maintained barrier. A spectator does not "assume" that risk because fans have reason to expect that these barriers will protect them. Clinton's recovery should not be affected.

    Answer (A) is incorrect because, as explained above, this risk is not inherent in sitting so close to the ice at a hockey game. Also, the facts do not suggest that Sidney's failure to repair the barrier was reckless. It appears Sidney was merely negligent.

    Answer (B) is incorrect because, if being hit by glass fragments was not an inherent risk of attending a hockey game, there is no basis for reducing Clinton recovery to any degree.

    Answer (D) is incorrect because merely choosing to attend the game does not amount to any form of assumption of risk. If the roof had caved in during the game, surely Clinton would have been able to recover.

97. **Answer (D) is correct.** Courts would find Natalie's rescue of Grandpa as morally impelled rather than a free choice comparable to recreational activity, where implied assumption of risk remains most vital.

    Answer (A) is incorrect because the voluntariness element is not present.

    Answer (B) is incorrect because it applies an "objective" reasonable person standard. Assumption of risk is subjective.

    Answer (C) is incorrect because a "teen granddaughter" like Natalie would know about the danger of fire, as is evidenced by her decision to rescue Grandpa.

98. **Answer (C) is correct.** Unlike the scenario of the previous question, here Natalie's behavior is objectively unreasonable with respect to her own safety. The fire had become severe enough that a reasonable dweller of the house would not have reentered it except for an urgently necessary rescue. The story fits negligence by the plaintiff—in this jurisdiction, comparative neg-

ligence—better than any of the alternatives. It expresses the "imprudent" rather than "inadvertent" kind of negligence: Natalie was paying attention, but acted unreasonably anyway.

Answer (A) is incorrect because when a plaintiff's conduct is objectively imprudent—in other words, unreasonable—in the face of a risk caused by a defendant, courts in a comparative-negligence jurisdiction classify her conduct as comparative negligence rather than assumption of risk. Answer (A) is the least wrong of the wrong answers.

Answer (B) is incorrect because express assumption of risk applies to dangers encountered deliberately by the plaintiff. It has no place in a claim based on a fire that started by accident.

Answer (D) is incorrect because "last clear chance" is a doctrine used only in jurisdictions that retain contributory negligence, and this jurisdiction has adopted comparative negligence.

99. Primary implied assumption of risk arises where the defendant did not breach a duty to the plaintiff; secondary implied assumption of risk arises where the defendant has breached a duty to the plaintiff and then, upon being sued by the plaintiff, raises "assumption of risk" as an affirmative defense. Often "secondary implied assumption of risk" claims strongly resemble claims of "contributory negligence." Before the onset of comparative negligence, courts were casual about distinguishing the two. The modern trend views implied secondary assumption of risk as equivalent to comparative negligence, and so the task of distinguishing them has returned to being relatively unimportant, although not for the same reason.

100. The mentally deficient plaintiff has hurt only herself; the mentally deficient defendant has hurt others. Because self-preservation is a powerful force, the courts can take a more relaxed stance about negligence that harms only the negligent party. This "inconsistency" also softens the harsh effects of contributory negligence.

101. First, contributory negligence is still the rule in a handful of jurisdictions. Second, most jurisdictions that have adopted comparative negligence limit its effect through the "not as great" or "not greater than" approach (both are sometimes called "modified" approaches), in effect holding plaintiffs to a more stringent standard of care. Like the original rule of contributory negligence, these versions of comparative negligence provide that a defendant whose share of fault was a significant factor in the plaintiff's injury (perhaps the defendant was 30 percent responsible, or even 50 percent) will completely escape liability because the plaintiff was also at fault.

102. **Answer (A) is correct.** The question asks you to consider why defendants are not entitled to invert the pro-plaintiff doctrine of negligence in their favor when they have complied with a statute. Of the four choices, Answer (A) notes the most important distinction: Negligence per se proves only breach, and plaintiffs have a lot of other work they must do before they can prevail; an inversion of negligence per se in favor of defendants, however, would take them straight to no liability. The other choices do not state any distinction between the hypothetical rule and negligence per se, and are wrong for additional reasons:

Answer (B) is incorrect because neither plaintiffs nor defendants need to know about the existence of a statute for that statute to make a difference in a negligence claim.

Answer (C) is incorrect because state-by-state variations on how to use negligence per se do not pertain to the question.

Answer (D) is incorrect because excuse is just as available to the hypothetical rule as it is to negligence per se.

Strict Liability and Nuisance

103. **Answer (A) is correct.** The "value to the community" factor was present in the Second Restatement but dropped in the Third.

    Answer (B) is incorrect because the Third Restatement includes this factor.

    Answer (C) is incorrect as explained above for answer B.

    Answer (D) is incorrect as explained above for answer B.

104. **Answer (B) is correct.** The common law uses a negligence standard for dog bites. Dog bite statutes, enacted in many states, but not all, impose strict liability.

    Answer (A) is incorrect because negligence is always available for dog bites, and strict liability is not available in this jurisdiction.

    Answer (C) is incorrect because, as explained above, strict liability is not available.

    Answer (D) is incorrect because, as explained above, negligence is available.

105. **Answer (A) is correct.** Though at one point some courts did not apply the strict liability rule to concussion damage caused by blasting, all courts now do.

    Answer (B) is incorrect because, as discussed above, strict liability applies.

    Answer (C) is incorrect because trespass by a physical object, such as a rock, need not have occurred for strict liability to apply. The shockwave caused by the blast brought about the damage.

    Answer (D) is incorrect because keeping a rickety old barn does not constitute assumption of risk that it will be blown down by a dynamite blast.

106. **Answer (A) is correct.** Under *Restatement (Second) of Torts* § 520, the easier it is to eliminate the risk of harm through the exercise of reasonable care, the less likely the court will classify the activity as abnormally dangerous. If Ahmid can lessen the noise and avoid spreading the dust simply by enclosing his work area, his activity is less likely to be classified as abnormally dangerous.

    Answer (B) is incorrect because the plaintiff's ability to avoid the harmful effects of the defendant's conduct by limiting her use of her own land should not matter to an action for carrying on an abnormally dangerous activity. Rosa should not be forced to choose between using her back porch and becoming ill, and not using her back porch and staying healthy.

    Answer (C) is incorrect because the plaintiff's ability to avoid the harm by spending money should not affect her recovery for harm caused by defendant's abnormally dangerous activity. While we must all accept certain dangers associated with everyday life, if the factors relevant to characterizing Ahmid's activity as abnormally dangerous suggest that the activity qualifies, it is not fair to force Rosa to limit the use of her own property to avoid the harm.

Answer (D) is incorrect because an activity is even more likely to be deemed abnormally dangerous if it affects a larger number of people. Thus, this factor probably increases, rather than reduces, Rosa's chances of success in her suit against Ahmid.

107. **Answer (A) is correct.** By making it easier for the plaintiff to recover, courts shift the costs of accidents to defendants. This shift has the effect of discouraging the activity.

Answer (B) is incorrect; it is a better answer than (C) or (D) but not as good as (A). In general, making an activity subject to strict liability has the effect of discouraging that activity. The shift is not neutral; it encourages potential defendants to abstain from the "ultrahazardous" or "abnormally dangerous" activity in question.

Answer (C) is incorrect because to the extent plaintiffs are encouraged to change their safety investments based on the onset of strict liability, they are encouraged to invest less rather than more. The cost-benefit tradeoff to them is not relevant to the question posed.

Answer (D) is incorrect for a similar reason: making an activity subject to strict liability rather than negligence does not encourage potential victims to invest in safety.

108. **Answer (D) is correct.** Nuisance is the substantial and unreasonable interference with plaintiff's use and enjoyment of property. It can be based on conduct that qualifies as intentional, negligent, or abnormally dangerous. Here, Peg Co.'s conduct interferes with Al's sleep to a degree that a jury might find substantial. In addition, a jury might find it unreasonable to impose this burden on Al. (This would be especially true if a reasonable company would make the alarms less sensitive or program them to stop making noise more quickly.)

Public nuisances are those that affect the entire community in much the same way. Al is especially vulnerable because his home is so close to the parking garage. Thus, the harm he suffers is greater than that which is suffered by the community. In fact, proximity is what makes the activity so much of an interference with Al's use and enjoyment. People who live even a little further away might not suffer "substantial" interference.

Answer (A) is incorrect for the reasons given above. The noise from Peg Co. vehicles affects Al differently than it affects other people. Of course, some other people might suffer in the same way as Al, but only those whose homes are as close to the garage as Al's. This is more a private matter than a community-wide matter.

Answer (B) is incorrect for two reasons. First, Peg Co.'s behavior is intentional. "Intent" may be shown either by a desire to bring about the event or by knowledge that the event is substantially certain to occur. Though Peg Co. probably does not want the alarms to go off when there is no criminal activity, it certainly is aware that this is happening. Second, an action for nuisance may be based on intentional conduct, but does not have to be based on such conduct.

Answer (C) is incorrect because there is no suggestion in the facts that creation of the noise is an abnormally dangerous activity. In fact, it would not qualify as such because most of the factors listed in *Restatement (Second) of Torts* § 520 are not satisfied. (For example, the risk (probability) of harm is not very great; the harm itself, while not negligible, is not as great as harm that normally qualifies as abnormally dangerous; car alarms are commonly used; and the risk can be eliminated or substantially reduced by the exercise of reasonable care.)

109. The *Restatement (Second) of Torts* offers multifactor balancing rather than a bright-line rule. Balancing is more familiar to negligence than strict liability, which seeks categories. Factor (a), which looks for a high risk of harm, and factor (d), which asks whether the activity is uncommon, raise questions that are integral to assigning strict liability to an activity, yet they are not dispositive. Other factors could outweigh these two. Thus, an activity that is neither especially risky nor especially common — that is, an activity that seems to fit within the more ordinary category of negligence — could fall within the *Restatement (Second) of Torts'* test for strict liability.

110. **Answer (B) is correct.** Conducting experiments with chemicals that can explode and release toxic chemicals to neighboring property is the kind of activity that historically qualifies for the strict liability "abnormally dangerous activities" claim. From the facts, we cannot tell how likely it was that the activity would lead to harm, nor the amount of harm that would likely occur if there was a mishap. But chemical experimentation can often be very dangerous. In addition, this was done in the basement of a house, probably in a residential neighborhood, which might not be common or appropriate for this location. Though unclear, the fact that the explosion was unexpected and inexplicable suggests that even the exercise of reasonable care would not prevent it from occurring. The potential social benefit from the activity might be relatively great, but whether that is true for an amateur scientist engaged in research that hasn't been particularly fruitful for professional scientists is somewhat doubtful. If the activity fits into that category, it will not be necessary to prove negligence, making it a preferred claim for Curly to assert.

Answer (A) is incorrect because this is a case of injury to the person of the plaintiff, not interference with plaintiff's use and enjoyment of property. Thus, this is not the type of harm that the law of private nuisance is designed to redress.

Answer (C) is incorrect because the facts suggest that negligence will be difficult to prove. Ari was being "careful[]," and the explosion was "inexplicabl[e]" and "unexpected[]," making it less likely that he was negligent.

Answer (D) is incorrect because trespass requires an *intentional* entry onto the land of another without permission. Here, the entry of the chemicals was not intentional. Ari neither wished this to happen nor knew it was substantially certain to happen. Thus, trespass is not a viable claim.

111. An activity governed by strict liability — for example, blasting with dynamite — can cause a variety of injuries, but in order to fall within strict liability, the injuries must relate to the dangerous propensities of the activity. This requirement resembles the "risk rule" (or risk analysis) of proximate cause, which limits liability for harms caused by the defendant's negligence. For example, not every harm caused by blasting is actionable in strict liability. The classic case of *Foster v. Preston Mill Co.*, 268 P.2d 645 (Wash. 1954), held that a defendant that engaged in blasting would not be liable for a particular result that appeared odd or un-

foreseeable to the court (minks killing their young), even though the court accepted that the defendant's blasting caused this result. For another example, consider the keeping of a wild animal. If the wild animal does something harmful that is related to its dangerous propensities (such as biting), the keeper is strictly liable, but if the wild animal does something harmful that is unrelated to its dangerous propensities, the keeper is not strictly liable. (The keeper might be found negligent, however.)

112. Although driving a truck along a highway is not an abnormally dangerous activity, driving a tanker truck filled with gasoline poses a risk of extremely great harm in the event of a mishap that causes the gasoline to spill and ignite. Reasonable care, whether in the manner of driving or in the maintenance of the truck and trailer, will not eliminate the risk of this great harm. Although tanker trucks are common on the highways, their use is not common among the general public (only special companies use them). For at least these reasons, the activity can be classified as abnormally dangerous, and GasCo should be strictly liable to Popper.

113. **Answer (C) is correct.** Coming to the nuisance means moving into an area where an activity that would otherwise constitute an actionable nuisance is occurring. Generally this newcomer cannot recover for nuisance when he arrived after the condition that offends him was already in place.

Answer (A) is incorrect because nothing has happened yet as far as nuisance law is concerned.

Answer (B) is incorrect because nobody came to a nuisance. (A newly erected tower that blocks someone's view is probably not a nuisance at all.)

Answer (D) is incorrect because it inverts the timing that "coming to the nuisance" envisions. Here the newcomer is the source of the offending condition rather than someone who objects to it, as in the correct answer C.

114. **Answer (A) is correct.** An abnormally dangerous activity is one that has to pay its own way, as it were. There are only very limited exceptions to the general rule that if the defendant engaged in the abnormally dangerous activity and caused harm, then the defendant is liable.

Answer (B) is incorrect because reasonable care does not defeat liability for an abnormally dangerous activity.

Answer (C) is incorrect because taking cost-justified precautions (which are reasonable precautions, in the economic sense of the term) does not defeat liability for an abnormally dangerous activity, either.

Answer (D) is incorrect because it references one of only six factors of the Second Restatement criteria for abnormally dangerous activities. If the jurisdiction follows the Second Restatement, then the defendant could qualify for strict liability by fulfilling several of the other factors. If the jurisdiction follows the Third Restatement, then this factor or criterion will not be included at all.

115. **Answer (C) is correct.** Nuisance requires a substantial interference with the plaintiff's use and enjoyment of property. Some courts hold that it also must be an unreasonable interference, partly in the sense that the benefits of the activity do not outweigh the gravity of the harm to the plaintiff. Darren's strongest defense is probably that seeing people in various states of

undress is not a substantial interference with Samantha's use and enjoyment of her land, and that the benefit of operating a facility of this kind (in which people unavoidably engage in somewhat strange activity from time to time) outweighs the offense Samantha suffers.

Answer (A) is incorrect because it is not enough to say that the plaintiff can look away. She has a right to keep her eyes open while on her property. The real question is the degree of offense/interference she suffers and the relative merit of First Step's activity as compared with the offense/interference.

Answer (B) is incorrect because a majority of courts hold that "coming to the nuisance" is not a per se defense to a nuisance action. The court may take into consideration that the defendant was there first when it decides the appropriate remedy (such as whether to enjoin the activity), but it does not affect the basic question of whether defendant is creating an actionable nuisance.

Answer (D) is incorrect because the public interest in allowing such facilities to operate, standing alone, does not provide a defense. As explained above, the court must weigh the value of the activity against the harm it causes ("unreasonable" interference), and must also consider the degree of harm suffered by the plaintiff ("substantial" interference).

116. Statutes and case law often make exceptions for *trespass*, when the plaintiff has unlawfully entered the defendant's land, and for *provocation*, when the animal was minding its own business and plaintiff instigated an unnecessary encounter with the animal. Statutes also will sometimes exempt dangerous police dogs from strict liability.

117. **Answer (D) is correct.** Justice Blackburn set forth a standard that held a party strictly liable for keeping something on one's property that can do harm if it escapes. This is what happened here. The instruction states the essence of Blackburn's standard: if MotorCo's testing posed a substantial risk of harm to those outside its property as a result of the escape of one of its cars, MotorCo is strictly liable for the harm caused.

Answer (A) is incorrect because this is not a case that fits into Blackburn's exception for "traffic on the highways." MotorCo was not engaging in normal highway traffic, and Potter did not voluntarily take to the road with MotorCo's experimental car.

Answer (B) is incorrect because Justice Blackburn did not frame his standard in terms of the "non-natural" use of land. (It was Cairns in the House of Lords who stated that standard.)

Answer (C) is incorrect because Justice Blackburn rejected this standard. As stated above, he viewed this case as one where strict liability could be imposed.

118. **Answer (C) is correct.** Recovery on an "abnormally dangerous activity" theory requires proof that the type of harm suffered was caused by a feature of the activity that made it abnormally dangerous. Here, that feature was the explosiveness of the fuel (greater than the explosiveness of regular automobile fuels). Because the harm was caused by a collision with Potter's car, and not by an explosion, MotorCo is not strictly liable.

Answer (A) is incorrect because it fails to account for the requirement that the harm be caused by the "abnormally dangerous" feature of the activity.

Answer (B) is incorrect because it assumes that if the balance of social benefit against risk favors the benefit, MotorCo may not be held liable. This is not correct. The six-part standard set forth in *Restatement (Second) of Torts* § 520 is not a categorical test; an activity need not meet each element. (Note that it is possible, though unlikely, that an activity that meets only one element of the standard could be classified as abnormally dangerous.) The court is to view the activity as a whole in light of all the elements, and decide whether it qualifies. Thus, even an activity the benefit of which outweighs the risk it creates can qualify as abnormally dangerous.

Answer (D) is incorrect because it has the element backward. Under the *Restatement* test, if the harm can be prevented by the exercise of reasonable care, it is *less* likely that it will qualify as abnormally dangerous.

119. **Answer (C) is correct.** Storing huge quantities of gasoline might be an abnormally dangerous activity, but liability will only extend to harm caused by the characteristic of that activity that makes it abnormally dangerous. Presumably, that characteristic is the explosiveness of gasoline vapor. Had Patty's car been destroyed by an explosion of the tank, Patty could hold OilCo strictly liable. But in this case, the damage was not caused by the explosive quality of gasoline. It was caused by a combination of the weight of the full tank and the defective steel in the platform. A collapse of this kind would have occurred with any heavy substance in the tank, including water. Weight alone does not make the activity abnormally dangerous, nor does the use of steel. Thus, unless facts appear that are not given in this question, it is not abnormally dangerous to store gasoline in a tank on top of a platform. Patty can only hold OilCo liable if OilCo was negligent.

Answer (A) is incorrect for the reasons just given.

Answer (B) is incorrect because violation of an industry custom is not negligence in itself. It is only some evidence of negligence.

Answer (D) is incorrect because OilCo need not have built the platform to be liable for damage it caused. It can be held liable if it negligently maintained the platform or failed to conduct reasonable inspections.

120. **Answer (B) is correct.** A major change of the Third Restatement was to remove the Second Restatement inclusion of location as part of the blackletter. Because Answer (B) refers to location, it is different from the others.

Answer (A) is incorrect because both Restatements support strict liability.

Answer (C) is incorrect because the claim would be equally weak under both Restatements. Courts seldom recognize emotional distress under either approach to strict liability.

Answer (D) is incorrect because both Restatements would view this type of conduct and consequence similarly.

Products Liability

121. **Answer (D) is correct.** The facts describe what is most probably a manufacturing defect involving a flaw in the adhesive or mounting of the handle.

    Answer (A) is incorrect because the problem says nothing about the role of a warning in this injury. Tony appeared to have handled the kettle correctly.

    Answer (B) is incorrect because it doesn't make sense as an alternative design. The top of the kettle was already occupied by a lid. Putting a handle on top seems to increase the risk of burns as steam rises.

    Answer (C) is incorrect because although under normal use a brand-new kettle handle does not break off, this result does not show that it was defectively designed. Answer (C) evokes res ipsa loquitur, but res ipsa loquitur is not used to prove design defect.

122. **Answer (C) is correct.** These facts give rise to a simple products liability case based on manufacturing defect. Courts hold that such cases may be brought on a strict liability theory, which is extremely easy to prove if the defect is known. Because the facts indicate that the handle was defective, this essentially leaves only the question of whether the defect was a cause in fact of her harm, and that will be simple in this case. It does not matter that Diane did not purchase the car.

    Answer (A) is incorrect because a negligence case is necessarily more difficult to prove, even aided by the doctrine of res ipsa loquitur. Diane will have to demonstrate that this is the type of defect that usually results from negligence in the manufacturing process, something she does not need to show under the strict products liability theory.

    Answer (B) is incorrect because the facts do not indicate that there was an express warranty covering this kind of situation.

    Answer (D) is incorrect because in the products liability context, "absolute liability" is more of an academic phrase than a cause of action. Courts do not purport to impose it on a defendant.

123. **Answer (B) is correct.** Under the Restatement, the plaintiff's own fault may be used to reduce her recovery in a products liability action. A jury might view plaintiff's having tried to skate down a hill the first time she donned a pair of in-line skates as an act of comparative fault. This will reduce her recovery against RollersInc.

    Answer (A) is incorrect because any negligence on the part of Joni's parents in buying the in-line skates does not affect the liability of RollersInc to Joni. Put differently, the negligence of Joni's parents, if any, will not be imputed to Joni so as to reduce her recovery.

Answer (C) is incorrect because a manufacturer is responsible not only for injuries to intended users, but also to others who might foreseeably use the product. This is an application of the "foreseeable misuse" doctrine.

Answer (D) is incorrect because the cost of the skates is irrelevant to whether they were defective.

124.   **Answer (D) is correct.** For strict products liability to apply, the defendant must be in the business of selling the product. If Megan's endorsement of the Gametendo could support a claim by Wilson, that claim would be for negligence or fraud, not strict liability. The claim against GamInc. is valid because GamInc. is in the business of selling the injurious product and strict liability applies to manufacturing defects.

Answer (A) is incorrect because the strict products liability claim against GamInc. is valid.

Answer (B) is incorrect because the strict products liability claim against Megan is not valid.

Answer (C) is incorrect because it reverses the correct result. The claim against GamInc. ought to go to trial and the claim against Megan ought not.

125.   **Answer (C) is correct.** Under the Restatement, comparative negligence is a partial defense in a products liability action. Here, Danny ran a red light, which appears to be negligent. The jury should reduce Danny's recovery.

Answer (A) is incorrect because current authority, including the Third Restatement, rejects the consumer expectations test of defect. Courts that follow the Restatement use a risk-utility balance.

Answer (B) is incorrect because compliance with safety standards is relevant evidence of reasonable care, but hardly dispositive. A car that meets federal standards still may be found to have been designed defectively.

Answer (D) is incorrect because Danny did not assume the risk. There is no suggestion in the facts that he knew the door's protective beams were not as strong as those used in other cars.

126.   **Answer (C) is correct.** A person who is injured by a defective product is a proper plaintiff even if she was not the purchaser (or even the user) of the product. The fact is irrelevant.

Answers (A), (B), and (D) are incorrect for the reason explained above. Answer (D) is extra wrong because what it says is categorically not correct.

127.   Requiring that a plaintiff prove a reasonable alternative design increases her costs of litigating. She has to find expert evidence in order to reach a jury. Fewer valid claims might reach the courts when this standard is used. Critics also fault the requirement for importing negligence reasoning into strict products liability, thereby harming the general "enterprise liability" project of making manufacturers internalize the costs of product-caused injury. The requirement is also at odds with "generic products liability," which condemns entire categories of products, like cigarettes, as unreasonably dangerous. Many observers favor generic products liability. However, comment *e* to section 2(B) of the *Third Restatement* recognizes the possibility of a

"manifestly unreasonable design" which might be extended to some general products liability claims.

128. The implied warranty of fitness for a particular purpose arises between a buyer and seller when the buyer communicates to the seller a particular need, and the seller understands that the buyer is relying on the seller's expertise and advice. For purposes of products liability, an unflawed product can become the basis of liability when the seller gives advice to the buyer about a product, the buyer purchases the product and uses it as the seller advises, and the buyer suffers injury.

129. **Answer (C) is correct.** The Food and Drug Administration requires that a drug be effective for something before it can be sold by prescription. Effectiveness equals utility for this purpose, and so the question for liability is almost always whether the manufacturer could have marketed or described the drug in a way to reduce the risk that harmed the plaintiff.

   Answer (A) is incorrect because statutes of limitation seldom distinguish between warning defect and design defect.

   Answer (B) is incorrect because the risk-utility test is a test for design defect, not warning defect.

   Answer (D) is incorrect because no such qualified immunity exists.

130. **Answer (C) is correct.** Both the Second and Third Restatements require that the defendant be in the business of selling the product in question. Stella might be liable for negligence or another tort, but not for products liability as provisioned in the Restatements.

   Answers A, B, and D are incorrect for the reason discussed above.

131. The post-sale duty to warn dates back to the case of *Comstock v. General Motors Corp.*, 99 N.W. 2d 627 (Mich. 1959). There, the court held that an automobile manufacturer had to inform owners of this product after a latent design defect was discovered. Courts accepting this duty find that it is owed to users of the product. The manufacturer must act reasonably to find these users and communicate with them. The standard in evaluating this claim is negligence, not strict liability.

132. **Answer (D) is correct.** Assumption of risk (particularly assumption of risk interpreted similarly to comparative negligence) is a recognized defense to a products liability action. Putting a muffin in your mouth after noticing that there is something sharp embedded in it is probably both the voluntary confrontation of a known hazard and unreasonably dangerous. Rodger's recovery is likely to be reduced as a result.

   Answer (A) is incorrect because a plaintiff in a products liability case need not have been the purchaser of the product.

   Answer (B) is incorrect because the seller of a product is a proper defendant in a product liability action.

   Answer (C) is incorrect because, even if the nail was placed in the muffin by a person other than Anyushka's, Anyushka's sold the defective muffin. Strict liability applies.

133. **Answer (C) is correct.** If the nail got into the muffin after Bart's sold it to the Anyushka's, Bart's did not sell a defective muffin. Thus, Bart's will prevail in the products liability action.

     Answer (A) is incorrect because, as noted already, a person need not be the purchaser to be a proper plaintiff in a products liability action.

     Answer (B) is incorrect because Anyushka's negligence is irrelevant to Rodger's case against Bart's. Rodger will win if the muffin left Bart's in a defective condition. Because it did not, Bart's is not liable.

     Answer (D) is incorrect because any entity in the chain of distribution is a proper defendant if the product left that entity's hands in a defective condition. Here, of course, it did not.

134. **Answer (A) is correct.** As the source of the skates, RollersInc played a role in bringing about the harm Sally suffered. Cause in fact is an easy test to satisfy: conduct involved in any way in bringing about the harm is a cause in fact of that harm.

     Answer (B) is incorrect because RollersInc might be successful in arguing that Sally's modification of the skates so fundamentally changed their design, and was so unforeseeable (given the difficulty of accomplishing it), that RollersInc should not be viewed as a proximate cause of Sally's injury.

     Answer (C) is incorrect because Sally might well have assumed the risk. She modified the skates for the purpose of achieving great speed. Her experience in skating for about an hour before her accident also probably added to her appreciation of the dangers posed by the modified skates. Thus, RollersInc has a viable argument that Sally voluntarily confronted a known and appreciated hazard.

     Answer (D) is incorrect because Sally's modification might constitute an unforeseeable misuse of the skates. Though sellers are responsible for foreseeable misuse, they are not liable for unforeseeable uses. Because the wheel brackets were welded in place and were very difficult to modify, it is likely that a reasonable manufacturer in the position of RollersInc would not think it very likely that someone would make this modification. If this argument is accepted, RollersInc will defeat Sally's case.

135. **Answer (A) is correct.** This is a manufacturing defect case. Under the *Restatement* and the law as it has developed in all jurisdictions, such cases may be brought on a strict liability theory. Section 2 of the *Third Restatement* provides that a product "contains a manufacturing defect when the product departs from its intended design even though all possible care was exercised in the preparation and marketing of the product." Thus, all Greg will need to prove is that the skate left the hands of Skatz with a deviation from its design that caused him harm.

     Answer (B) is incorrect because Skatz will be held strictly liable even if it would not be economically feasible for it to institute additional quality control procedures that would have caught this defect. This is the essence of strict liability in the present context.

     Answer (C) is incorrect because it does not matter that Skatz uses quality control measures that exceed reasonable care. It is strictly liable for a manufacturing defect.

     Answer (D) is incorrect because the law permits an injured person to recover from any seller along the chain of production, including the original manufacturer. Of course, if a product has been altered before it reaches the plaintiff, entities earlier in the chain might not be liable for the alteration (though sometimes they are responsible), but that is not the case here in any event. When the skate left Skatz's hands, it was in a defective condition. Skatz is liable even though others, such as the store from which Greg bought the skates, might also be liable.

Defamation

136. **Answer (B) is correct.** Severe emotional distress is not an element of the prima facie case for defamation.

    Answer (A) is incorrect because a false statement about a person's embezzlement tends to lower the reputation of that person, and harm to reputation is a central element of the prima facie case for defamation.

    Answer (C) is incorrect for the same reason.

    Answer (D) is incorrect because "publication," or the revelation of the defamatory communication to third parties, is an element of the prima facie case for defamation.

137. **Answer (A) is correct.** As a public official, Bumpkin must show that the Succotash *Times* acted either with a desire to lie or with reckless disregard for the truth of the statement it published. If its reporter should have been able to tell that Magoo was mentally incompetent, publishing Magoo's comments may satisfy the "actual malice" requirement of this tort.

    Answer (B) is incorrect because any "right to privacy" that Bumpkin asserts, or holds, does not affect his status as a defamation plaintiff.

    Answer (C) is incorrect, even though it may appear to show "actual malice." The requirement of "actual malice" is not fulfilled by proving animus, however. Rather, the defendant must have either intended to tell a lie or been reckless about the truth.

    Answer (D) is incorrect because media defendants do not become more liable, or less liable, when they choose to employ fact-checkers or print Corrections notices.

138. **Answer (A) is correct.** Defamation law reluctantly recognizes that litigation often has the effect of hurting a person's reputation, as a side consequence of the matter being litigated. It tries to mitigate this harm by requiring a reasonable relation to the issues raised in the proceeding.

    Answer (B) sounds good, perhaps, but says almost nothing. Defamation in a judicial proceeding often has nothing to do with "a matter of common public concern," to the extent that phrase refers to government.

    Answer (C) is incorrect, even though it is not far from the correct Answer (A). It exaggerates the speaker's duty, and suggests a negligence standard that is not in fact used.

    Answer (D) is incorrect: The privilege applies to civil cases.

139. **Answer (C) is correct.** This question addresses what courts used to call "innuendo"—the meaning of an ambiguous statement. Given what Gay is famous for and the subtext sur-

rounding the reporters' question, a listener would infer that Gay was saying that McHew throws spitballs.

Answer (A) is incorrect because we don't know whether McHew has consented to anything.

Answer (B) is incorrect because the words are not innocuous and could harm McHew's reputation.

Answer (D) is incorrect because (among other reasons) we don't know whether Gay was offering an opinion on a matter of public comment.

140. **Answer (B) is correct.** Under the common law of defamation, the dead cannot be defamed.

Answer (A) is incorrect because the defendant made no claims about Shipley Shipping.

Answer (C) is incorrect because we have no information on the amount of time that has passed since publication.

Answer (D) could be correct, but we do not have enough information to so conclude. It is possible that the behavior of Channel 7 was sufficiently egregious to overcome the limited protections of the First Amendment.

141. **Answer (C) is correct.** The First Amendment, like the rest of the Bill of Rights, presents limits to government power. The opportunity to criticize government officials is more fundamental to free speech than the opportunity to criticize the more eclectic, often apolitical, "public figures." Accordingly, public officials have more onerous obstacles when they sue for defamation.

Answer (A) is incorrect for the reasons just stated above.

Answer (B) is incorrect for the same reasons; in addition to being unsuccessful to support the point, this claim is probably not true.

Answer (D) is incorrect because even though public officials do enjoy relative immunity from defamation liability, the rationale for the relative immunity does not support making them suffer as plaintiffs.

142. **Answer (A) is correct**—a categorically accurate statement.

Answer (B) is incorrect because justification (or lack thereof) is not part of defamation law.

Answer (C) is incorrect because even actual malice is not sufficient to support a defamation claim, if the statement is true.

Answer (D) is incorrect because invasions of privacy do not generate defamation liability.

143. This situation arises where the defendant has a defamatory message and packages it with other words that make the statement formally or literally not false. For example, "I say she committed adultery with Rick Samson." "Ask yourself whether he looted twenty thousand from his company." "If I'm not mistaken, these books don't add up and she hid the money in her own private checking account." "In my opinion, he is an unregistered child molester with a 2010 conviction for felony sexual assault;" and so forth. Speakers cannot escape liability by intoning a few "magic words" along with the defamatory message.

144. Some citizens are so famous and powerful that they are all-purpose public figures, and the First Amendment protects a wide range of commentary about them. According to *Gertz v. Robert Welch, Inc.*, 418 U.S. 323 (1974), such a person must enjoy either "pervasive power and influence" or "fame and notoriety." A larger number of potential plaintiffs are limited-purpose public figures, who may be discussed freely with respect to the issue or controversy for which they gained fame. Typically, the defendant in such a defamation claim would have to show that the plaintiff sought this public role and participated voluntarily in a controversy.

145. **Answer (A) is correct.** Slander per se is a rule that eases the plaintiff's burden of proof. It rests on the premise that, as was stated, certain common accusations have predictable effects. Making each plaintiff prove individual harm would be costly.

Answer (B) is incorrect even though it is generally accurate: This sentence does not offer an argument in favor of slander per se.

Answer (C) is incorrect for similar reasons. This sentence offers an argument in favor of treating libel and slander differently, while the slander per se rule treats slander more like libel.

Answer (D) is incorrect because slander per se applies to both business activity and the plaintiff's private life.

146. **Answer (C) is correct.** Lawrie enjoys a broad privilege to speak freely (and even defamatorily) in the well of the legislature.

Answer (A) is incorrect because a legislator's remarks need not relate reasonably to a legislative endeavor in order for the speaker to escape liability.

Answer (B) is incorrect because Milton may not be a public figure, and if he were, his defamation would be *harder* to prosecute, not easier.

Answer (D) is the least incorrect of the three incorrect answers. Answer (C) is better than (D) because it identifies Lawrie's status as a legislator. Without reference to that status, Lawrie's safe harbor to engage in defamation becomes much more questionable. To the extent Answer (D) implies some general privilege to defame in the context of debate on a matter of public interest, it is incorrect.

147. Not entirely satisfactorily. The class of potentially defamatory statements is nearly infinite. Courts modify the *Restatement* formulation slightly to hold that a statement is *not* defamatory unless it is likely to cause a substantial number of people to avoid the plaintiff or hold her in less esteem. Although this approach does not resolve the definitional question, it does spare courts from having to hear eccentric claims of defamation.

Invasion of Privacy

148. **Answer (D) is correct.** An invasion of privacy claim of this kind—intrusion upon seclusion—turns on whether the plaintiff had a reasonable expectation of privacy.

    Answer (A) is incorrect because truth is a defense to defamation, not to invasion of privacy.

    Answer (B) is incorrect because overnight guests have a legitimate expectation of privacy that covers this problem. Their rooms can be entered for cause, but not wiretapped for no good reason.

    Answer (C) is incorrect because whether disclosure is "repugnant" or not is not at issue in privacy claims.

149. **Answer (A) is correct.** The two versions of the privacy tort that might be used here, "disclosure of private facts" and "intrusion upon seclusion," both require an invasion into the plaintiff's private space. If the video camera had entered her home surreptitiously, Benita's claim would be stronger.

    Answer (B) is incorrect because Benita associates injury—harm related to "professional disgrace"—with the disclosure.

    Answer (C) is incorrect because the television station could have been liable if it had in fact intruded into Benita's private life.

    Answer (D) is incorrect because courts do not examine the gathering and dissemination of private facts under a reasonableness standard.

150. **Answer (C) is correct.** A corporation cannot bring a claim for invasion of privacy. Its rights to privacy are protected by trade secrets law and similar special categories.

    Answer (A) is incorrect because deceit is not an element of invasion of privacy.

    Answer (B) is incorrect because "privilege" has nothing to do with this problem. Tarpala made her way onto the factory floor with a ruse. Her deceit might relate to a trespass claim, but not a privacy claim.

    Answer (D) is incorrect because the problem states that Tarpala's client used the information for competitive advantage against the plaintiff.

151. **Answer (A) is correct.** Packaging of consumer goods falls within the traditional heart of this tort, which has focused on using the plaintiff's likeness for purposes of advertising.

    Answer (B) is incorrect because courts give magazines broad license to use photographs in their reporting of "newsworthy" events.

Answer (C) is incorrect because giving a character in a work of fiction the name of a real person does not, without more, give rise to liability for invasion of privacy, even if the character is unattractive.

Answer (D) is incorrect because of the same notion of "newsworthiness" mentioned above with respect to Answer (B). Neither the ex-lover nor Infotainment Tonite would be liable to Hilda-May for appropriation of her likeness.

152. **Answer (D) is correct.** To prosecute this version of the privacy tort—disclosure of private facts—a plaintiff must show "publicity" (*Restatement (Second) of Torts* § 652D, comment *a*), which means publication to the public at large or to a large group of people. Gossip within a limited circle does not satisfy this element.

Answer (A) is incorrect because even if this "legitimate public concern" criterion is fulfilled, the "publicity" criterion remains fatal to the claim.

Answer (B) is incorrect because the "highly offensive to a reasonable person" criterion is not used in the disclosure version of the privacy tort.

Answer (C) is incorrect because the "public figure" criterion is not used in the disclosure version of the privacy tort.

153. Like various freedoms—of speech, mobility, and conscience among others—privacy is a cherished human right. If tort law were to be indifferent to privacy, most people would agree that it had failed to recognize something important. A legal concept of privacy also helps indirectly to check the power of other actors. Such a concern may underlie the Fourth Amendment condemnation of unreasonable searches and seizures—government would become a menace if it did not have to respect privacy. Privacy could be legislated as a public law, with tort law kept out of it. Statutes and the Constitution do in fact protect privacy. Adding a tort remedy strengthens these protections by empowering citizens to enforce their privacy rights.

154. **Answer (B) is correct.** By filing a claim, Mulcahy disclosed her own private facts. The Supreme Court has held in several cases that the media are not liable for invasion of privacy when they obtain information about individuals lawfully, through public records, and publish it.

Answer (A) is incorrect because Mulcahy's privacy claim is unlikely to prevail. Her being a minor doesn't strengthen her claim.

Answer (C) is incorrect because news disclosed need not be a matter of public significance in order for a media defendant to escape liability.

Answer (D) is incorrect because Mulcahy did not consent to the publication.

155. **Answer (B) is correct.** Privacy law is generally unconcerned with the distinction between true and false disclosures.

Answer (A) is incorrect because the privacy tort overlaps with other torts, and can be redundant.

Answer (C) is incorrect because individuals' interests in privacy is a major justification for the tort.

Answer (D) is incorrect because "newsworthiness" is salient to many privacy cases, especially those involving media defendants.

156. "Appropriation" refers to the exploitation of the plaintiff's likeness or identity for commercial gain, without the plaintiff's consent. FanRagZine has made money from the identity of Gothika without her consent. This tort denies recovery to plaintiffs, however, when what defendants appropriate is "newsworthy." Gothika is a celebrity and her experiences have news value. The appropriation tort does not compel defendants to share their profits with newsworthy plaintiffs.

Emotional Distress

157. **Answer (D) is correct.** A jury is very likely to find that Doyle's act was "extreme and outrageous" in the sense that it is utterly intolerable. Even if Doyle did not want Crane to suffer serious emotional distress, but only to see it as a joke, it is hard to imagine that a jury will not view her conduct as having been undertaken with reckless disregard for causing such distress. This was not a private practical joke, and Doyle probably realized that many people would think Crane really was a "deadbeat parent." As such, Doyle's conduct seems reckless. In addition, Crane suffered what the facts describe as serious emotional distress.

Answer (A) is incorrect because Doyle probably acted with reckless disregard for causing serious emotional distress, as explained above. This meets the intent requirement for intentional infliction of emotional distress.

Answer (B) is incorrect because malice is not required for this tort.

Answer (C) is incorrect because bodily harm is not required when the intended victim is the one who suffered the serious emotional distress.

158. **Answer (A) is correct.** Though Parker appears to have suffered severe emotional distress, and though Dawn probably intended to cause at least some embarrassment, this kind of behavior is sufficiently common among seventh graders that it probably does not rise to the level of "extreme and outrageous."

Answer (B) is incorrect because intent to injure is not an element of intentional infliction of emotional distress. The element is intent to create severe emotional distress.

Answer (C) is incorrect because assumption of risk is not a defense to the tort of intentional infliction of emotional distress. In addition, even if it were a defense, it is very unlikely that prior acts of kidding around amounted to consent to this sort of conduct on Dawn's part.

Answer (D) is incorrect for the reasons stated above.

159. Liability of this kind is rare. Courts are not eager to extend liability for negligent infliction of emotional distress to benefit hypersensitive plaintiffs. In exceptional situations, liability would be proper: A defendant aware of the plaintiff's sensitivity who could, through reasonable care, avoid causing the plaintiff distress, might be liable for negligent infliction of emotional distress even though the plaintiff is hypersensitive. A psychotherapist-patient relationship provides an example of this potential liability.

160. **Answer (A) is correct.** Kanye's behavior is cowardly and tacky, perhaps, but not outrageous.

Answer (B) is incorrect because Kim's symptoms are sufficient to show severe distress.

Answer (C) is incorrect because courts interpret the intent requirement for this tort to include either intent (desire or substantial certainty of causing) severe emotional distress or reckless disregard for the possibility of causing it.

Answer (D) is incorrect. Kim need not suffer physical injury to succeed on an intentional infliction of emotional distress claim.

161. The oldest cases upheld liability for "fright and shock" associated with nearby trauma. Liability for this type of injury continues. Among the emotional consequences that can be compensated are anguish (suffered by relatives located near the body of a person who suffers physical impact, for instance), fear (of becoming ill in the future, sometimes compensable when the plaintiff has been exposed to a hazardous substance), anxiety (if sufficiently severe), deep revulsion (caused by negligent mishandling of corpses, for instance). One might also include consortium, which covers harm to familial intimacy.

162. **Answer (B) is correct.** The injuries of assault and battery happen immediately. Emotional distress can unfold slowly, sometimes over a period of years.

   Answer (A) is incorrect because even if the injury is more subjective, subjectivity of an injury does not affect its timing.

   Answer (C) is incorrect because IIED requires the same causal connection as battery or assault.

   Answer (D) is incorrect because it is not true.

163. **Answer (D) is correct.** To prevail in an action for intentional infliction of emotional distress, Park must prove (1) that Smith's conduct was extreme and outrageous; (2) that Smith acted with intention to cause severe emotional distress or with reckless disregard for that consequence; and (3) that Park suffered severe emotional distress. A jury might well find that Smith's conduct was "extreme and outrageous." This was an employment context, and he was Park's immediate boss. Park is unlikely to have felt free to complain directly to Smith in that situation. In addition, several courts have found that racial/ethnic slurs go beyond mere insults, and are particularly obnoxious in our society. The second element is probably satisfied even if Smith did not intend to cause severe emotional distress. At the very least, a jury is likely to find that he acted with reckless disregard for that consequence. Finally, Park's distress might well have been severe. She felt the need to quit her job, suggesting that the situation was particularly difficult for her.

   Answer (A) is incorrect because the facts reveal that Smith believed he was promoting employee morale. Thus, the "motive" test for scope of employment seems to be satisfied.

   Answer (B) is incorrect because most courts do not require proof of physical injury in actions for intentional infliction of emotional distress.

   Answer (C) is incorrect because, as discussed above, Smith's actions probably satisfy the standard for recklessness, which is sufficient for this tort.

164. **Answer (B) is correct.** Dan's best hope of defeating Laureen's intentional infliction of emotional distress claim is to argue that what he did was not "extreme and outrageous." This is not necessarily a winner; a jury might find that performing invasive surgery on a person with-

out disclosing your HIV-positive status is so inappropriate as to be outrageous. But there are countervailing considerations. For one thing, Dan took steps to avoid cutting himself, which minimized the risk of transmission of the virus. Also, society respects people's right to privacy about their medical conditions. Still, Dan did place Laureen at risk, and Dan's privacy interest might have to give way when his medical condition places an unsuspecting patient at risk.

Answer (A) is incorrect because the tort of intentional infliction of emotional distress does not require malicious intent. One need only intend to cause serious emotional distress (not present here; on the contrary, Dan hid his HIV-positive status, which would both protect his own privacy and prevent Laureen from becoming distressed) or act with reckless disregard for causing serious emotional distress (and again, his acts show that he exhibited some care with respect to that matter, not recklessness).

Answer (C) is incorrect because the tort does not require any physical contact. Many successful cases of intentional infliction of emotional distress involve no contact at all between the defendant and the victim.

Answer (D) is incorrect because it is not alone a reason to deny Laureen recovery. True, there is concern about fakery, and this is part of the reason why the plaintiff must show severe emotional distress. But the possibility of fakery does not in itself defeat an otherwise valid claim.

165. **Answer (C) is correct.** Because Diego did not know that Paddy was close friends with Risa and her wife, it appears that Diego neither intended to cause Paddy severe emotional distress nor acted with reckless disregard. According to *Restatement (Second) of Torts* § 46, someone other than the intended target of the defendant's behavior may only recover if the person is present at the time of the conduct and was either a member of the target's immediate family or suffered bodily injury. Though Paddy suffered severe emotional distress, the facts do not indicate that he suffered any bodily injury.

Answer (A) is incorrect because, as explained above, Paddy's claim appears weak.

Answer (B) is incorrect because there is little doubt that a jury will consider this sort of behavior "extreme and outrageous." Telling a person a knowingly false story that her spouse has been in an accident and probably will not survive is exceptionally cruel behavior.

Answer (D) is incorrect because reasonable foreseeability of harm to a bystander is not an element of intentional infliction of emotional distress. The bystander element is discussed above.

166. **Answer (B) is correct.** To be liable for intentional infliction of emotional distress, the defendant must have intended to cause serious emotional distress or have acted in reckless disregard for causing it. The facts state that the captain accidentally played the crash announcement. The facts do not suggest any recklessness in doing so.

Answer (A) is incorrect because, according to the "thin skull" rule, if conduct would be tortious toward a normally constituted person, one who happens to be particularly sensitive or vulnerable may still recover for his entire damages. Thus, Daphne's extra sensitivity would not assist the airline's defense.

Answer (C) is incorrect because it is difficult to argue that playing the tape was not extreme and outrageous. It is very likely to cause extreme distress to just about any passenger. And of course, there was no good reason for this recording to be played.

Answer (D) is incorrect because physical injury is not an element of intentional infliction of emotional distress.

167. **Answer (A) is correct.** The most common test, sometimes called the "zone of danger" test, is incorporated in Restatement (Second) of Torts § 313(2), which provides that one may not recover for "emotional distress arising solely from harm or peril to a third person, unless the negligence of the actor has otherwise created an unreasonable risk of bodily harm to the other." From the facts, it does not appear that the employee created an unreasonable risk of bodily harm to Pauline. She was behind a thick glass window.

Answer (B) is incorrect because the "impact" rule required the plaintiff to have suffered some physical injury from impact. Pauline did not suffer impact, so her claim would fail under that test.

Answer (C) is incorrect because at least one type of test, represented by *Dillon v. Legg*, 441 P.2d 912 (Cal. 1968), *Thing v. La Chusa*, 771 P.2d 814 (Cal. 1989), and other cases, allows a bystander to recover even if the bystander was not in the "zone of danger" of physical impact.

Answer (D) is incorrect because, as explained above, Pauline will lose under several theories.

168. **Answer (C) is correct.** Because the employee's negligent handling of the equipment was a cause in fact and proximate cause of Peter's bodily injury, he may recover for that injury in a simple negligence action. When emotional distress occurs as a result of the same event that caused bodily harm to the plaintiff, all courts allow recovery of damages for emotional distress as "parasitic" to the damages for bodily harm. Because the same incident that caused Peter's bodily injury also caused the injury to Padua, Peter may recover for the emotional distress he suffered.

Answer (A) is incorrect because Peter's recovery for his own bodily injury does not depend on whether he observed his son's impaling by the equipment. Also, for the reasons stated above, Peter may recover for emotional distress.

Answer (B) is incorrect because the foreseeability of emotional distress does not matter when there is liability for physical injury. In addition, in all likelihood emotional distress *is* a reasonably foreseeable outcome of the kind of accident caused by the employee's negligence.

Answer (D) is incorrect because, as discussed above, the jurisdiction's test for negligent infliction of emotional distress will not affect Peter's recovery in this situation.

169. **Answer (B) is correct.** Because there was no physical impact, Peter does not satisfy the "impact" test. However, the jury will probably find that he was in the zone of danger from the negligent handling of the equipment because, as an occupant of the car, he, too, was a reasonably foreseeable victim of the negligent handling of the equipment.

Answers (A) and (D) are incorrect for the reasons just stated.

Answer (C) is incorrect because even if Peter did not have sensory awareness of the injury to Padua as it was happening, Peter was in the zone of danger created by the negligent handling of the equipment. Where the zone of danger test is satisfied, courts using *Dillon*-type tests would allow plaintiff to recover.

170. **Answer (D) is correct.** Consortium opens recovery to another plaintiff, someone directly touched by the tortious conduct. The other three choices all keep people out of court.

    Answer (A) is incorrect because the impact rule is a criterion that not all distressed people can meet.

    Answer (B) is incorrect for the same reason that makes A incorrect.

    Answer (C) is incorrect because the zone of danger rule says that distressed persons outside this zone cannot recover.

Topic 13

Harm to Economic Interests

171. **Answer (A) is correct.** It is usually hard to know or predict the consequences of a false statement. If ignorance about the consequences was sufficient to defeat the claim, most of the tort would disappear.

    Answer (B) is incorrect. Knowledge that the statement made was false is a crucial element of intentional (as contrasted with negligent) misrepresentation.

    Answers (C) and (D) are incorrect. Most courts consider Answers (C) and (D) to be crucial elements of the tort as well.

172. **Answer (C) is correct.** Dolly committed both the intentional and the negligent versions of the misrepresentation tort. When the bank official asked Dolly whether she had personally chosen the accounting firm and Dolly said yes, she made a false statement—and it is fair to infer that the statement was material (at an interview, the questions frequently matter to the questioner) and that it induced reliance. Thus the elements of the intentional tort are satisfied. Regarding negligent misrepresentation, the problem says that Dolly sincerely believed her net worth to be more like $10 million rather than less than $1 million, suggesting she probably assumed that the crony's "audited financial statement" was accurate, or close to accurate, and also that she was careless to hold this belief and not verify what Madison gave her before submitting it as part of a loan application.

    Answers (A), (B), and (D) are incorrect because under these facts, both intentional and negligent misrepresentation are available claims.

173. **Answer (B) is correct.** The Hoof & Mouth partners fulfilled the elements of the tort of fraud (or intentional misrepresentation).

    Answer (A) is incorrect because it does not state a correct rule of law. Hoof & Mouth is a wrongdoer.

    Answer (C) is incorrect. Although it may be true, it does not explain why Metrobank should prevail.

    Answer (D) is incorrect. The "representations of Regiment" were not unlawful; the fraudulent behaviors of Regiment and Hoof & Mouth were unlawful.

174. **Answer (C) is correct.** The statement is accurate, and it explains the rule of no liability in this situation.

    Answer (A) is incorrect. Answer (A) says the defendant was negligent, which may well be a correct conclusion. But when the financial consequences of negligence to the plaintiff are only lost benefits or opportunities pursuant to a contract, these losses are not recoverable.

175

Answer (B) is incorrect. Answer (B), like Answer (A), may well be true but does not suffice to support the claim.

Answer (D) is incorrect. The answer is somewhat obscure, but seems to assert that the plaintiff's losses are covered by contract. This conclusion has no support in the facts.

175. **Answer (D) is correct.** Louisa seems to be a cheater whose dumb cheating cost her partner money, but she did not commit a tort against her partner. She made the misrepresentation (tampering with the offer document) to the seller, not to Bonnie Blue. The only contracts she interfered with were (in part) her own, and a defendant cannot be liable for tortious interference with her own contractual relations.

Answers (A), (B), and (C) are incorrect because under these facts, both misrepresentation and tortious interference with contract are *not* available to Bonnie Blue.

176. A claim for tortious interference with contract requires an existing, enforceable contract; tortious interference with economic opportunity or prospective economic advantage does not. Courts agree that the prerogative to interfere with another person's business is stronger when the interest at stake is mere "opportunity" rather than the more definite, fixed "contract." In the infamous case of *Texaco, Inc. v. Pennzoil Co.*, 729 S.W. 2d 768 (Tex. App. 1987), the court made a crucial ruling that an agreement intended to lead to a future merger constituted a "contract," thus putting the plaintiff, Pennzoil, in a much stronger position to recover.

177. **Answer (D) is correct.** The topic here is *spoliation*: the destruction of evidence necessary to pursue a claim. Most jurisdictions do not provide a tort remedy for spoliation. One exception to the no-liability stance is made when there is a bailment-like contract between the plaintiff and the defendant to take care of the physical evidence. No such contract was made here.

Answer (A) is incorrect. It is belied by the facts. We have seen nothing to suggest that Timeshare assumed a duty of care.

Answer (B) is incorrect. It is obscure. A defendant that has "exceeded the terms of its employment" has done nothing to incur tort liability. We would need to know something more, and having "caused financial loss" is not enough.

Answer (C) is incorrect. It is irrelevant to a spoliation claim.

178. **Answer (B) is correct.** Of all the choices, Answer (B) eliminates fault and negligence the most decisively. In Answer (B), the defendant behaved as carefully as he could. In general, courts disfavor strict liability for misrepresentation. Violations of labeling statutes constitute one of the few vital corners of this tort. (Note that the customer might also have a valid strict products liability claim against Alfred. Even though it appears that Alfred inspected the vegetables, even a reasonable inspection will not constitute a defense to a strict liability claim for selling dangerous foodstuffs.)

Answer (A) is incorrect. While Genevieve also seems not to be at fault, she probably did not make a misrepresentation. She said something like, "According to this map that I have had commissioned, my land has unobstructed access to a lake." That statement appears to be true. There is no suggestion of her withholding any material information from Barton, nor of her intending to induce reliance.

Answers (C) and (D) are incorrect because both showcase careless persons, neither of whom would be strictly liable. In Answer (C), Dalma appears to have committed negligent misrepresentation when she presented financial statements prepared by an auditor whom she knew to be dubious. Answer (D), like Answer (B), probably contains no misrepresentation of any kind. Instead, this is an instance of an ignorant buyer meeting an ignorant seller.

179. Yes, S is wrong. Although the plaintiff will often have a claim against the breaching party (for breach of contract), she need not pursue it in order to bring a claim against the interferer. Courts regard the two actions as separate and independent.

180. **Answer (B) is correct.** Courts agree that contributory or comparative negligence is available in legal malpractice claims, just as it is available in medical malpractice claims—that is to say, sparingly applied, because of the heightened duty of care that the professional holds, but not categorically precluded either.

    Answer (A) is incorrect because it categorically precludes consideration of Carmen's behavior, and that is wrong.

    Answer (C) is incorrect because it brings in an irrelevant reference to causation in fact, which is usually part of the plaintiff's case, not the defendant's.

    Answer (D) is incorrect because it is both factually and legally dubious. The wording of the problem suggests that Llewellyn had several other opportunities to catch the error after Carmen missed it. As a statement of law it is equally wrong; "last clear chance" is a doctrine used against defendants (to soften the harsh effects of contributory negligence), and does not limit a plaintiff's opportunity to recover. In addition, most jurisdictions eliminated the doctrine of last clear chance when they moved to systems of comparative fault.

181. **Answer (A) is correct.** Although the question is written on a rather theoretical plane, it ought to be clear that Answer (A) is different from the other choices. Answers (B), (C), and (D) all militate *in favor* of liability for economic loss. Answer (A)'s point about "nearly infinite chain reactions" suggests that courts have a difficult time administering liability for economic loss. This administrative difficulty is an argument against liability.

    Answers (B), (C), and (D) are incorrect for the reasons just given.

182. Courts are divided on this issue, but several cases recognize claims for emotional and reputational harm. They usually require that the emotional or reputational harm be foreseeable. One type of tortious interference with contract that seems well suited to this kind of damages award is the unlawful obstruction of an employment contract. The supporting rationale is that the claim is one of tort, and tort law recognizes these interests. The contrary rationale is that the claim is linked to a contract, and contract law does not generally recognize these interests.

Damages

183. **Answer (C) is correct.** The collateral source rule, a common law doctrine, provides that the defendant must pay for the injuries it caused even if the plaintiff has received compensation from these injuries from another source, such as private or public health insurance. With no discount reflecting the insurance funds that Vincent received, Celeste is liable for the full judgment. The sum of $15,000 and $40,000 is $55,000.

     Answer (A) is incorrect because it apparently rejects the collateral source rule, giving Vincent only the unreimbursed $5,000 of his medical expenses (rather than the full $40,000) plus the $15,000 of lost income. This answer could be correct if Lympet had rejected or modified the collateral source rule.

     Answer (B) is incorrect because it apparently tosses out the $15,000 of lost income, which has nothing to do with the collateral source rule.

     Answer (D) is incorrect because the collateral source rule does not disqualify a plaintiff from receiving a tort judgment.

184. Because punitive damage awards are noncompensatory, some observers believe there is no good reason for the plaintiff to keep them. In principle, compensatory damages rectify her injury. Other observers favor disallowing plaintiffs from retaining punitive damages awards in the belief that tort judgments are simply too high, and need to be reduced before adverse, hard-to-reverse social consequences ensue. The contrary stance urges that plaintiffs be allowed to keep their punitive damages awards on the ground that even though in principle the plaintiff does not "need" or "deserve" these sums, the defendant "needs" or "deserves" punishment. If plaintiffs could not collect punitive damages, they would be less willing to bring claims, and defendants would enjoy a windfall. Others argue that punitive damages help to compensate for the percentage of recovery that the plaintiff turns over to her lawyer as a fee.

     If punitive damages are to be taken from the plaintiff, one might argue that the most appropriate public purpose would address one of two general categories: the awards should go to either (A) some tort-like need, such as compensation for personal injuries inflicted by insolvent defendants or perhaps for health insurance, or to (B) a public need that cannot be met adequately through taxation, perhaps to benefit a politically unpopular but deserving class. An alternative approach would simply turn the money over to the state treasury as general revenue.

185. **Answer (B) is correct.** Of the four choices, these expenses are the least open-ended.

Answer (A) is incorrect because emotional distress is open-ended and thus hardest for a conservative court to constrain.

Answer (C) is incorrect because child-rearing expenses are hard to assess. They also might or might not stop at age 18.

Answer (D) is incorrect because offsets are not awarded to plaintiffs; instead they function to limit the amount recoverable.

186. **Answer (C) is correct.** The purpose of discounting damages to present value is to prevent a plaintiff from collecting more than she would have collected if she had not been injured. Lost future earnings relate to income that the plaintiff would have collected in the future, without an injury. Because she would not have received all of this income at the time of judgment, she would be overcompensated if she received it all at this point. She'd get to invest it and collect not only the principal but interest.

Answer (A) is incorrect because the collateral source rule is unrelated to this question. It refers to additional sources of compensation.

Answer (B) is incorrect because damages for past pain and suffering are fully realized at the time of judgment; they have no "future," and only future losses are subject to discounting to present value.

Answer (D) is incorrect because the purpose of punitive damages is not compensatory, and not closely related to the plaintiff's future losses. Punitive damages are set at an amount to punish and motivate the defendant.

187. **Answer (A) is correct.** Wrongful formation claims seek the expenses of pregnancy and childbirth, and sometimes for child rearing. Typically a plaintiff cannot reduce these costs after wrongful formation occurs. When childrearing expenses are sought, the way to mitigate the harm is either by relinquishing the baby for adoption or terminating the pregnancy. Courts generally view these measures as too burdensome. Such options are available to prospective parents before negligent sterilization occurs; the reason they chose sterilization was to avoid going through the measures.

Answers (B), (C), and (D) are incorrect because although mitigation is not always possible, scenarios can arise under all of them where the plaintiff has an opportunity to lower the cost of the injury through reasonable conduct.

188. This argument, sometimes called the "per diem" approach, has been disapproved by some judges and permitted by others. *Pro*: It expresses pain and suffering in relatively concrete, specific terms. It reminds the jury that the plaintiff will not live forever, possibly placing a cap on reckless excess. Although it is far from ideal, if rigid specificity is required, future pain and suffering would be impossible to recognize in terms of money damages, and under non-recognition would unfairly enrich defendants. *Con*: It is imprecise and encourages false quantification. It is inaccurate in that the 'curve' of suffering is probably not linear: victims will often experience intense distress at first, then adjust somewhat. It might inflame the jury into an exaggerated measure of damages.

189. **Answer (D) is correct.** It may be helpful to think of a numerator and a denominator. Caps on damages address the denominator (the total amounts of judgments and settlements), not the numerator (the percentage of a judgment or settlement that the lawyer would collect as a fee). The problem in Answer (D) is one of finding the right percentage to pay a lawyer—a 'numerator' problem, if you will, rather than a denominator problem. Thus it does not relate closely to the 'denominator' concern of the question.

   Answer (A) is incorrect because a wide range of recoverable damages makes the pricing of insurance more difficult.

   Answer (B) is incorrect because if the amount that a plaintiff can recover is unlimited, a personal injury lawyer is more likely to file a weak claim than would be the case if recovery is limited.

   Answer (C) is incorrect because the risk of paying high damages affects the profitability of products sold in the market. This threat to profits might induce a manufacturer not to offer a product for sale.

190. **Answer (B) is correct.** The three criteria mentioned are the ones provided in the decision, and they are met under these facts.

   Answer (A) is incorrect because the decision does not discuss actual malice. A similar concept is included in the reprehensibility criterion, but "actual malice" is a term of art not used here.

   Answer (C) is incorrect because there is no separate rule for personal injury cases. (Ira Gore, the plaintiff in *BMW of North America Inc. v. Gore*, suffered only financial loss based on property damage.)

   Answer (D) is incorrect because punitive damages claims are not preempted by "lemon laws."

191. **Answer (D) is correct.** Damages for a death caused by negligence may include such things as future earnings, but if the person's expected lifetime was already likely to be shorter than average, it is not appropriate to calculate damages based on figures for an average lifetime. Thus, damages for Arni's death must take into account the likelihood that he would have died earlier than an average person.

   Answer (A) is incorrect because it misconceives the "eggshell skull" or "thin skull" rule. Under that rule, a defendant may not defend the action on the basis of the plaintiff's extra sensitivity. *If* the defendant's behavior would have caused harm to a healthy person, then defendant is liable for the full damages suffered by a person whose health made her particularly susceptible to harm from defendant's activity. Arni fell into this class. His weakened immune system was more affected than that of the average person, but as the facts show, many people (including, presumably, otherwise healthy people) were injured by the contaminated water. Their injuries were not permanent, but they were harmed nonetheless.

   Answer (B) is incorrect because the facts make clear that the contaminated water was a cause in fact of Arni's death. Other factors (such as the weakened immune system caused by illness) were also causes, but this does not mean the water contamination was not a cause.

   Answer (C) is incorrect because Arni did in fact suffer damage. His life was shortened even more than it would have been as a result of his illness.

192. **Answer (B) is correct.** It presents a claim for trespass to land, the cause of action where courts are most receptive to an award of nominal damages.

     Answer (A) is incorrect because it suggests carelessness on the part of Empire, not actual malice, generally understood to mean an intentional lie or reckless disregard of the truth. As a public figure, Estevez could not recover in this defamation claim without proving actual malice.

     Answer (C) is incorrect because it is a claim for nuisance, which requires actual damages.

     Answer (D) is incorrect because it is a claim for negligent infliction of emotional distress, which requires actual damages.

193. The connection rests on two facts: Most plaintiffs who file personal injury actions pay their attorneys with a contingent fee, and most elderly people do not earn significant wage income. A contingent fee rests on a fraction: the more damages the plaintiff receives, the more money the attorney earns. Conversely, the less damages the plaintiff receives, the less money the attorney earns.

     Noneconomic damages occupy a larger fraction of the total damages when a plaintiff is elderly. Caps on noneconomic damages reduce the value of a tort claim when the plaintiff lacks wage income. Potential advocates are more likely to reject the case, leaving the injured elderly person less able to obtain a lawyer.

Multiple Defendants and Vicarious Liability

194. **Answer (A) is correct.** Superseding cause can exist in a multiple-defendants scenario, but the liability for each defendant is not "vicarious," which means indirect or derivative.

    Answer (B) is incorrect because one who aids and abets another can be liable for the other's intentional tort.

    Answer (C) is incorrect because respondeat superior—liability imposed on "the master," i.e., an employer—is an example of vicarious liability.

    Answer (D) is incorrect because drag-racing liability as described is indirect.

195. **Answer (C) is correct.** Dr. Medvedev will be liable for the back injury because it was caused by his own negligence. Vlad will be liable because his original negligence in causing the accident was a cause in fact and proximate cause of the back injury. Courts hold almost unanimously that a tortfeasor is liable for enhanced injury caused by a rescuer, medical personnel, or others who render aid to the victim. Under a "directness" or "intervening cause" theory of proximate cause, the doctor is not treated as a "superseding cause." Under a scope of risk analysis, additional harm suffered at the hands of a rescuer or medical personnel is within the foreseeable scope of risk created by the original act of negligence. (Some courts explain that the harm was within the scope of risk by noting that the dust had not yet settled from the original accident when Barry suffered further injury.)

    Answers (A) and (B) are incorrect because, as explained above, both Vlad and Dr. Medvedev are liable for the back injury.

    Answer (D) is incorrect because there is no need to apportion responsibility for the back injury; both Vlad and Dr. Medvedev will be liable for the full injury (though Barry may not recover more than the amount of that injury). This is a situation in which the court will impose joint and several liability.

196. Jury. The question is typically fact-specific. Unfortunately for employers, scope-of-employment disputes often cannot be resolved in summary judgment proceedings.

197. **Answer (A) is correct.** Under the doctrine of joint and several liability, each negligent defendant is responsible for the full amount of the judgment. The judgment, however, must reflect a reduction of the plaintiff's damages in accordance with the plaintiff's own fault. Here, if Ermintrude's fault was 35 percent of the total, and she suffered $10,000 of damages, she can only recover $6500. She will receive a judgment in that amount against both Link's and Needlenose, and may recover that amount (and no more) from one of the defendants or a combination of the two.

Answer (B) is incorrect because joint and several liability allows Ermintrude to receive a judgment for the full amount against both defendants (even though her recovery will be limited to $6500 in total).

Answer (C) is incorrect because Ermintrude's judgment must be reduced according to the degree of her own fault.

Answer (D) is incorrect because, under a pure system of comparative fault, a plaintiff may recover even against a defendant whose negligence was less than plaintiff's.

198. *Respondeat superior*, which is liability imposed on employers for those torts of their employees that are within the scope of the employees' employment. This liability has been described as "strict," meaning that the plaintiff need not prove fault on the part of the employer. *Respondeat superior* does not transfer liability away from the employee. She too is liable for her own torts; she and the employer are jointly and severally liable to those she injures in the scope of her employment.

199. An example of contribution would describe an action by one defendant against another person or entity who shares legal responsibility for the injury. An example of indemnification would describe a voluntary agreement by one person or entity to pay the damages attributable to tortious conduct of another.

200. Both *respondeat superior* and strict products liability are forms of "enterprise liability," generally understood to mean strict liability of business enterprises for the harms that their activity causes as part of "doing business." Both types of liability are paid for by customers of the business, in a kind of insurance. The overlap between the set of customers and the set of plaintiffs is usually stronger in products liability than *respondeat superior*—especially when the product is one devised for individual consumers—but both doctrines spread costs to a customer base in order to compensate injured persons and create incentives to safety.

201. **Answer (D) is correct.** The presence or absence of comparative fault in a particular case is a separate question that does not pertain directly to the debate over whether to retain or abolish joint and several liability. The other arguments are frequently mentioned by critics.

     Answer (A) is incorrect because it argues that the arrival of comparative fault (as a doctrine, not in a particular case) has made courts and juries familiar with fractional apportionment, and so it makes sense to apply this practice toward "proportional," rather than joint and several, liability.

     Answer (B) is incorrect. It is a fairness argument that critics often raise.

     Answer (C) is incorrect. This argument comes up frequently in the context of workplace injury, where an employer is much more to blame than a product manufacturer, but because of employer immunity, the product manufacturer is saddled with the worker's damages.

202. Parents are liable for the torts of their children when the parents were at fault: for example, when they fail to control a dangerous child. (Note that this liability is usually imposed only when the parents knew about the dangerousness of the child and had the ability to control him or her.) They can be liable under ordinary principles of vicarious liability: when they employed the child and the child committed a tort in the scope of his employment, or when

they were in partnership with the child and the child committed a tort pursuant to the activities of the partnership. Some states hold them liable by statute as owners of a motor vehicle that the child drives negligently.

203. **Answer (B) is correct.** (Easy if you have a flair for math. Hard for some people. Others can't "show their work" but can pick the correct answer.) If Justin weren't insolvent, the damages would be awarded as follows: $400,000 from Zach, $300,000 from Bradley, $200,000 from Justin, and $100,000 from Ed. Under state law, Mike should receive the full $1,000,000 in damages. The Justin shortfall means that the other three defendants have to make up the share that Justin would have paid.

The ratio of liability among Zach, Bradley, and Ed assigned by the jury is 4:3:1. In the new distribution, Zach should be paying four times as much as Ed, and Bradley should be paying three times as much as Ed. The total amount to be paid is $1,000,000.

Or, algebraically: $4x + 3x + 2x + x = \$1,000,000$.

Thus, $8x = \$1,000,000$.

That means $x = \$125,000$.

Zach pays $4x$ ($500,000). Bradley pays $3x$ ($375,000). Ed pays x ($125,000).

Answer (A) is incorrect because it ignores the fact that Justin is insolvent.

Answer (C) is incorrect because it deprives Mike of the missing $200,000, a result that the state law rejects.

Answer (D) is incorrect in that it seems to be imposing an additional 20 percent on each remaining defendant for no particular reason. Close but no cigar.

204. **Answer (B) is correct.** The question does not ask you to determine liability, only to consider whether this instance of careless behavior by an employee is attributable to his employer under respondeat superior.

Answer (A) is incorrect because even though it is a true statement, it does not speak to what the question asks about *respondeat superior*.

Answer (C) is incorrect because it does not address the connection between Willis's carelessness and his employment.

Answer (D) is incorrect for the same reason as Answers (A) and (C).

205. **Answer (A) is correct.** Workers' compensation precludes negligence claims. The facts are not 100 percent certain on the question of whether Lorelei is an employee; they say she worked "on a flexible basis" for Scudder Gardens, suggesting that her work status might have been informal.

Answer (B) is incorrect. The conditions that permit workers' compensation preclude tort claiming, and vice versa. Injured employees do not elect one remedy or the other; they may receive no more than one.

Answer (C) is incorrect because it assumes too much. It could be true, but we don't know. A person can be both a law student and an employee for purposes of workers' compensation.

Answer (D) is incorrect because workers' compensation does not exclude toxic exposure (although for workers who want workers' compensation, toxic exposure claims can be hard to prove), and because its description of what happened is inaccurate: falling into poison ivy *is* a source of traumatic injury.

206. **Answer (C) is correct** because it describes the difference between contribution and indemnity.

Answer (A) is incorrect because both contribution and indemnity ask whether a second tortfeasor played a role in causing the harm.

Answer (B) is incorrect because although negligence is the context in which both most claims of contribution and indemnity are considered, there is no rule limiting either of them to negligence alone.

Answer (D) is incorrect because it does not identify a difference between contribution and indemnity.

207. **Answer (A) is correct.** Darren is not vicariously liable for Endora's attack. Endora was not Darren's agent. To be liable to Jade, Darren must have been negligent in some respect, probably in supervising the residents to prevent them from doing things such as this.

Answer (B) is incorrect for the reasons just given.

Answer (C) is incorrect because, even if Darren negligently supervised the residents, he might be liable for Endora's conduct. The reason is that Endora's attack on Jade is one of the things Darren's supervision is designed to prevent.

Answer (D) is incorrect because the facts simply do not support the conclusion that Darren "permitted" Endora to escape. Perhaps other evidence will provide support for this conclusion, but facts given in the problem do not.

Answers

Practice Final Exam

208. **Answer (B) is correct.** This action blames a rule-writing authority for an injury that might have been prevented by the enactment of a more stringent rule. The defendant could argue that it ought not to be liable because legislatures are not liable for failing to enact safety legislation.

    Answer (A) is incorrect because defendant-choreographers work directly with plaintiffs, whereas RBUS was a remote institution.

    Answer (C) is incorrect because it discusses liability for intentional torts rather than negligence and because, as in Answer (A), the defendants and plaintiffs there interact closely rather than remotely.

    Answer (D) is incorrect because workers' compensation is dissimilar to liability, and because it presents no allegation of wrongdoing by any defendant.

209. **Answer (C) is correct.** The question has moved away from the duty point that the defendant raised and asks you to consider which facts would pertain or not pertain to the claim. Because these plaintiffs were injured in a community-league game rather than at school, conditions inside a high school have nothing to do with their injury.

    Answer (A) is incorrect because if RBUS rules are routinely ignored, then the actual cause element of the plaintiffs' claim becomes weaker.

    Answer (B) is incorrect for similar reasons as Answer (A): if RBUS rules are idle and ignored, then their content has little or nothing to do with the plaintiffs' injury.

    Answer (D) is incorrect because if the defendant could not have done what the plaintiffs say it should have done, then the defendant did not breach its duty. The scenario does say that RBUS rules had been changed once in the past. So what the plaintiffs wanted the defendant to do is probably not impossible. If what they want is very difficult, however, then this difficulty is relevant to their claim—certainly more relevant than what goes on in high schools.

210. **Answer (D) is correct.** A victim of negligence who acts out of a desire for self-preservation, and in the course of doing so suffers further harm, is not viewed as a superseding cause that ends the wrongdoer's liability even if the victim's conduct, viewed in the context of the emergency situation, is negligent. However, if the jury believes that the victim acted unreasonably (even given the exigent circumstances), the jury may reduce the victim's recovery according to the jurisdiction's comparative fault rules.

    Answer (C) is incorrect because it assumes that contributory negligence will have no effect on Pearl's recovery.

Answer (A) is incorrect because it assumes that the victim's effort at self-preservation will be a superseding cause of her harm. This is contrary to the law as discussed above.

Answer (B) is incorrect for the same reason as Answer (A) and because it wrongly suggests that the emergency circumstances may not be taken into account in judging the reasonableness of Pearl's actions.

211. **Answer (A) is correct.** Winkle's case fails on the cause in fact element. Very likely, the fire started by Rocky *would have* destroyed Winkle's house if it had been there, but the Whatsamatta U fire got there first. Thus, Rocky's fire did not harm Winkle.

Answer (B) is incorrect because it doesn't matter what Rocky's fire would have done. We already know that it did not, in fact, burn down Winkle's house.

Answer (C) is incorrect because it assumes that a party who has breached a duty of reasonable care is liable even if other elements of the cause of action are not satisfied. The nature of a cause of action is otherwise: all elements must be met, or the action fails completely.

Answer (D) is incorrect because Whatsamatta U's insolvency, while unfortunate, does not give Winkle a valid claim against a party who did not cause Winkle harm. The same is true for the fact that Winkle is innocent. True, the outcome will be that Winkle will have no one from whom to recover, but that is not sufficient to make another party responsible in the absence of a valid cause of action against that party.

212. **Answer (B) is correct.** The issue here is whether Gary performed the surgery in accordance with the applicable standard of care. That makes it a negligence case, and it appears to be strong because the facts indicate that he used too large a tube, and that it caused permanent damage.

Answer (A) is incorrect because the surgery, even if negligently performed and even if it took place against Cara's wishes, was not an unconsented contact. Cara is too young to give consent to surgery. Her parents have that responsibility, and they made their decision after learning the nature of the surgery.

Answer (C) is incorrect because, even if Cara did suffer apprehension of imminent harmful or offensive contact, her apprehension was not caused by any unlawful act of Gary. She may have been apprehensive, but that stemmed from the prospect of surgery to which her parents lawfully consented.

Answer (D) is incorrect because a common surgical procedure is not abnormally dangerous. The furnishing of medical services by physicians is never governed by strict liability.

213. **Answer (C) is correct.** The issue here is one of duty. Adam is a trespasser. Although he was legally on campus, this fenced-off part of the campus no doubt was out of bounds for students. At common law, a possessor of land owed no duty of reasonable care toward a trespasser. (Most states held that there was only a duty to refrain from willful and wanton conduct toward trespassers; this case involved only a condition on the property, and no overt conduct that harmed Adam.)

Answer (A) is incorrect because it assumes a duty was owed.

Answer (B) is incorrect because any negligence by Wynona (here, leaving the mixer where the wind could blow it and the cable could snap) was a "but-for" cause of Adam's injury.

Answer (D) is incorrect because we have sufficient facts to decide the duty question at common law. Note that the issue of "attractive nuisance" does not arise here because Adam was not a child.

214. **Answer (D) is correct.** If the common law rule limiting the duty of land possessors toward trespassers has been abolished, the possessor will owe a general duty of reasonable care regardless of the entrant's status. Satisfying that duty, however, requires a close look at the circumstances of the case. Here, we are not provided with sufficient information to judge the reasonableness of leaving a cement mixer suspended in the air at this site. It is not uncommon for contractors to suspend valuable equipment when the site is shut down, but there are some situations in which doing so poses an unreasonable danger. This might be one of them, but we can't tell without more facts.

Answer (A) is incorrect because, as indicated above, the reasonableness of Wynona's acts cannot be determined without more facts.

Answer (B) is incorrect because any negligence on Wynona's part was a "but-for" cause of Adam's injury.

Answer (C) is incorrect because Wynona did owe Adam a duty of reasonable care.

215. Drucilla's conduct toward the psychiatrist was negligent. Because the facts do not reveal that Walden suffered physical harm, a typical negligence action is not cognizable, but an action for negligent infliction of emotional distress might be. Cases involving mistaken identity have traditionally qualified, albeit in different contexts. For example, a telegraph company that sends a telegram notifying next-of-kin of a person's death, but directed to the wrong family, can be held liable for negligent infliction of emotional distress. And a funeral home that places the wrong body in the casket for an open casket funeral has also been held liable. The present situation seems analogous because it also involves mistaken identity and also is the type of situation that is likely to cause very real emotional distress—in this situation, embarrassment and humiliation.

Intentional infliction of emotional distress does not suit the facts for at least three reasons. First, as to psychiatrist Walden, Drucilla's conduct was negligent, not intentional. Second, even if Drucilla acted with the intent to cause serious emotional distress in the other Walden (which might well have been her purpose—to induce him to catch up on his child support payments), her intent to cause such distress was probably not unlawful. Walden was a wrongdoer, and a jury might not view Drucilla's method (albeit a very public one) of getting him to pay up as "extreme and outrageous." Third, even if the jury views it as extreme and outrageous, courts do not treat intentional infliction of emotional distress as a trespassory tort that allows for application of the "transferred intent" doctrine except in situations in which an unintended victim, present when the act occurs, suffers physical harm in addition to emotional distress. *See* Restatement (Second) of Torts § 46. Because Dr. Walden did not suffer physical harm, he may not recover for intentional infliction of emotional distress.

216. **Answer (B) is correct.** Shakira refused consent to surgery. Shamrock's proceeding in defiance of this refusal was an intentional offensive touching.

    Answer (A) is incorrect. Negligence is used for accidental injury and this injury did not arise by accident.

    Answer (C) is incorrect. Conversion is an interference with one's property, not one's person.

    Answer (D) is incorrect. Assault requires apprehension of imminent physical contact which, due to having her eyes closed, Shakira did not experience.

217. **Answer (B) is correct.** "Serious emotional harm," a more modern concept than existed at the time of the Second Restatement, is new to the Third.

    Answer (A) is incorrect because the Third Restatement retains the "extreme and outrageous" criterion.

    Answer (C) is incorrect because the Third Restatement, like the Second, permits recovery even without physical manifestations.

    Answer D is incorrect because both Restatements accept recklessness as a mental-state standard.

218. Richards, for whose acts the city will be vicariously liable, undertook to advise Demetria about her options. Though he told Demetria about the witness protection program, he left out some very important facts about Frank's dangerousness that might have led Demetria to enter the program. By his acts, Frank arguably created a special relationship, and thus had a duty to act reasonably for her safety.

219. **Answer (C) is correct.** The question of breach is left to the jury unless a reasonable jury could reach only one conclusion. Here, on the given facts, it is not absolutely clear that the city's confinement of Frank satisfied its duty of reasonable care to Demetria. That appears likely, but it is not so clear that the judge should take the case away from the jury.

    Answers (A) and (B) are incorrect because, as explained above, the breach issue is not so clear.

    Answer (D) is incorrect because none of the rationales for burden shifting apply here.

220. **Answer (D) is correct.** The only form of assumption of risk that might have any application in a fact pattern such as this is the "secondary" form, which requires the voluntary confrontation of a known and appreciated hazard. Had Demetria been warned that she would be murdered at the bus stop, and had she gone there despite the warning, assumption of risk might apply. But here, she received a warning about the consequences of testifying, something that had not yet happened. The facts clearly show that she did not confront a specific hazard about which she knew. The court should therefore decide the question as a matter of law.

    Answer (A) is incorrect because this would not be a case of "primary" assumption of risk. Demetria was not involved in an activity with the killers such as a sporting event. Thus, it would make no sense to speak of accepting hazards inherent in the activity.

    Answer (B) is incorrect because, as explained above, there are no facts supporting assumption of risk in its secondary sense.

Answer (C) is incorrect because assumption of risk and contributory (comparative) negligence are separate doctrines. Whether she acted reasonably in waiting for the bus is a question to be addressed under comparative negligence, not assumption of risk. (You should be aware, however, that some courts conflate the two defenses, and hold that under a system of comparative fault, the doctrine of secondary assumption of risk disappears because it is completely subsumed by comparative negligence. This assumes that assumption of risk in its secondary sense requires unreasonable conduct — contributory negligent conduct. That was not the case at common law. Courts would hold that a plaintiff who voluntarily confronted an appreciated hazard assumed the risk, even if their decision under the circumstances was not unreasonable.)

221. **Answer (D) is correct.** Diva appears to have run toward Pluto with the intention of creating in him the apprehension of suffering imminent harmful or offensive contact. It was unlawful for her to do this, especially when her object was to steal his concert ticket. Pluto appears to have suffered the apprehension. This is an assault.

    Answer (A) is incorrect because an action may generate a claim for both battery and an assault. There is some overlap between the two.

    Answer (B) is incorrect because "fright" is not an element of assault. Pluto need only have been "apprehensive," which means he need only have believed Diva was going to contact him harmfully or offensively.

    Answer (C) is incorrect because assumption of risk is not a defense to assault. *Consent* can be a defense, but the facts do not support it. Pluto did not consent to having Diva take his concert ticket.

222. **Answer (B) is correct.** A person has a privilege to use reasonable force to protect himself from what he believes to be an imminent unlawful contact. If the jury finds that Pluto reasonably believed Diva was about to strike him, and if the jury finds that the amount of force Pluto used to repel the attack was not excessive under the circumstances, Pluto has a good self-defense claim.

    Answer (A) is incorrect because whether Pluto reasonably believed Diva was going to batter him, and whether the force Pluto used was reasonable under the circumstances, are questions for the jury (unless the facts are so clear that a reasonable jury could only reach one conclusion).

    Answer (C) is incorrect for two reasons. First, it fails to take account of the "reasonable mistake" aspect of self-defense. As long as Pluto's error in thinking Diva was going to strike him was reasonable, self-defense is still available to him. Second, the question is one of fact for the jury, not for the judge (unless the facts are so clear that a reasonable jury could only reach one conclusion).

    Answer (D) is incorrect because, as indicated above, what matters is whether Pluto reasonably believed Diva was going to batter him, not what Diva actually believed.

223. **Answer (C) is correct.** Eliot's strongest claim is that James did not exercise the care of a reasonable person in deciding to stand up while the bus was moving. The court will allow the

jury to take into account that James was elderly, because age affects one's stability and strength. While it might have been reasonable for a younger person to do what James did, it might not have been reasonable for a person of his age to do it.

Answer (A) is incorrect because it misstates the required mental state for battery and because James did not possess that mental state. It is not enough to say that James "should have realized" he was substantially certain to fall. The law of battery requires proof that James did in fact realize it. The facts do not support this conclusion.

Answer (B) is incorrect because, even if James knew he was more prone to fall than a younger person would be, this is not the same as saying he knew he would strike another person when he fell. (Of course, nothing suggests that he desired to strike another person.) The requisite intent is missing.

Answer (D) is incorrect for the reason given above. The jury should take James' age into account when deciding the reasonableness of his conduct.

224. **Answer (A) is correct.** Jon acted intentionally in a way that tended to deprive Kermit of a prospective economic opportunity, the chance to purchase the bakery.

Answer (B) is incorrect because the problem specifies that no contract existed between Augustine and Kermit.

Answer (C) is incorrect because the story is true.

Answer (D) is incorrect because the formal disposition of criminal charges is generally considered to be public information, whose revelation cannot generate liability for disclosure of private facts—the only branch of the privacy tort that could apply here.

225. **Answer (D) is correct.** Under principles of vicarious liability, an employer may be liable for an employee's conduct even if that conduct violates explicit instructions. The question is whether the conduct is considered within the "scope" of employment. Different tests are used to decide that question. Some courts apply the *Restatement of Agency* test that imposes vicarious liability for an employee's acts done out of a desire to serve the master. It is unclear whether that would be true here; stopping the bus to adjust an uncomfortable uniform does not appear to be something done with that intention. Other courts apply a foreseeability test, asking whether the negligent act or omission is a reasonably foreseeable event given the nature of the job and the circumstances. Under that test, the driver's act is much more likely to be seen as within the scope of employment, especially if drivers do this sort of thing fairly often. In all, courts tend not to place a great deal of emphasis on the fact that the act or omission was in violation of established rules or instructions. Instead, they focus more on the timing of the act (while performing a work-related job or not) and other similar factors. In all, the court is likely to hold in this case that the driver's conduct was within the scope of employment.

Answer (A) is incorrect for the reasons just noted.

Answer (B) is incorrect because the more foreseeable the act or omission, the more likely a court will be to rule that it was within the scope of risk. Here, the omissions appear to be reasonably foreseeable.

Answer (C) is incorrect because the driver's conduct was not an intentional tort. The driver did not want a collision to occur, and did not know that a collision was substantially certain to happen. Finally, even if this was an intentional tort, that does not automatically mean the Bus Co. cannot be held liable; an employer may be liable for intentional torts if they are within the scope of employment.

226. **Answer (D) is correct.** Even though Gilles' shot was in desperation, what he did was still something inherent in the game: fire a puck at high speed. And pucks fired at high speed often leave the ice and sometimes even fly into the stands. This is a risk inherent in attending a hockey game, and courts hold that spectators lose the right to sue for injuries caused by such a risk. Put differently, Gilles did not have a duty to refrain from hitting the puck into the stands during the game. This is considered by most courts to be a case of "primary" assumption of risk, and completely defeats recovery.

Answer (A) is incorrect because nothing suggests that Gilles had substantial certainty that the puck would hit anyone if it did not go into the goal. This answer simply misreads the facts.

Answer (B) is incorrect because "should have known with substantial certainty" is not sufficient to meet the intent requirement for battery.

Answer (C) is incorrect because the facts do not suggest that Gilles' shot was negligent. And even if it was, this is precisely the purpose of the primary assumption of risk doctrine. Gilles did not have a duty toward fans to refrain from negligently striking the puck.

227. **Answer (A) is correct.** The doctrine of primary assumption of risk operates regardless of the plaintiff's actual knowledge of the dangers she faces. Here, it is true that Vorch did not know that pucks could fly into the stands. But being hit by pucks flying into the stands is an inherent risk of attending a hockey game, and Vorch is held to "assume" that risk when he voluntarily attends the game. As a result, his claim is completely defeated. Had the barrier been shorter than those used by other teams, Vorch might have a reasonable argument that he did not assume the risk of being struck while in the seat he took, but the facts indicate that HockeyCo had constructed a barrier of the same height used in all other stadiums where professional hockey teams play.

Answer (B) is incorrect because the primary assumption of risk will completely defeat Vorch's claim, not provide a basis for reduction. HockeyCo did not owe Vorch a duty to prevent this accident from happening.

Answer (C) is incorrect because even if Vorch did not keep a lookout for flying pucks, there is no reason to address the comparative negligence issue. That is because there is no negligence of HockeyCo with which to compare Vlad's negligence.

Answer (D) is incorrect because, as explained above, the doctrine of primary assumption of risk applies to these facts.

228. **Answer (D) is correct.** An employee of a newspaper, through carelessness, caused an injurious false statement to be published.

Answer (A) is incorrect because the word "desiring" demonstrates the intent to do harm, and negligent defamation involves unintended harm.

Answer (B) is incorrect because the injury described is not actionable in defamation unless the statement was false, and answer (B) does not say that the statement was false.

Answer (C) is incorrect because Gabriel's defamation-by-omitting-praise contention is more far-fetched — one might say "paranoid" — than courts will accept. It is hard to see anything defamatory in this omission.

229. **Answer (D) is correct.** The claim appears well founded: the elements of duty and breach are present.

Answer (A) is incorrect because a reasonable jury could find that retaining obsolete, now-dangerous glass in doors evinced negligence.

Answer (B) is incorrect because the owner of Shamarina Hall did owe Brenda a duty of care. Shamarina Hall is open to the public, and renters who lease it for a private function are not in possession of it.

Answer (C) is incorrect because it doesn't quite make sense. It seems to rest on a premise that if Brenda were entirely responsible for her own injury, then the owner of Shamarina Hall would be entitled to judgment as a matter of law. The facts say too little about Brenda's contribution to her own injury to justify any conclusions about its effect.

230. **Answer (A) is correct.** In actions for negligence against land possessors involving the shattering of old glass, when the plaintiff can show that newer glass was available and would have been more shatterproof, courts permit introduction of this evidence. *See* Trimarco v. Klein, 436 N.E. 2d 502 (N.Y. 1982).

Answer (B) is incorrect because the condition of contemporary glass is relevant to the question of whether the defendant was negligent for not replacing it.

Answer (C) is incorrect because reasonable care may include replacing dangerous fixtures like door glass when safer alternatives become available.

Answer (D) is incorrect because it is too quick to side with the plaintiff. We don't know whether the standard of care required replacement of old glass.

231. **Answer (C) is correct.** This was a game. The players impliedly consented to suffering apprehension of being touched. Thus, Steve was privileged to create the apprehension.

Answer (A) is incorrect because it fails to take account of Steve's privilege to create the apprehension in Rose.

Answer (B) is incorrect because "apprehension" exists even when the plaintiff knows she can avoid the contact. As the *Restatement* commentary states, apprehension is not the same as fear. Thus, if defendant aims a rock at the plaintiff, and plaintiff knows she can avoid being hit by ducking behind a door, plaintiff still has a valid assault claim because plaintiff knows she has to take this evasive action to avoid the contact. And it is wrong for defendant to place plaintiff in such a position. Here, plaintiff might have had a way to avoid contact, but she was still "apprehensive." (Of course, as noted above, Steve was privileged to create the apprehension, so there was no assault.)

Answer (D) is incorrect because we have enough facts to conclude that Steve is not liable for assault.

232. **Answer (D) is correct.** Norm's conduct of driving 45 mph instead of 25 mph might have been unlawful, and he might be liable to Ronnie for negligence, but he did not intend to strike Ronnie. That is because he neither desired to strike her nor, *at a time when he could have done something to prevent striking her*, did he know to a substantial certainty that he would strike her. This is a negligence case, not a battery case.

Answer (A) is incorrect because intentionally driving the car is not the same as intentionally striking Ronnie, even if he knew at some point that he would in fact hit her.

Answer (B) is incorrect because "should have known the grave risk of striking a child" is not sufficient for battery. The intent required is either to desire contact or to know with substantial certainty that a contact will occur.

Answer (C) is incorrect because the "negligence per se" concept that is used to establish a duty in negligence law does not apply to the law of battery. It was unlawful to drive faster than 25 mph in that place, but Norm did not have the unlawful intent to strike Ronnie.

233. **Answer (C) is correct.** Deterrence as a rationale encourages potential defendants to consider taking precautions against a foreseeable injury. One who is judgment proof has inadequate incentive to do so, according to the deterrence concept. Vicarious liability of an employer able to pay a judgment provides an incentive to take reasonable care.

Answer (A) is incorrect because access to insurance does not affect deterrence.

Answer (B) is incorrect because it is a fairness rationale for this kind of vicarious liability, rather than a deterrence argument.

Answer (D) is incorrect because though it might be true, its fatalistic futility ("there's no hope") conflicts with a deterrence rationale. Deterrence as a rationale optimistically proceeds as if taking care will reduce harm.

234. **Answer (D) is correct.** Even though Elinor was mentally ill, she could still be found comparatively negligent for walking onto the highway. The facts will have to be investigated, of course, but this claim seems viable.

Answer (A) is incorrect because defendants did have a duty to inform Serene Chateau of Elinor's tendencies. The state was in a special relationship with Elinor. This imposed a duty of reasonable care for her safety. A reasonable social worker would have realized that Elinor presented certain risks to herself that might not be apparent to the new facility, at least for a while. Reasonable care toward Elinor therefore would require informing Serene Chateau of her tendency to walk away and become disoriented.

Answer (B) is incorrect because a jury is very likely to find that defendants breached their duty. There is nothing in the facts to suggest a cognizable excuse for their failure to inform Serene Chateau of Elinor's tendencies.

Answer (C) is incorrect because the failure to notify Serene Chateau of Elinor's tendencies was almost certainly a "but-for" cause of Elinor's harm. That is, it is very likely that had the state notified Serene Chateau of the relevant facts, the facility would have taken steps to monitor Elinor more carefully, and perhaps limit her freedom to leave the facility.

235. **Answer (B) is correct.** The "directness" approach to proximate cause basically asks whether any harm was reasonably foreseeable from defendant's conduct, and if so, whether the chain of events from the negligent act to the harm was unbroken (direct). Answer (B) states that test.

Answer (A) is incorrect because the "directness" approach does not require that the harm that occurred be what one might expect. In fact, an important feature of the approach as articulated by Andrews and the decisions of the courts of which Andrews approved is that the type of harm that actually occurs is of minor, if any, importance.

Answer (C) is incorrect because even under a "directness" approach, the plaintiff's own negligence does not cut off the liability of the originally negligent actor, especially if it was reasonably foreseeable (as was the case here).

Answer (D) is incorrect because it states a risk-type of approach, not a directness approach.

236. **Answer (A) is correct.** Scope of risk approaches tend to look at whether the victim was within a class of persons to whom harm was reasonably foreseeable, and at whether the type of harm that occurred was of the kind one might reasonably expect. Answer (A) embodies these principles.

Answer (B) is incorrect because courts do not require that the precise chain of events have been reasonably foreseeable. Even rather convoluted chains of events can be considered within the scope of risk created by the defendant's carelessness if the victim and type of harm the victim suffered were reasonably foreseeable. (Note that the same is true in courts using a directness approach; the precise manner in which the harm comes about need not be reasonably foreseeable.)

Answer (C) is incorrect because it states a directness type of test rather than a scope of risk test.

Answer (D) is incorrect because courts do not require the *extent* of injury to be reasonably foreseeable. (Note that the same is true under a directness approach.)

237. **Answer (B) is correct.** According to *Restatement (Second) of Torts*, in order to be liable the land possessor must know or have reason to know that a trespasser is actually present.

Answer (A) is incorrect because there is no reason to suppose that Tommy assumed any risk.

Answer (C) is incorrect because Muskrat owed Tommy no duty.

Answer (D) is incorrect because foreseeability of a trespasser's presence is insufficient to support liability.

238. **Answer (C) is correct.** Most likely, Louise's entry onto Walter's property was justified by the doctrine of private necessity. A person has a privilege to commit what would otherwise be a trespass if the action appears necessary to prevent imminent harm to person or property.

That was Louise's reason for entering Walter's land. She had reason to believe that the child was injured and needed help.

Answer (A) is incorrect because Louise's entry was voluntary. She was not coerced into going onto the property.

Answer (B) is incorrect because Louise was lawfully present on the property.

Answer (D) is incorrect for the reason stated above.

239. False light. The false light claim is similar to defamation, except that under false light doctrine the statement can be actionable even if it is true, whereas for defamation it cannot be actionable unless it is false. Other elements are held in common: the false light must be offensive (similar to defamation's criterion of "harmful to the plaintiff's reputation") and the defendant must have publicized (cf. "published") the communication. Because the standard for false light is more inclusive, many defamation claims can be actionable as false light claims as well.

240. **Answer (C) is correct.** Most American courts hold that physicians are required to reveal only information that a reasonable person in the patient's position would have considered material in deciding whether to have the surgery. This does not give each patient the greatest right of self-determination, but it is a realistic standard that avoids requiring the physician to reveal a huge amount of information that most people simply would not consider important.

Answer (A) is incorrect because one of the physician's obligations is to reveal possible side effects of the surgery. Patients consider this information to be important as they consider their options.

Answer (B) is incorrect because the success of Kevin's case does not depend on a weighing of the benefits of the surgery against the harm it did to Kevin. True, Kevin must have suffered harm as a result of the doctor's failure to disclose material information, but the mere fact that the surgery was otherwise successful does not exonerate McAllister from the possibility he might be liable for the pain and suffering Kevin endured as a result of the side-effects.

Answer (D) is incorrect because most American courts do not allow medical custom to set the standard for proper disclosure in informed consent cases.

241. **Answer (D) is correct.** Most courts allow a narrow exception to the informed consent standard. If the physician reasonably believes that this particular patient is so sensitive that providing certain information will cause such anxiety that it actually will harm the patient, then the physician need not provide that information.

Answer (A) is incorrect because, as explained above, a narrow exception allows the physician to withhold information if she reasonably believes the patient will be harmed by the anxiety caused by that information.

Answer (B) is incorrect because it fails to take account of the exception.

Answer (C) is incorrect because it grossly overstates the applicability of the exception. A doctor may not withhold information merely because she thinks the patient will make the "wrong" decision if the information is provided. Such an exception would overwhelm the patient-centered informed consent standard.

242. **Answer (B) is correct.** Courts tend to hedge on the causation issue. If courts wished to give the greatest effect to a patient's right of self-determination, they would establish a causation standard that would be met by proof that this particular patient would not have agreed to the surgery if he had been told about the possible side-effects that occurred. Thus, even if a reasonable patient would have agreed to the procedure, the plaintiff could prevail. But courts have chosen instead to establish an objective test of causation: plaintiff must prove that a reasonable person would not have undergone the procedure if she had known of these possible side effects.

One reason courts adopt the objective standard is that the subjective standard would be too easy to meet. A patient who has suffered horribly would almost always believe, in hindsight, that she would not have agreed to the procedure had she known this might happen. But that might not always be true as a matter of foresight; a patient told that she will benefit from a particular procedure might choose to undergo the procedure even if she knows that certain side effects might occur. Answer (B) is correct because it states the objective standard.

Answer (A) is incorrect for the reasons just given.

Answer (C) is incorrect because it deals with the problem of proximate cause or scope of liability, not cause in fact.

Answer (D) is incorrect because proof of duty and breach does not establish causation. In a negligence case, the plaintiff must also prove that the breach caused harm.

243. **Answer (B) is correct.** The Port Authority has a duty to keep the walkway clean and clear of litter, and to act reasonably with regard to foreseeable risks. This duty does not require it to eliminate every possible danger. Since the apple core had only been on the ground three minutes, it is unreasonable to expect the Port Authority to have cleared the danger.

Answer (A) is incorrect. Although the Port Authority does have a duty to Crowbar as an invitee, this situation falls outside the scope of this duty.

Answer (C) is incorrect. The Port Authority does have a duty to use reasonable efforts to prevent harm to people such as Crowbar.

Answer (D) is incorrect. Although the area was marked Designated Lunch Area, Crowbar did not assume the risk of risk of tripping over an apple core. However, the fact that Crowbar did not assume a risk does not mean that the Port Authority is liable for his injuries.

244. **Answer (D) is correct.** Most courts agree that when two negligent forces combine to cause damage, and either force standing alone would have been sufficient to cause all of the harm, the parties responsible for both agencies are treated as causes of the harm, and are jointly and severally liable for it. If one of the agencies of harm is not attributable to negligence, the party responsible for the other force is liable for the full extent of the harm. Here, the facts indicate that Wingnut City negligently maintained the dam, and that the water from the dam would have been sufficient by itself to cause all of Abel's harm. Thus, Wingnut City is liable for all of the harm.

Answer (A) is incorrect for the reasons just stated.

Answer (B) is incorrect because, as long as either force would have been sufficient to cause all of the damage, it does not matter if more water from the river flood reached Abel's gallery than from the dam.

Answer (C) is incorrect because, as stated above, Wingnut City is liable for all of the harm.

245. Wingnut City has a reasonable argument that it should only be liable for the value of any goods Abel could have saved if he had had an extra hour to remove some of his goods from the building. The analogy is to the wrongful death of a person who, due to other factors, had only a short time to live. Here, some of Abel's goods were about to be destroyed by the river water. Thus, Wingnut City may argue that it is only liable for the value of any goods Abel would not have had time to save. Note that the court might not accept this idea. After all, Wingnut City *did* destroy all of the art. In addition, such an argument is not availing in the scenario described in Question 244, where an argument by Wingnut City that it should not be responsible because Abel's goods would have been destroyed anyway was not considered valid. The outcome is not clear.

246. In this toxic tort case, Platt must prove two things to prove cause in fact: *First*, Platt must prove that it is more likely than not that the chemical that leaked from the tank *was capable of causing* this type of cancer. *Second*, Platt must prove that it is more likely than not that the chemical *actually did cause* Platt's case of cancer. This, in turn, will require Platt to show that the chemical reached his property (perhaps through ground water), and that it reached his body and caused the disease. Much of Platt's proof might have to be in statistical form, and, of course, he will need expert testimony to establish both basic points.

247. **Answer (D) is correct.** The facts state that the lift snapped "[d]ue to factors of which CE had not reason to be aware." If that is true, this appears to have been an accident without fault. Even though harm occurred, CE is not liable for negligence in the handling of the drum. (Perhaps Diane could make a different kind of claim, such as a claim that CE should not have been using a forklift to move the drum. But that is not the claim stated in the problem.)

Answer (A) is incorrect because, as explained above, the evidence strongly suggests that CE exercised reasonable care in its handling of the drum.

Answer (B) is incorrect because CE's experience with handling chemicals did not impose on it a "higher duty." The jury would be entitled to consider CE's experience in deciding whether CE in fact breached its duty, but the duty is the same as it would be even if CE did not have the experience: reasonable care under the circumstances. CE appears to have exercised reasonable care, even taking account of CE's experience.

Answer (C) is incorrect because using procedures that meet or exceed industry standards is not a per se test for reasonableness. It is some evidence of reasonable care, but not conclusive proof.

248. **Answer (D) is correct.** An attorney-client relationship, which a plaintiff must prove in order to recover for legal malpractice, sets a duty of care that includes vigilance about financial risks. This contractual relationship takes legal malpractice out of the economic loss rule.

Answer (A) is incorrect because legal malpractice claims are overwhelmingly about financial loss. It is rare for a client to attribute physical injury or property damage to this form of negligence.

Answer (B) is incorrect because it is overbroad. Lawyers frequently impose economic losses on clients without incurring liability. Duty and breach are both elements of the claim: merely causing a financial injury is not enough.

Answer (C) is incorrect because there is no such distinction between legal malpractice claims by clients and claims by nonclients.

249. The two torts overlap most frequently where the defendant's behavior combines "outrage" and "intrusion." Stalking might give rise to both claims. When the defendant has power over the plaintiff and can control her mobility to some extent—for instance, the defendant might be a high school principal and the plaintiff a high school student; the defendant might be an employer and the plaintiff an employee—both claims could arise when the defendant repeatedly hounds the plaintiff with intimate, personal questions. *Snyder v. Phelps*, a 2010 decision by the U.S. Supreme Court, also combined the two.

250. **Answer (D) is correct.** Gretchen's claim satisfies the elements of negligence per se. There is no excuse for the statutory violation, and the bite was both the cause in fact and the proximate cause of her injury.

Answer (A) is incorrect. Gretchen's keeping a chinchilla in violation of the statute suffices to establish negligence; whether she gave Maureen permission to handle it is irrelevant.

Answer (B) is incorrect. Negligence per se, the doctrine at issue here, eliminates the need to prove breach of duty. The conditional "if" makes this choice incorrect.

Answer (C) is incorrect. Keeping a chinchilla locked in a cage in one's home does not necessarily constitute negligent behavior. Under these facts, the statute made it negligence.

251. **Answer (B) is correct.** "Serious emotional harm," a more modern concept than existed at the time of the Second Restatement, is new to the Third.

Answer (A) is incorrect because the Third Restatement retains the "extreme and outrageous" criterion.

Answer (C) is incorrect because the Third Restatement, like the Second, permits recovery even without physical manifestations.

Answer (D) is incorrect because both Restatements accept recklessness as a mental-state standard.

252. *Criticism*: Many people do not read warnings. Some people read warnings but misinterpret the information conveyed. If warnings proliferate, perhaps consumers would suffer from "information overload" and become unable to absorb everything warned about. Some warnings state the obvious. *Critique of the criticism*: If consumers process warnings ineffectively, that might mean that sellers should figure out how to warn more effectively, rather than just escape liability. Warnings can convey not only news of a risk but ways to reduce the risk—helpful information that the user might not know. The effort to compose a warning makes a product seller keep dangers in mind, and might foster safety-related innovation.

Answers

Essay Issue-Spotter Answers

253. Battery, assault, and intentional infliction of emotional distress are relatively apparent here. Your instructor might approach the claim of *Latham v. Travolta* as either trespass to land or trespass to chattel.

Latham v. Travolta — trespass

A. <u>Allegation</u>: Travolta caused property damage when he clung to the beam.

B. <u>The tort</u>: (1) <u>Trespass to land</u>: Travolta traveled into, and chose to remain in, a portion of the Urban Cowboy bar where he was expressly not welcome by the possessor. (2) <u>Trespass to chattel</u> means intentional interference with a possession that belongs to the plaintiff, in a way that causes harm. The chattel here is the valuable antique beam.

C. Initial contact with the beam does *not* fulfill the elements of either type of trespass because Travolta was flung onto it; he did not land there intentionally. The tort occurred when Travolta refused to let go.

D. All elements appear present. Travolta acted by clinging to the beam. We know he acted intentionally because he said as much. Clinging to the beam, according to the story, caused it to splinter due to Travolta's weight.

Two ways to analyze the question of responsibility: confirm which your instructor favors:

A. Prima facie case of trespass to chattel coupled with the <u>privilege</u> of **necessity.** (A majority of instructors would endorse this approach.)

   1. Travolta harmed the beam to save himself from falling.

   2. In a 'lesser evils' analysis, compare the $1800 damage to the beam against what its damage avoided: a crushed pelvis and two broken legs. Travolta's decision makes good economic sense. However ...

   3. ... Travolta has only a *qualified privilege*, which means that he has to compensate Latham for the value of the beam.

B. Alternative analysis: a <u>simple trespass</u>. (Favored in Goldberg, Sebok, and Zipursky, *Tort Law: Responsibility and Redress.*) Note that both alternatives lead to the same dollar amount owed by Travolta to Latham.

   1. All elements of trespass to chattels or trespass to land are met.

   2. Travolta accordingly is liable for the value of injury he caused.

Travolta v. Winger — battery

A. <u>Volitional act</u>: Winger pulled a control lever to increase the electric current flowing into Bucko.

B. <u>Intent</u>: Winger desired to make the Bucko ride at a speed that was much harder for Travolta to stay on.

C. <u>Harmful consequence</u>: Winger's act caused Travolta to suffer a broken ankle.

So far so good.

Travolta v. Winger — the <u>defense</u> of consent?

A. <u>Defendant's argument supporting a defense</u>: Travolta climbed aboard a mechanical bucking bronco knowing full well that an electric current routinely causes its riders to fall. Like the name "Flopper" in *Murphy v. Steeplechase Amusement Co.*, the famous 1929 decision authored by Cardozo, the name "Bucko" might be understood as a "warning to the timid."

B. The defense should <u>fail</u>. Travolta consented to a normal quantity of electric current, not the doubling that Winger imposed without his knowledge.

Winger v. Travolta — assault

A. <u>Allegation</u>: Travolta acted intentionally to cause Winger to apprehend imminent harmful bodily contact.

B. <u>Volitional act</u>: Travolta's slipping on a pair of brass knuckles and then waving his fist while making a threat.

C. <u>Intent</u>: Travolta's words, "I'll smash your face in, you rotten little creep," reveals a desire to inflict harmful contact on Winger. There is no reason to suppose that Travolta was joking; Travolta saw Winger come up through the basement door and likely figured out that Winger had caused the electric current to reach a harmful level.

D. <u>Apprehension of harmful contact</u> is likely *not* present. We know that Travolta "tried to get up, but couldn't." A reasonable person would understand that harmful contact imposed by Travolta was not imminent.

The claim should <u>fail</u>.

Winger v. Redford — battery

A. <u>Allegation</u>: Redford intentionally caused Winger to suffer offensive contact.

B. <u>Elements and application:</u> The plaintiff must show a <u>volitional act that causes intentionally inflicted harmful or offensive contact</u>: Redford's patting Winger on the head and kissing her cheek was offensive to Winger given what appeared to be a sarcastic, cruel agenda: after this touching, Redford promptly played a song that he knew held painful emotional association for Winger.

C. <u>Analysis</u>: Both sides have arguments to raise. Winger would concede that she experienced the contact as benign when it happened, and only later realized that Redford desired the contact to be offensive. Redford would argue that a kiss and a pat on the head, in response to which the touched person speaks friendly words, was not offensive contact.

A case on point might be *Neal v. Neal*, decided by the Idaho Supreme Court in 1994. The plaintiff was a wife and the defendant her husband. The couple had uneventful sexual intercourse that the wife later characterized as a battery because, unknown to her, the husband had been sexually unfaithful. In her perspective the touching of her body would have been welcome and inoffensive if the husband had not withheld the truth about his recent sexual past. The court found that the wife's allegation stated a valid claim. Here, similarly, the light of hindsight suggests that the defendant withheld information that the plaintiff found important. This withholding, like that of *Neal*, may be enough to characterize as a battery a touching that seems quite inoffensive.

Winger v. Redford — intentional infliction of emotional distress

A. <u>Allegation</u>: Redford played the song "Rabbit" with the goal of causing distress to Winger.

B. <u>Elements of the tort</u>: (1) Outrageous conduct by the defendant that (2) causes the plaintiff to suffer severe emotional distress.

C. <u>Analysis</u>: Debatable.

  (1) <u>The outrage element</u>:

  <u>How the defendant would describe the action</u>: A joke, not very funny perhaps but trivial. The defendant could note that courts set the outrage bar rather high.

  <u>How the plaintiff would describe the action</u>: Gratuitously cruel for no reason. Furthermore, the defendant knew that the plaintiff had been mentally fragile with respect to her husband's suicide. Courts are relatively willing to agree that conduct is outrageous when it exploits a weakness of the plaintiff's psyche known to the defendant. The action was done in public, at a bar, which might have added to the humiliation and distress suffered by Winger.

  (2) <u>The severe-distress element</u>:

  This one looks bad for the plaintiff and good for the defendant. All we know about the plaintiff's emotional response is "Winger wanted to sob, but she kept stoic." Sounds like distress but not severe distress.

  The claim probably should <u>fail</u>.

254. Note that negligence is the only tort available.

(A) Bobby v. Steverino

1. <u>Alleged negligent act</u>: Arranging to conduct conference call on cell phone and then answering cell phone while driving, causing Steverino to lose concentration and nearly hit Bobby.

2. <u>Duty</u>: Care that would be exercised by reasonably prudent driver under same or similar circumstances.

  a. No statute forbids, so use ordinary common-law analysis.

  b. Custom among business people to use a cell phone might be evidence of reasonable care, but court can decide that custom is unreasonably dangerous.

3. Breach: Did Steverino exercise reasonable care? Thoughts:

   a. Hand formula (try to learn whether your instructor welcomes this analysis): Probability of accident is greater than when not using phone, but still not extremely high. Loss if accident occurs could be very high, as was the case here (we don't know monetary value of Bobby's leg injury or other consequences, but in total it's pretty high). Burden of avoiding harm would probably mean not conducting business on cell phone, which can be costly in terms of lost productivity. But maybe society would rather have greater safety than higher productivity. Result? Other alternatives?

   b. Note, however, that Steverino hadn't even begun to talk on cell phone when accident happened. Had only looked down to answer the phone. Looking down or away from road momentarily is something drivers do for many good (and not so good) reasons (tuning radio, checking for positions of other cars, looking at street signs, etc.). So if the real focus here is on simply looking away to answer cell phone, act doesn't look particularly unreasonable, if unreasonable at all.

4. Cause in fact: But for Steverino's looking away, would he have hit Bobby anyway? Need more facts because we can't really tell if the momentary loss of eye contact with the road ahead and to the sides made any difference here. Seems likely the answer is yes.

5. Proximate cause:

   a. Risk-type approach: Pedestrians are obvious potential victims of drivers becoming distracted. Harm that occurred (personal injury) is the type of harm one would expect to occur. Manner in which it came about (injury from jumping out of the way), though not likely important, is maybe not the most foreseeable manner, but it's certainly one of the ways one would expect a person to be harmed. Bobby's act of self-preservation is certainly within the scope of risk created by Steverino's negligent act. Proximate causes is likely no real problem.

   b. Directness-type approach: Some harm foreseeable from failing to pay attention to the road ahead and to the sides. The harm appears to have been a direct consequence because the chain was broken only by Bobby's act of self-preservation, which would not be deemed superseding.

6. Damages: Bobby suffered leg injury.

(B) Lois v. Steverino

1. Two possibilities: (a) For using the cell phone; (b) for swerving. These two are connected, because the allegation essentially is that using the cell phone began the sequence of events that led to the need to swerve, and thus the striking of Lois's car.

2. Using cell phone: Analysis much the same as in *Bobby v. Steverino* for negligence. Certainly, as another driver on the road, Lois is another reasonably foreseeable victim of increased rate of accidents while using cell phone. This set up situation that forced Steverino into a choice between striking Bobby and swerving out of the lane.

3. Swerving

<u>Duty</u>: Steverino owed Lois, as another driver, a duty to act care that would be exercised by reasonably prudent person under same or similar circumstances.

<u>Breach</u>: Normally, when there is an emergency in which the person must act, that emergency can be taken into account in determining reasonableness of actions. But when the actor is responsible for creating that emergency, courts tend not to allow consideration of that factor. Whether that is true here depends on whether use of the cell phone (or more exactly, whether looking down to answer the cell phone to pick up a pre-arranged call) is a negligent act.

a. If the emergency can be considered, Steverino is unlikely to be held in breach because of the need for immediate action. Even reasonable people sometimes don't check for other cars if there's an imminent collision with a pedestrian ahead and there's no virtually time to think.

b. If the emergency can't be considered in Steverino's favor, he's likely to be held in breach because reasonable people in non-emergency situations check before changing lanes.

<u>Actual cause</u>: But for failing to check, Steverino probably would not have hit Lois's car. May need more facts, because this conclusion assumes he would have been able to see the car if he had checked. There are some blind spots, and she might have been in one momentarily. (Even then, however, maybe reasonable drivers should take account of blind spots and check more closely.)

<u>Proximate cause</u>:

a. Under a risk-based approach, Lois is a reasonably foreseeable victim, the harm that occurred (personal injury and damage to the car) is the type one would expect, and even the manner in which it occurred (if that matters) is what's to be expected normally.

b. Under a directness-type approach, same result. Some harm from Chain was unbroken with intervening causes. Some harm from failing to check for other cars is foreseeable, and the chain was unbroken? No intervening acts, passage of much time, etc.

<u>Damages</u>: Lois suffered personal injury and damage to the car.

(C) Chris's Estate v. Steverino

1. Was Steverino negligent toward Chris and liable for his initial injuries as well as his death?

2. <u>Analysis of elements</u>

<u>Duty</u>: Steverino owed Chris, a passenger in another car, a duty to act as would a reasonably prudent person under same or similar circumstances.

<u>Breach</u>: See *Lois v. Steverino* for negligence. Same issue as to emergency that was raised in Lois v. Steverino for negligence.

<u>Actual cause</u>:

<u>Initial personal injury</u>: See *Lois v. Steverino* for negligence. Same issues.

<u>Death</u>: This raises a probability problem. We know Chris was already suffering a heart attack when Steverino came along. But we also know that the accident delayed Chris's arrival at a hospital, and that this reduced substantially his chances of survival. (The facts state that Chris "would have had a much better chance of surviving" had he reached the hospital without delay.) So, what chance did he have anyway? This is important because of the "chance of survival" cases.

a. Traditional view is that unless Chris had a better than even chance of survival from the heart attack had he not been delayed, Steverino can't be held responsible for his death because he probably didn't cause it.

b. But some courts have held that defendant's negligent reduction of even a less than even chance of survival is actionable, though damages would only be represented by the percentage chance of survival the person would have had without the negligence.

c. We don't know what position the courts in this jurisdiction take.

<u>Proximate cause</u>:

<u>For initial injuries</u>: See *Lois v. Steverino* for negligence.

<u>For death</u>:

a. Steverino takes his victim as he finds him, so he can't argue that a normal person wouldn't have suffered harm from the delay in treatment.

b. If courts (regardless of general approach) hold an initially negligent actor liable for harm even when caused by later negligence of doctors, then they would surely hold that the initially negligent actor is liable when doctors do a good job of treating the patient. Here, we're told that the doctors "performed admirably," which probably means reasonably.

c. Thus, proximate cause is satisfied regardless of the general approach the court might take to proximate cause analysis.

<u>Damages</u>: Steverino will be liable for the initial harm he caused Chris. As for Chris's death, extent of damages (if any) would depend on the jurisdiction as explained above.

(D) Peggy v. Steverino

1. Is Steverino liable to Peggy for the damage to her café as a result of the car crashing through the window?

2. <u>Duty</u>: To act as would a reasonable person under same or similar circumstances.

   <u>Breach</u>: See above claims by Bobby, Lois, and Chris for discussion of possible breach in using cell phone and in swerving to avoid collision with Bobby.

   <u>Actual cause</u>: But for Steverino's crashing into the café, none of the damage, including the flooding, would have occurred.

   <u>Proximate cause</u>:

   <u>Initial damage from crashing through the window</u>: No problem regardless of approach. A merchant whose business is along a street is a foreseeable victim of careless driving.

This is the kind of harm one would expect. And in case it matters (which it probably doesn't), the harm occurred in the usual way. A car careening out of control and striking the building. Nothing intervened except the natural actions of vehicles in motion.

Flood damage: A little more difficult.

a. Risk-based approaches:

i. Peggy is a foreseeable victim, but some courts also require that the type of harm be foreseeable (*Wagon Mound* is an example). Would one expect a <u>flood</u>? Maybe not, though severing of water lines is a common feature of some accidents in which cars go off the road. (For example, it's not unusual to strike a fire hydrant.) Close call.

ii. Under the "dust settling" idea of proximate cause there's probably liability. Because the cars were still in motion and out of control, the consequences of the careless act were still unfolding.

b. Directness-type approaches: The *Polemis* court would have little trouble with this case because some harm (to Peggy, in case that matters) would be a reasonably foreseeable consequence of negligently losing control of a car in a business district. Thus, liability would be for all "direct" consequences. Because there were no intervening actors or forces other than those of nature carrying a vehicle in motion past the point of impact, and because no appreciable time passed between careless act and the severing of the water line, a directness analysis would consider this consequence close enough to be attributed legally to Steverino.

Damages: Property damage, perhaps including damage caused by the flood.

255. **(A) Danny v. Ron—assault**

1. Allegation: By chasing him in his car under these circumstances, Ron committed assault leading to several harmful consequences. (Note: It is possible that Ron committed an assault at some point before he began chasing Danny in his car, but the facts do not reveal any support for such a conclusion.)

2. Assault elements: (a) Defendant commits an overt act (generally required); (b) defendant unlawfully intends to cause apprehension of imminent harmful or offensive contact in plaintiff or another person; (c) plaintiff suffers apprehension of imminent harmful or offensive contact.

a. (Overt) act: Ron chased Danny with his car.

b. Intent:

Basic: We don't know exactly what Ron was thinking, but it is not unreasonable to believe that he either acted with the purpose of causing Danny to suffer apprehension that he'd be battered imminently or that he knew that this apprehension was substantially certain to result. There is also the possibility of intent of battery, through the "transferred intent" fiction, but the facts suggest that Ron hadn't yet actually tried to contact Danny. This aspect of the intent requirement is perhaps a bit unclear, but is probably satisfied.

<u>Unlawfulness</u>: There is no doubt that it's highly inappropriate to do what Ron did. Even if Ron believed he was acting properly to protect his territory, he was wrong to protect it by threatening violence in this way.

<u>Suffering of apprehension</u>: Certainly, Danny suffered apprehension of imminent harmful contact. He ran away to avoid being killed or badly hurt. Most likely, the harm Ron threatened was imminent because it appeared that Ron could inflict it almost immediately.

3. <u>Recoverable damages (including extended liability)</u>: Ron never did catch Danny, so did not *directly* cause actual harm. If this was all that happened, Danny would recover only nominal damages and, perhaps, punitive damages because of the elevated wrongfulness of Ron's conduct. (Trying to hurt someone is a bad thing for which punitive damages are appropriate.)

But Danny did suffer physical harm, albeit not immediately. Danny was eventually hit by Fran's car. Courts often say that an intentional tortfeasor is liable for all harm resulting from her conduct. This can't be literally true, of course; there must be some limit. But it's possible a court will say that that limit had not been reached when Danny was still reacting to the situation caused by Ron's pursuit. Still, Danny was hit by the car many hours after Ron's pursuit presumably ended, so perhaps the limit was reached before that occurred.

It is also possible that Danny could try to hold Ron responsible for any damages Danny has to pay Bumble for destroying Bumble's flowers. We can't be sure how such a claim would be received, however.

4. <u>Defenses</u>: None appear.

Ron's effort to eject Danny from turf claimed by Ron's gang would not be recognized by the court because the law would not recognize the gang's claim to exclusive possession. Danny had a right to be where he was.

The facts do not support an inference that Ron reasonably believed Danny posed a threat of harm. Thus, Ron was not acting in self-defense.

Consent is not present here, either. Even if Danny's membership in a street gang leads to the conclusion that he understood that he would be subjected to certain risks, that fact does not amount to consent to those things happening. And the facts do not state that he knew Ron would be present at the store. Finally, some courts do not allow "consent" to illegal acts (such as being chased by a car).

<u>Bottom line</u>: Danny has a strong assault claim against Ron.

<u>Note</u>: Danny's effort to claim damages for being struck by Fran's car could also be seen as a battery claim. That claim will not be addressed separately because the same considerations (attenuated contact, etc.) are involved. It's duplicative.

Danny v. Ron — false imprisonment

Note: This is a weak claim unless one can use transferred intent principles because Ron was not trying to confine Danny to an area set by Ron. The facts do not indicate that Ron knew Danny was in Bumble's yard.

Note: Ron's desire to *exclude* Danny from his gang's "territory" is not considered "confinement" under most definitions used for false imprisonment purposes.

1. Elements of false imprisonment: (1) Defendant acts; (2) Defendant unlawfully intends to confine plaintiff or a third person to a limited area set by defendant; (3) Plaintiff is in fact confined; (4) Plaintiff is either aware of the confinement or is harmed by it.

2. Act: Ron's chasing Danny was a volitional act.

3. Intent: This is the weak link. Ron did not act with the purpose of confining Danny; he probably wanted to kill him, not confine him. Because the facts do not suggest that Ron knew Danny was in Bumble's yard, he did not have the intent to confine Danny there.

    However, doctrine of "transferred intent" applies here. A desire to commit one type of trespassing intentional tort will suffice to fulfill the intent element should another result occur. So if Ron had the intent required for assault or battery, and Danny establishes the rest of the prima facie case, there would be false imprisonment.

4. Effect on plaintiff: Danny probably believed he needed to stay in Bumble's yard in order to avoid being killed. This qualifies as confinement.

5. Awareness of harm: Danny was aware of the confinement.

6. Recoverable damages: Danny was not harmed directly by the confinement, but if he suffered emotionally, this would be a recoverable type of damage. If not, nominal damages are available. Punitive damages are also available; see discussion in assault claim above.

    The extended liability principle might apply to entitle Danny to damages from being struck by Fran's car. See discussion in assault claim above.

7. Defenses: None. See assault discussion.

8. Bottom line: This is a weak claim without using "transferred intent" principles. But the claim is probably superfluous anyway; any damages suffered as a result of the confinement would be awardable in the assault claim anyway.

(B) Pixie v. Danny — battery

1. Allegation: When Danny shot Pixie, he committed the intentional tort of battery.

2. Elements: (1) Defendant commits a volitional act; (2) Defendant unlawfully intends to bring about a harmful or offensive contact; (3) Plaintiff suffers harmful or offensive contact.

3. Act: Danny intentionally fired his gun, intending to do so.

4. Intent:

    a. Basic: Danny was trying to hit Ron or Ron's car. If the former, this satisfies the requirement. Even if the latter, it qualifies because the car was closely associated with

Ron at the time, meaning that trying to hit the car is tantamount to trying to hit Ron. Anyone who is hit has a claim by "transferred intent" principles.

  b. <u>Unlawfulness</u>: Normally, of course, it is wrong to try to shoot someone or a car the person is driving. But Danny was acting in self-defense, which will be discussed below. If his act is deemed within his right of self-defense, the act will be viewed as justified.

5. <u>Contact</u>: Pixie was struck by the bullet from Danny's gun.

6. <u>Defense</u>:

  a. <u>Self-defense</u>.

   Danny has a privilege to use reasonable force to repel or prevent an attack if he reasonably believes such force is necessary for that purpose.

   Reasonable belief: Danny believed Ron was going to seriously injure or kill him. Under the circumstances, that belief was certainly reasonable. The two were members of rival gangs. Danny was in territory claimed by Ron's gang. Ron was chasing Danny in his car. These facts, together with a history of violence between the gangs (if any) would make Danny's belief reasonable.

   Reasonableness of the force used: If it was reasonable to believe that Ron was going to try to seriously injure or kill Danny, Danny was privileged to use whatever force was necessary to prevent that from happening. Shooting Ron under the circumstances appears to qualify, though this will be up to the jury to decide. The jury may consider whether Danny had any alternatives, however. If, even under these stressful circumstances, a reasonable person would have seen a way to avoid using the gun, the jury might find that Danny did not act reasonably.

  b. <u>Unintended victim</u>: The cases seem to suggest that if someone other than the purported attacker is hit, that person does not have a battery action against the person acting in self-defense, as long as the element of self-defense are satisfied. This is a harsh result, but it doesn't foreclose the possibility of a negligence action if the defender's conduct was sufficiently careless. And of course, the victim may also sue the attacker who created the need for self-defense in the first place.

7. <u>Bottom line</u>: Pixie's claim is weak because of Danny's right to exercise self-defense.

Pixie v. Danny — negligence

1. <u>Allegation</u>: Danny failed to use reasonable care (even under the emergency circumstances) when he fired his weapon.

2. <u>Elements</u>: Plaintiff must prove (1) Defendant owed plaintiff a duty of reasonable care; (2) defendant breached that duty by failing to act as the reasonable person in the same or similar circumstances would act; (3) plaintiff suffered physical harm (injury or damage to property); (4) defendant was the cause in fact of that harm; and (5) defendant was the legal or proximate cause of the harm.

3. <u>Duty</u>: A person owes a general duty of reasonable care toward those whom a reasonable person would foresee might be affected by her behavior. As a person using the public

streets, Pixie is a reasonably foreseeable victim of any careless conduct on Danny's part. Danny owes Pixie a duty of reasonable care.

4. <u>Breach</u>: The jury will be permitted to take into account that Danny was acting in a sudden emergency situation. (Whether a specific jury instruction about this is permitted is jurisdictional.) We need more facts to determine whether Danny's shot was so far off his intended target that even under these circumstances, it was unreasonable. This is the biggest issue in the case, and it will be a question for the jury to resolve.

5. <u>Damages</u>: Pixie suffered personal injury when struck by the bullet.

6. <u>Cause in fact</u>: Danny's act of firing the gun was a cause in fact of Pixie's harm. But for firing the gun, Pixie would not have been harmed.

7. <u>Proximate cause</u>: Not to be discussed.

8. <u>Defenses</u>: Not to be discussed.

(C) Bumble v. Danny — trespass to land

1. <u>Allegation</u>: Danny entered Bumble's back yard without privilege; even if he had had a privilege, he remained after the emergency. The privilege had ended.

2. <u>Elements</u>: (1) Defendant volitionally acts to enter plaintiff's property; (2) Defendant does not have a privilege to be on the property, or if she had a privilege, she remained after the privilege ceased.

3. <u>Act</u>: Danny meant to go onto the property. He was hiding from Ron, and he chose to go where he did.

4. <u>Privilege</u>: <u>Necessity</u>

Rule: When an emergency occurs endangering a person's life or property and it is necessary to occupy another's property to avoid the harm, she has a privilege to do so for as long as necessary. What would otherwise be a trespass is a justified entry.

Applied: A jury is likely to find that the circumstances forced Danny to hide *somewhere* to avoid Ron, and his choice of Bumble's property seems to have been reasonable. He thus had a privilege to commit what would otherwise be a trespass. However, that privilege ended when the emergency ceased. When Danny fell asleep, he remained for several hours after Ron gave up the search.

Nevertheless, would Danny be a trespasser when he did not *consciously* remain? It seems inappropriate to hold him so. By analogy to the "act" requirement, he did not volitionally remain on the property after the necessity ceased; though remaining on the property isn't exactly an "act," the fact that he did not consciously remain might be seen as not blameworthy.

5. <u>Recoverable damages</u>: If Danny became a trespasser at any point, Bumble is entitled to recover at least nominal damages for that trespass.

The real problem here is that while he was on the property, Danny killed some valuable flowers. Normally, a person privileged to enter land by reason of necessity must still pay for damage caused (necessity is an "imperfect" defense). But Danny did not consciously cause the damage; he rolled over the flowers while sleeping. Would he be liable under those circumstances? This is unclear; the analysis is similar to that noted above, but with one difference: whereas Bumble only suffered nominal damages from Danny's merely remaining beyond the end of the emergency, he suffered real physical harm when Danny killed his flowers. Perhaps, a social policy favoring compensation would require Danny to pay for the flowers, but if Danny is blameless (because he did not act volitionally), requiring compensation would violate another policy: holding liable only those who are at fault.

6. <u>Bottom line</u>: This is a very uncertain case. Danny probably has a good chance of defeating Bumble's claim.

Bumble v. Danny — conversion

1. Another weak claim. <u>Allegation</u>: Danny's destruction of the flowers was conversion.

2. <u>Note</u>: You may not have studied whether flowers growing on a person's land are a chattel or are part of the real estate. We'll assume they're a chattel for our purposes.

3. <u>Elements</u>: (1) Defendant volitionally acts; (2) defendant intends to exercise substantial dominion over the chattels of another; (3) defendant in fact exercises such dominion.

   <u>Note</u>: If Bumble's trespass action is successful, he would be permitted to recover damages for the loss of his flowers (their value at the time of destruction). If the trespass action fails because Danny never became a trespasser or his destruction of the flowers was not an "act," Bumble would not recover their value. The same issues would affect his conversion claim. Thus, the conversion claim is superfluous and will not be discussed further.

(D) Danny v. Fran & Corey — negligence

1. <u>Allegation</u>: Fran and Corey were concurrent tortfeasors. They combined to cause a single indivisible injury. Both are therefore jointly and severally liable, or if this is a "several liability" state, each will be liable for damages represented by his or her degree of fault.

   <u>Note</u>: No battery claim is possible against Fran because she did not see Danny before she hit him. Nothing in the facts indicates that she either acted with the purpose of striking anyone or knew to a substantial certainty that she was going to strike someone. So, even if it was wrongful to hit Danny under the circumstances, Danny's battery claim will fail for lack of the requisite intent. (A similar analysis would preclude an assault claim.)

2. <u>Elements</u>: See *Pixie v. Danny* for negligence, above.

   a. <u>Duty</u>: As drivers, Fran and Corey owe pedestrians a duty of reasonable care because their failure to exercise reasonable care would endanger the pedestrians. Danny is a pedestrian. Thus, he is owed a duty of reasonable care.

   b. <u>Breach</u>:

      i. <u>Fran</u>: The facts state that Fran was distracted trying to program her navigation system, causing her not to notice Corey until it was too late. What we don't know is how long Fran's distraction lasted. It is not always unreasonable to look away briefly to do such things as pick up a phone or change a radio station. But a reasonable person would only do so very briefly. Any "custom" to spend more than a miniscule amount of time looking away from the road would be mere evidence of reasonable care, and in fact a jury might well decide that it is unreasonable. In addition, because programming a navigation system is more complicated than changing a radio station or picking up (and even dialing) a phone, a reasonable person might well program the system before taking off, or perhaps would pull over to the side of the road to perform this task. If (and the facts do not state this) Fran had some sort of sudden emergency requiring her to change her destination to an unfamiliar one, she still could have pulled over to do this unless it would have been unreasonable under the circumstances. There is a good chance the jury will consider Fran's behavior to be negligent.

ii. <u>Corey</u>: The facts only say that Corey had crossed the center line. They do not say why. Did Corey simply fail to pay attention? Did he suffer a sudden physical illness such as a heart attack? Was there some other reason for his crossing the line that would be deemed not his fault? Danny will have to prove to the jury that Corey was at fault (negligent) for crossing the center line.

3. <u>Negligence per se</u> might apply to establish Corey's duty and breach. A statute probably forbids crossing the center line of a roadway. The statute is designed in part to prevent collisions or near-collisions that harm both other drivers/passengers and pedestrians. Thus, Danny is in the class of persons designed to be protected by the statute. Of course, Corey is in the regulated class because he is a driver. And the harm, though perhaps not the most usual kind, is certainly one of the types the statute was designed to prevent. We do not know if an excuse would apply (see above).

4. <u>Damages</u>: Danny was injured.

5. <u>Cause in fact</u>: In most situations, the issue is whether, "but-for" the negligence of defendant, plaintiff would not have been harmed. For present purposes, we'll assume that Fran's negligence was failing to pay proper attention to the road ahead of her, and that Corey's negligence was in crossing the center line. Depending on how the facts are interpreted, there are two possibilities:

   a. If Fran had been paying proper attention, she would have seen Corey crossing the center line and heading in her direction sooner, allowing her to take safer evasive action. On this interpretation of the facts, the negligence of both parties combined to cause the harm. Both are "but-for" causes.

   b. Even if Fran had been paying proper attention and seen Corey sooner, she still would not have been able to avoid the accident. On this interpretation of the facts, Corey is a "but-for" cause because his act led to Fran's swerving and hitting Danny. Fran, however, is not a "but-for" cause. This is because there is no connection between her *negligence* and the accident. True, she hit Danny, but not because of negligence.

We do not know which of these scenarios accurately describes the facts. If scenario (1) is accurate, Fran and Corey are concurrent tortfeasors who caused a single, indivisible injury. They will be jointly and severally liable (see below).

6. <u>Proximate cause</u>: Not to be discussed.

7. <u>Joint and several liability</u>: Most states hold that concurrent tortfeasors who cause a single, indivisible injury are each jointly and severally liable to plaintiff. This means plaintiff may recover one full judgment from one or the other, or part from one and part from the other. It's up to plaintiff. Generally, these states also allow contribution in some form. (Note that if plaintiff recovers from one defendant and the other is insolvent, the right to contribution will be of little value to the defendant who paid.)

   a. <u>Several liability</u>: Some states hold concurrent tortfeasors liable to plaintiff only for their proportionate share of fault. Plaintiff must prove each defendant's share. In these systems, it is generally the plaintiff who suffers if one party is insolvent, missing, immune, etc.

   b. <u>Application</u>: Depending on the system of contribution used in the state, the jury might be asked to decide each defendant's degree of fault. The facts given in the problem do not provide sufficient information to guess what those degrees might be.

8. <u>Defenses</u>: Not to be discussed.

9. <u>Bottom line</u>: Danny has a strong case against Fran. The strength of his case against Corey is uncertain because of the absence of detail in the facts.

256. (A) **Dirk v. Bee—assault**

1. <u>Volitional act</u>: Bee's jumping out of the bushes.

2. <u>Intent</u>: Bee intended to frighten Abe. Is this the same thing as intending to cause apprehension of imminent harmful or offensive contact? Probably. It is likely that Bee's idea of a practical joke was to startle Abe into thinking he was about to be struck. If so, the requisite intent can be found by showing that Bee desired plaintiff to suffer apprehension of imminent harmful or offensive contact. Even if not, it would be fairly easy to show that Bee knew it was substantially certain that Abe would suffer apprehension of imminent harmful or offensive contact. This would be much easier to show. Even if the victim had been Abe (as Bee intended), Abe at least momentarily might well have believed he was about to suffer such contact.

   If Bee harbored the requisite intent, there is still a question whether the intent is unlawful under the circumstances. Abe and Bee were kids horsing around. Though we would need more facts to reach a clearer conclusion, it is possible that in their horsing around, the kids impliedly consented to this sort of thing. We allow children to play games of this kind.

   Kids are liable for intentional torts based on the same standards as adults. If they harbor the requisite intent, and the other elements are present, they are liable.

   If the jurisdiction adheres to a "dual intent" rule, plaintiff would also have to demonstrate that Bee knew it was "unlawful" to do the act. Given that Bee is a child, it is not likely that this requirement could be satisfied.

   If Bee had the requisite intent, it does not matter that the person affected was not her intended victim. The intent would "transfer" to Dirk. But if the act would not be unlawful as to Abe, there is no unlawful intent to "transfer" to Dirk.

3. <u>Apprehension of imminent harmful or offensive contact</u>: The facts indicate that Dirk lost control when he heard Bee's yell and saw Bee appear suddenly in front of him. At least it can be said that Dirk was startled, and indeed enough to fall off his skateboard. But whether he believed he was about to suffer harmful or offensive contact is not clear. Perhaps this will not be hard to prove.

4. <u>Defenses</u>: None appear. Bee has a very weak argument that Dirk impliedly consented to this sort of thing by riding a skateboard on the sidewalk where many people, including children, were playing that day. But there is a difference between going out among people and consenting to being intentionally placed in apprehension of imminent harmful or offensive contact. Dirk did not consent to this. Other defenses are inapplicable.

5. <u>Bottom line</u>: The difficult element here would be intent, particularly demonstrating its unlawfulness. If intent can be proven, Dirk will probably prevail.

Dirk v. Bee — battery

1. <u>Volitional act</u>: Bee's lunge from the bushes is a volitional act because she meant to perform it.

2. <u>Intent</u>: The facts strongly suggest that Bee did not desire any contact with her victim (whom she thought would be Abe), or that she knew such contact was substantially certain to occur. Thus, the battery form of intent does not seem to be provable here. Because of doctrine of "transferred intent," however, Dirk could get over this hurdle by showing that Bee possessed the intent for assault. Still, however, it is possible that the intent to commit this act would not be unlawful.

3. <u>Contact</u>: Contact need not occur directly between plaintiff and defendant. As we saw in the case of the boy who pulled the chair out from under the old woman, contact can be indirect. Here, Dirk's contact with the ground is probably sufficient. Because the tort of battery does not require physical injury, Dirk's failure to suffer injury does not matter.

4. <u>Defenses</u>: None likely apply. See *Dirk v. Bee* for assault, above.

5. <u>Bottom line</u>: This claim is about as strong as the assault claim.

(B) Carol v. Abe — assault

1. <u>Volitional act</u>: Abe deliberately rounded the corner at high speed on his skateboard. This was an overt act, but it did not accompany any intention to create apprehension in Carol of imminent harmful or offensive contact because at the time he did it, Abe probably did not know Carol was present. Abe probably did see Carol after he rounded the corner, however, and he continued to ride the board toward her. This would constitute the requisite act.

2. <u>Intent</u>: At some point as he approached Carol, Abe probably became aware both of Carol's presence and of the likelihood that Carol would think Abe was going to run into her. If at that point, Abe could have stopped or steered his skateboard away from Carol, and he failed to do so, he probably would have had knowledge to a substantial certainty that he would come in contact with Carol. Abe was a 10-year-old, but a child of that age almost certainly can put two and two together in this way.

Unlawfulness of the act (and thus unlawfulness of the intent to perform the act) also appears to be present. It is one thing to skate toward a friend in play, but another to aim your fast-moving board at a stranger on the sidewalk. As adults in a crowded, diverse society, we must accept certain inconveniences and annoyances, but being intentionally placed in apprehension of imminent harmful contact arguably is not one of them. A jury is likely to find that at some point as he neared Carol, Abe possessed unlawful intent.

If the jurisdiction uses a "dual intent" rule, Carol would run into the same sort of difficulty that Dirk faces in his action against Bee. See that discussion.

3. <u>Apprehension of imminent harmful or offensive contact</u>: The facts make clear that Carol believed Abe was going to skate into her; that is why she dove into the bushes. Apprehension exists even when one knows she can avoid contact by taking evasive action; as long as Carol believed that she would suffer imminent contact if she did not get out of the way immediately, the apprehension element is satisfied.

4. <u>Extent of liability</u>: Though the principle probably has some limit, we have read that an intentional tortfeasor is liable for "all" the consequences of her tortious conduct. If Carol suffered injuries from her dive, Abe therefore would be liable for those even if some of them would not have been suffered if not for the negligence of a third party (Ocean City Power Co.'s placement of the wooden box covering the high voltage lines).

Given Abe's age and the fact that he probably did not *desire* to create apprehension or to strike Carol, punitive damages probably would not be awardable.

5. <u>Defenses</u>: None appear.

6. <u>Bottom line</u>: This looks like a relatively strong case for assault.

Carol v. Abe — battery

This claim would be similar to the assault claim, except that Carol would not have to demonstrate that Abe meant to cause contact. The "assault" intent, if present, would suffice for battery, and the requisite touching would be Carol's contact with the ground. Certainly, Abe set in motion the chain of events that led to this contact.

Carol v. Abe — negligence

1. <u>Duty</u>: A skateboarder using public sidewalks certainly has a duty to take reasonable care for the safety of others. If Cardozo's limitation of foreseeable plaintiffs, articulated in *Palsgraf*, applies, that rule would also be satisfied. A reasonable skateboarder, even a child, would anticipate the presence of adults on the sidewalk. This would create a duty to exercise reasonable care for their protection. Carol falls into that class.

2. <u>Breach</u>: Skateboarding is an activity in which children often participate. Though it is dangerous, it is probably more dangerous to the skateboarder than to others. Also, the nature of the activity gives notice to those around that the actor is probably a child. For all of these reasons, the court almost certainly will allow the jury to take Abe's age into consideration when determining whether his speed and manner of managing the skateboard reached the level of reasonable care.

If riding skateboards on the sidewalk is customary, this would be some evidence that doing so is not unreasonable. But compliance with custom is only evidence of reasonable care. It is not reasonable care per se.

Because it appears that Abe was an inexperienced skateboarder, a reasonable person in his position might not have tried to ride the board that fast on the first day he owned it. So it is quite possible that the jury will conclude that Abe breached the duty of reasonable care he owed to Carol. Certainly, there is enough evidence of breach to go to the jury. On the other hand, where else could Abe ride? Riding on the street would pose significant danger to himself and perhaps others. Perhaps he could have ridden in a parking lot or vacant lot, but the availability of these places is not specified in the facts. In addition, he could forgo the activity of skateboarding altogether, but society benefits from children gaining experience of many types, so the burden of forcing kids to stop skateboarding is probably too great.

3. <u>Cause in fact</u>: No problem here. But for Abe's riding at warp speed straight toward Carol, Carol would not have been injured.

4. <u>Proximate cause</u>: The general type of harm Carol suffered—physical injury from diving out of the way—is probably within the scope of the risk created by Abe's negligence. Abe need not be in a position to foresee the extent of harm or the precise mechanism by which it occurred.

A court that takes a narrow view of the "risk" created by Abe's negligence might hold that the risk was of bruises or broken bones caused by a fall, not being punctured by a nail. But courts are unlikely to take such an extremely narrow view of the risk. After all, one who falls on the ground might well be punctured by glass or other objects on the ground. So the harm that occurred is almost certainly within the risk.

5. <u>Damages</u>: Carol suffered significant physical injury.

6. <u>Defenses</u>: Instructions state that defenses should not be discussed.

7. <u>Bottom line</u>: This looks like a strong negligence case.

(C) **Carol v. Ocean City Power Co. (OCPC)—negligence**

<u>Note</u>: OCPC would be liable for the torts of its employees committed within the course and scope of employment.

1. <u>Negligent act or omission</u>: It is important for Carol to specify the negligent act or omission. If Carol had suffered injury from contact with the electric current, she could argue persuasively that the negligent act was failing to take better precautions to prevent such harm. But here the harm came from nails that held the wooden box together. As a result, she might want to claim that the negligent act was placing a box constructed in such a way so close to the public sidewalk. She could also claim that the negligent act or omission was leaving the box there at all—that OCPC should have finished the job rather than leave it unfinished for all or part of a weekend. (She might assert that if OCPC did not wish to finish the job before the weekend, it should have posted a guard at the site, but this is not likely to be a strong argument because of the cost of doing so.)

2. <u>Duty</u>: OCPC owes a duty of reasonable care not to act in a way that causes unreasonable risk of harm. Because OCPC is a power company, and power companies have expertise relevant to this case, OCPC would be required to exercise the care and skill of a reasonable power company that possesses that expertise.

Cardozo might add "to reasonably foreseeable plaintiffs." As a pedestrian, Carol is in the class of persons who are foreseeable victims of a dangerously constructed object placed next to the public sidewalk.

3. <u>Breach</u>: What could OCPC have done to lower the risk of harm to an acceptable level? It probably had other means of protecting the high voltage lines during construction. Some sort of cover over the high voltage lines was certainly called for. Perhaps a heavy metal cover would have been better. Though it would have created certain dangers of its own (such as possible injury to a person whose head strikes the cover), it's a common way of protecting excavations, it is probably available at low cost, and it probably would have been effective to prevent the harms suffered by both Carol and Abe. A fence around the area in addition to the cover over the wires might have been helped as well, but it might not have prevented a falling person from striking the box. So even if a fence were used, due care might have required the use of a better cover than the box.

All of these considerations, and others, could be fed into a test such as the Hand formula to determine whether the precaution would have been cost-justified. If the cost of the precaution would have exceeded the harm discounted by its probability, Hand would say OCPC was not negligent for failing to take the precaution. If the alleged negligence of OCPC was leaving the work uncompleted for all or part of the weekend, Carol would have to show that the cost of completing the work would not have been prohibitive.

Without more information, we can't be sure if OCPC breached its duty of care to Carol.

4. <u>Cause in fact</u>: But for the way in which the box was constructed, Carol would not have suffered the precise injury she suffered. Though she might have been injured in some other way, there was a "but-for" relationship between OCPC's negligence and Carol's harm.

Even if it is not possible to say that "but for" OCPC's negligence, Carol would not have been injured (because Abe's act was what caused Carol to dive out of the way), OCPC's act or omission was a substantial factor in causing her injury. It certainly changed a possibly dangerous dive into a very dangerous one.

5. <u>Proximate cause</u>: Remembering that the allegation of negligence concerns the use of this type of cover over the high voltage wires, the harm that occurred (piercing by nails) was of a type one might reasonably expect a person to suffer if she falls on top of the box. Some courts would also consider whether Abe was an 'intervening' actor whose conduct 'superseded' that of OPCC, but these courts almost certainly would hold that Abe's conduct did not "break the chain" of events. OPCC arguably maintained a condition that posed a risk of harm to people walking along the sidewalk. There are many reasons why a pedestrian might end up coming in contact with the box, but one reasonably foreseeable way is for the pedestrian to have to move to the side in order to avoid a collision with an-

other person. In a general way, this is what happened. The precise *manner* in which the harm occurs need not be foreseeable; as long as harm is reasonably foreseeable under the circumstances, the conduct of a third party will not absolve the original wrongdoer. (Some courts hold that the *criminal* acts of a third party cut off the original wrongdoer's liability *per se*, but that is a minority rule, and it doesn't apply here anyway because Abe was not acting criminally.)

6. <u>Damages</u>: Carol suffered significant personal injury from the puncture wound to the chest. Her damages would likely include medical bills, lost future earnings, and compensation for pain and suffering.

7. <u>Defenses</u>: Instructions state that defenses should not be discussed.

8. <u>Bottom line</u>: Probably a weak case. The foreseeable risk of harm to a person in Carol's position is not likely very great. Unless the cost of avoidance is extremely low, it is unlikely that a reasonable power company would have acted differently, at least to avoid this harm.

Note also that this might be a case in which OCPC and Abe would be treated as independent tortfeasors each of whom was a substantial factor in bringing about a single, indivisible injury. In that situation, most courts would hold the two tortfeasors jointly and severally liable for the injury.

(D) Abe v. OCPC for negligence

1. <u>Negligent act or omission</u>: Abe will allege that OCPC's negligence consisted of loosely covering high voltage lines, which resulted in their exposure more easily than was justified. As in Carol's action against OCPC, Abe might assert that OCPC's negligence was failing to complete the work before the weekend.

2. <u>Duty</u>: See *Carol v. OCPC*. The analysis is the same.

3. <u>Breach</u>: Loosely covering exposed high voltage lines with a wooden cover, and not taking other precautions to protect the public using the sidewalk, does not seem reasonable. Because it is next to a public sidewalk, many people are likely to be close to it, and it is reasonable to expect that children will be among them. (The facts do not state explicitly that this was a residential neighborhood, but they suggest as much. Even if it was not a residential area, it is reasonable to foresee many people, including children, being near the excavation.) In all likelihood, a means of covering the wires was available at reasonable cost that would not have given way so easily and exposed the wires. Breach is much easier to prove here than in Carol's action against OCPC.

If OCPC's negligence was failing to complete the work before the weekend, the analysis of breach would be the same as in Carol's action against OCPC.

4. <u>Cause in fact</u>: Abe's injury resulted from the combination of Carol's dive and the (possibly) inadequate cover. (Abe was also a causal factor, because it was his act that led Carol to fall in the first place. But that would most likely be a matter to be considered under the defense of comparative negligence, which is not to be discussed on this exam.) Both events were required before Abe's injury could occur, and thus both are "substantial factors" in bringing about Abe's injury.

5. Proximate cause: Note that Abe is a foreseeable victim, and that the harm that occurred is of the type that one would expect from inadequately covering high voltage lines. Moreover, if "danger invites rescue," it probably also invites spectators or others who might not wish to help but certainly wish to find out what happened. So even if Abe only approached Carol to find out if she was okay, Cardozo would likely say that Abe's act is foreseeable as a matter of law, placing him within the zone of risk. (On the other hand, Abe did start the chain of events that led to Carol's injury, and if he did so tortuously, he might not be given the benefit of the "rescue" doctrine. This would make sense from the standpoint of policy, because we do not want to offer this protection to the person who created or substantially participated in the creation of the need to rescue in the first place.)

6. Damages: Abe suffered significant personal injury from contact with the high voltage line.

7. Defenses: Instructions state that defenses should not be discussed.

8. Bottom line: This is a strong case.

    Note: If Abe is held liable and Carol chooses to collect from him more than his fair share of damages, he might seek contribution from OCPC. The contribution rules of the state would come into play to determine whether this would be permitted.

257. Note: *Respondeat superior*: Under the doctrine of *respondeat superior*, the University would be liable for the torts of its employees committed within the course and scope of employment. For *respondeat superior* to apply, Jugala must have been acting under the scope and course of his employment; his "undercover operation" must have been within the bounds of his employment as a University security guard.

(A) Jillian v. University of Edgemo — negligence

Officer Jugala will be held to the standard of a security officer.

1. Duty: Jugala had the duty to act as a reasonable security officer. Plaintiffs will have to show that officer Jugala had an obligation to take care not to cause the type of injury suffered under these or similar circumstances.

2. Breach: Did Jugala act as a reasonable security officer would under the same or similar circumstances? Officer Jugala probably did not when he shot at Jillian out of a mistaken belief that Jillian was Lindsay attempting to shoot Madding. As a trained professional, Jugala should have taken more care to figure out who was standing up and whether that person was holding a weapon. Jugala's action was especially dangerous because he pulled out his weapon in a classroom filled with students.

3. Cause in fact: Officer Jugala's act of firing the gun was a cause in fact of Jillian's harm. But for firing the gun, Jillian would not have been harmed.

4. Proximate cause: It is foreseeable that the firing of a gun will result in a bullet wound. It is likely that the other persons in the classrooms will be foreseeable victims when firing a gun.

5. Damages: Jillian would likely be able to recover damages for the cost of her wound. *Respondeat superior* compels the university to pay these damages, although Jugala can also be held liable himself.

Jillian v. University of Edgemo — battery

1. <u>Volitional act:</u> Jugula's shooting the first shot that hit Jillian.

2. <u>Intent:</u> Jugala intended to shoot Lindsay, but whether that contact was lawful depends on whether or not officer Jugala was privileged.

   Note: *Transferred Intent:* Although officer Jugala did not intend to shoot Jillian, he did intend to shoot someone and this intent is transferred to the ultimate victim.

3. <u>Harmful contact:</u> The bullet shot from officer Jugala's gun that struck Jillian.

4. <u>Damages:</u> As above.

5. <u>Defense:</u> Privilege of a security officer acting in <u>defense of another</u>. Jugula would be entitled to use deadly force to save Madding's life if the circumstances warranted. Debatable. The privilege demands reasonable conduct from the defendant, and Jugula's actions appear unreasonable. See the negligence discussion above. If, contrariwise, the privilege is present — meaning that Jugula acted reasonably when he shot Jillian — then Jugula's shooting the wrong person would leave Jillian uncompensated. Mistake as to the identity of the harmed person does not defeat the privilege of defense of others.

6. *Respondeat superior* <u>for an intentional tort.</u> Although employers are typically held liable for employees' negligence rather than intentional torts, *respondeat superior* also extends to intentional harm if the employee committed it in the scope of his employment. In *Fisher v. Carrousel Motor Hotel,* for example, an employer was held liable for a battery committed on a guest of the hotel by a staffer. Negligence + *respondeat superior* fits the facts better as a route to impose responsibility on the university, however, because Jugula's actions appear more careless than intentional. Jillian can collect only once for the same injury, and she collects no less by characterizing her injury as an unfortunate accident rather than the harder-to-win battery.

(B) Madding v. University of Edgemo — negligence

Same as *Jillian v. University of Edgemo* for negligence.

Madding v. University of Edgemo — battery

Same as *Jillian v. University of Edgemo* for battery.

(C) Negligence by Jillian and Madding against Dr. Bigbrain

Note that the analysis is the same for both plaintiffs.

1. <u>Duty:</u> Following the *Tarasoff* decision, a mental health professional has a duty of care toward some victims of violence when the mental health professional had a therapeutic relationship with the assailant.

2. <u>Breach:</u> Did Bigbrain breach his duty of reasonable care of a psychiatrist by not detaining Lindsay? Possibly. Individuals competent to evaluate Bigbrain's inaction have said that the decision was unreasonable.

3. <u>Cause in fact:</u> Other psychiatrists have stated that, in hindsight, reasonable care might have included confinement of Lindsay, but as it turned out Lindsay did not inflict violent

harm on Madding or anyone else. Breach of duty, assuming it is present, did not cause the harm that occurred.

4. <u>Proximate cause</u>: The plaintiffs could try to argue that, but for Bigbrain not detaining Lindsay, officer Jugala would not have gone undercover and mistakenly shot Jillian and Madding, but this contention is probably too far of a stretch. Under a directness test, the stance might prevail, but it is unsound according to modern doctrine. Even if the *Tarasoff* limitation on the duty of care to cover only known, identified potential victims is ignored so that Dr. Bigbrain would we reasonable care to a wider set of persons, the breach of duty does not align with the harm that occurred. The risk rule (or scope of the risk) approach to proximate cause would defeat this element of the prima facie case.

5. <u>Bottom line</u>: Madding and Jillian will likely not recover damages from Bigbrain. *Tarasoff* relates to the claim, but does not support a judgment in favor of either plaintiff.

258. This question is inspired by *Weirum v. RKO General, Inc.*, 539 P.2d 36 (Cal. 1975), which spent some time as a proximate-cause note case in several casebooks.

(A) Liability of KDDD and the Dragon — negligence

1. <u>Duty</u>: Plaintiffs would have to show that the defendants had an obligation to take care not to cause the type of injury that the plaintiffs have suffered. A court could view the KDDD promotion as a kind of incitement with a monetary reward; it was foreseeable to the Dragon and KDDD that their stunt would put pedestrians and drivers at risk of injury. The court has agreed that this promotion was conduct that created a foreseeable risk of physical injury to Flora and Eddie.

2. <u>Breach</u>: Plaintiffs fulfill the breach element by showing that the defendants failed to act with the degree of care that they were duty-bound to exercise. An action inciting negligent behavior will almost certainly be viewed by a jury as a negligent act in itself. Telling contestants to hit the rear bumper of the Dragon's car and letting it be known that the Dragon would not "pull over easy" encourages listeners to drive dangerously in an attempt to tap the back of the Dragon's bumper and win the prize money. A reasonable jury could readily find that the Dragon and KDDD breached their duty to act with ordinary care.

3. <u>Cause in fact</u>: This element of the prima facie case requires that the plaintiff show that but for the defendants' actions, the plaintiff's injuries would not have occurred. In the present case, Eddie would not have accelerated through the green light, injuring Flora and himself, were it not for the Dragon and KDDD's promotional give-away.

4. <u>Proximate cause</u>: Because the injuries were physical, under the "risk rule" approach, foreseeability of injury will be key to meeting this requirement. (It is difficult to sustain the cause of action under a "directness" approach.) Proximate cause introduces an alignment concept that requires that the defendant's breach caused the plaintiff's injury in a "natural" rather than fortuitous way. More modern formulations of this standard require the plaintiff to show that their injury was within the "scope of risk" posed by the defendant's carelessness. One way a claim can fail where actual causation existed but proximate causation did not is when the superseding negligence of another party overshadows the negligence of the defendant such that it relieves the defendant of responsibility.

In the present case, the question is whether Eddie's intervening action of accelerating through the green light was sufficient to absolve the Dragon and KDDD of all responsibility for the incident. Here the jury had the option to determine that the negligence of the defendants encouraged the third party's negligence. Since the Dragon and KDDD encouraged the reckless driving of Eddie, the jury could have found that this intervening negligence was consistent with what the Dragon and KDDD intended and as such did not absolve them of liability.

5. Injury: Both Flora and Eddie must prove they suffered injuries to satisfy the prima facie case for negligence, which will not be a problem in the present case.

(B) Why do you think Gloria was ridiculed for allowing the claims of Flora and Eddie against the Dragon and KDDD to proceed?

Most likely the media felt that Dragon, a popular local celebrity, and KDDD were not at fault for the injuries. They may have focused on Eddie as the true source of all injuries here. The media might have been incensed that Gloria would allow Eddie to go forward with his case against the Dragon and KDDD; trying to hit the Dragon's car, he appears dangerous rather than a victim of dangerous conduct by another. Flora appears more "innocent" than Eddie, but she was a pedestrian who stood outside the crosswalk. The media probably ascribed responsibility to these two individuals, Eddie in particular.

(C) Why might the jury have reasoned as it did?

Flora's claim is one of negligence whose elements are listed above duty, breach, causation, damages. As a driver, Eddie owed a duty of care to persons who covered by injured by his careless driving. The facts indicate that he drove carelessly when he hit Flora "not looking at anything but the Bug fender," which constitutes unreasonable behavior. Causation is straightforward.

As for apportionment, the jury could have attributed some responsibility to her for her presence outside the crosswalk. This posture might have been comparative negligence per se. The facts do not indicate whether Flora was deemed 0 percent responsible, or some larger fraction: you may assume that this issue is relatively unimportant, though present.

(D) On what basis could the Dragon bring an action against Eddie? Why did the lawyer advise him not to?

Eddie's touching of the Bug falls in a gray area between careless and intentional conduct. One might describe the touching as an intentional one that exceeded the bounds of consent. The intentional tort available would be either trespass to chattels or battery.

1. Trespass to chattels: Trespass to chattels is the intentional interference with the right of possession of personal property. The defendant's acts must intentionally damage the chattel, deprive the possessor of its use for a substantial period of time, or totally dispossess the chattel from the victim. Eddie did not intend to damage the Bug, but his intent to contact the Bug may be sufficient.

2. Battery: Battery occurs when a defendant perpetrates (a) a voluntary act (b) intending to cause a contract with plaintiff of a type that is harmful or offensive and (c) causes such

a contact. Eddie intended to contact the Bug, which was so closely connected with the Dragon so as to constitute contact with his person. However, the Dragon had expressly invited the contact which Eddie intended. A battery claim would fail either on a shortfall in the prima facie case, i.e., no intent to commit harmful contact, or a defense of consent. (Courts and the *Restatement* leave some room for debate as to which source of failure would govern.)

3. <u>Defenses</u>: The lawyer's advice likely recognized the strength of "acceptance" defenses: consent for the intentional tort if the prima facie case were deemed fulfilled, express assumption of risk for the negligence claim. Eddie could argue that the Dragon consented since he had invited the touching and ought to have anticipated that the contact necessarily would go beyond the bumper. Alternatively, the Dragon could describe the contact as accidental. Eddie executed his bumper tap poorly and instead hit the side of the Bug. Hence, the elements of negligence are present: duty, breach, causation, damages. But the Dragon accepted this risk.

4. <u>Bottom line</u>: The Dragon made it clear that he would accept the touching of his Bug by another automobile. Even if these defenses would not defeat his claim, the Dragon might look silly or worse if he brought a lawsuit complaining about behavior that he had openly encouraged. Better to play the individual-liberties card, and focus blame on Eddie as a bad driver than invite scrutiny into whether the promotion was a good idea.

(E) Why was KDDD a defendant in the lawsuits?

Under *respondeat superior*, an employer is vicariously liable for the wrongful acts of its employees committed within the scope of their employment. Thus, even if KDDD had no knowledge of the promotional giveaway (which is virtually impossible) and were careful in supervising the Dragon, it could still be found liable for the negligence of the Dragon. In the present case the promotion was clearly within the scope of the Dragon's employment, which would make KDDD vicariously liable for any negligence claims brought against the Dragon.

(F) What would a corrective justice theorist say about Flora's experience as a plaintiff?

Corrective justice, a complex subject fraught with academic controversy, can be given only brief treatment here. It emphasizes rectification: a repair of unjust harm. Corrective justice in tort law focuses on the injury the plaintiff suffered and the correlative remedy that the defendant must provide.

A corrective justice theorist would be displeased by Flora's experience in this litigation. This theorist would probably accept the correctness of the jury's determination that Flora had been wrongfully injured and deserved compensation. Flora won a judgment so stating. Because of the inadequacy of Eddie's insurance, she did not receive a full measure of her entitlements.

Some corrective justice theorists are troubled by liability insurance. In their view, a tort judgment requires payment from wrongdoers themselves, not third parties. But even a theorist offended by liability insurance would prefer the rendering of an insurance payment to nothing. The facts state that Eddie had no assets to pay damages to Flora. Judgment-proof defendants defeat a crucial element of corrective justice, the payment of one's own money to repair one's own wrong.

Index

Topic	Question
Firefighter's rule	51
First Amendment	141, 144, 146, 154
Foreseeability	49, 77, 87
Fraud	32, 172, 173
Hand formula	57, 70
Hypersensitive plaintiff	159, 166, 183
Implied warranty	128
Indemnity	199
Informed consent	240, 241
Insolvency, effect on enforcement of judgment	76, 203
Intent: In general	4, 9
Intentional infliction of emotional distress (*See* Emotional distress)	
Intoxication	67
Invasion of privacy	148, 149, 150, 151, 152, 153, 154, 155, 156, 239, 249
Invitee	45, 50, 89
Joint and several liability	194, 195, 197, 201, 202, 255
Joint social venture	41, 194
Jury, role of	13, 75, 196, 219
Land possessors (*See* Limited duty)	
Licensee	45
Limited duty: Economic loss	43, 48, 78, 181, 224
Limited duty: Land possessors	45, 50, 51, 89, 213, 214, 237
Limited duty: Non-negligent actors	53
Limited duty: Reasons for limits	44
Limited duty: To control dangerous third parties	53, 218, 219, 250
Limited duty: To rescue (*See* Rescue)	
Limited duty: To the unborn	54
Limited duty: Undertaking	42
Malpractice: Architectural	46, 47
Malpractice: Legal	180, 248
Malpractice: Medical	52, 59, 212, 240, 241, 242